FREEDOM AND MORAL SENTIMENT

FREEDOM AND MORAL SENTIMENT

Hume's Way of Naturalizing Responsibility

PAUL RUSSELL

OXFORD
UNIVERSITY PRESS

OXFORD
UNIVERSITY PRESS

Oxford   New York
Athens   Auckland   Bangkok   Bogotá   Buenos Aires   Cape Town
Chennai   Dar es Salaam   Delhi   Florence   Hong Kong   Istanbul   Karachi
Kolkata   Kuala Lumpur   Madrid   Melbourne   Mexico City   Mumbai   Nairobi
Paris   São Paulo   Shanghai   Singapore   Taipei   Tokyo   Toronto   Warsaw

and associated companies in
Berlin   Ibadan

Copyright © 1995 by Paul Russell

First published in 1995 by Oxford University Press, Inc.
198 Madison Avenue, New York, New York 10016

First issued as an Oxford University Press paperback, 2002

Oxford is a registered trademark of Oxford University Press

Library of Congress Cataloging-in-Publication Data
Russell, Paul, 1955-
Freedom and moral sentiment : Hume's way of naturalizing
responsibility / Paul Russell.
p.   cm.
Includes bibliographical references and index.
ISBN 0-19-509501-4; 0-19-515290-5 (pbk.)
1. Hume, David.   1711-1776—Ethics.   2. Free will and determinism.
3. Responsibility.   I. Title.
B1499.E8R87   1995
123'.5—dc20   95-1110

1 3 5 7 9 8 6 4 2

Printed in the United States of America
on acid-free paper

For Katherine Bell,
who was brought up beneath
the slopes of Calton Hill,
where Hume lies buried.

Acknowledgments

My general interest in Hume's philosophy and problems of freedom and responsibility owes much to my undergraduate education at Edinburgh University in the late 1970s. An early version of the book was presented in my 1986 Cambridge University Ph.D. thesis ("Moral Sentiment and the Rationale of Responsibility"). Since then it has been substantially revised and expanded. I have benefited from many suggestions and comments from a number of friends and colleagues—more than I can mention on this occasion. However, I am especially grateful to the following: Páll Árdal, Annette Baier, G. A. Cohen, Jim Dybikowski, Don Garrett (a reader for Oxford University Press), Ross Harrison, Neil MacCormick, Terry Penelhum (also a reader for Oxford), and David Raphael. Above all, I am grateful to Bernard Williams, who supervised my graduate studies at Cambridge. I would also like to thank the editorial staff at Oxford University Press—particularly, Angela Blackburn, Robert Miller, and Grace Suh—for all their help in bringing this book into print.

A number of institutions have provided me with generous financial support. From 1980 to 1983 the Scottish Education Department awarded me a Major Scottish Studentship, which enabled me to pursue my graduate studies at Cambridge. In 1984 I was elected to a Junior Research Fellowship at Sidney Sussex College, Cambridge, which I held until 1987. During 1989–90 Stanford University awarded me a Mellon Postdoctoral Fellowship, and a position as visiting assistant professor. The Social Science and Humanities Research Council of Canada provided me with further research time for 1990–91. I have also benefited as a Fellow of the Institute for Advanced Study in the Humanities at Edinburgh University during the summer of 1991. I am deeply grateful to all these institutions for the support that I have received from them.

Parts of this book have appeared in the following journals: "On the Naturalism of Hume's 'Reconciling Project'", *Mind*, 1983; "Hume's 'Two Definitions' of Cause and the Ontology of 'Double Existence'", *Hume Studies*, 1984; "Hume's 'Reconciling Project': A Reply to Flew", *Mind*, 1985; "Causation, Compulsion and Compatibilism", *American Philosophical Quarterly*, 1988; and "Hume on Responsibility and Punishment", *Canadian Journal of Philosophy*, 1990. I am grateful to the editors of these journals for permission to use this material.

My greatest and most personal debt is indicated in the dedication.

Contents

Abbreviations

All references to the following works are to page numbers unless otherwise indicated.

T   David Hume, *A Treatise of Human Nature* [1739–1740], edited by L. A. Selby-Bigge, 2nd rev. ed. P. H. Nidditch (Oxford: Clarendon Press, 1978).

A   David Hume, *An Abstract of a Treatise of Human Nature* [1740], reprinted in T above (T, 641–62).

ESY   David Hume, *Essays: Moral, Political and Literary* [1741–1777], edited by Eugene F. Miller (Indianapolis: Liberty Classics, 1985).

LG   David Hume, *A Letter from a Gentleman to his friend in Edinburgh* [1745], edited by E. C. Mossner and J. V. Price (Edinburgh: Edinburgh University Press, 1967).

EU/EM   David Hume, *Enquiries concerning Human Understanding and concerning the Principles of Morals* [EU=*Enquiry concerning Human Understanding;* EM=*Enquiry concerning the Principles of Morals*], edited by L. A. Selby-Bigge, 3rd rev. ed. P. H. Nidditch (Oxford: Clarendon Press, 1975).

DP   David Hume, "A Dissertation on the Passions" [1757], reprinted in *Essays: Moral, Political and Literary*, 2 vols., edited by T. H. Green and T. H. Grose (London: Longmans, Green, 1875), vol. 2, 137–66.

D   David Hume, *Dialogues concerning Natural Religion* [1779], edited by N. Kemp Smith, 2nd ed. (Edinburgh: Nelson, 1947).

LET   David Hume, *The Letters of David Hume*, 2 vols., edited by J. Y. T. Greig (Oxford: Clarendon Press, 1932).

TMS   Adam Smith, *The Theory of Moral Sentiments* [1759], edited by D. D. Raphael and A. L. Macfie (Oxford: Clarendon Press, 1976).

FR   P. F. Strawson, "Freedom and Resentment", in G. Watson, ed., *Free Will* (Oxford: Oxford University Press, 1982), 59–80.

SN   P. F. Strawson, *Skepticism and Naturalism: Some Varieties* (London: Metheun, 1985).

FREEDOM AND MORAL SENTIMENT

. . . the question of liberty and necessity; the most contentious question of meta-physics, the most contentious science . . .

Hume, *An Enquiry concerning Human Understanding*

Introduction

Happy, if we can unite the boundaries of the different species of philosophy, by reconciling profound enquiry with clearness, and truth with novelty!

Hume, *An Enquiry concerning Human Understanding*

The nature and conditions of human freedom and moral responsibility are matters of perennial philosophical importance and controversy. The questions raised in this sphere concern nothing less than the basis of moral life and our understanding of the place of humankind in the natural order of things. These are issues that straddle both metaphysics and morals. The positions that we take on such matters deeply shape our fundamental philosophical outlook. In this book, I am concerned with David Hume's contribution to our understanding of these matters.

In modern times, problems of freedom and responsibility have been considered with particular reference to the narrower issue of "free will". This more specific problem may be expressed as follows: Can human freedom and moral responsibility be reconciled with causal determinism or the necessitation of all human thought and action? The philosophical literature on this subject is vast. There are, however, a few seminal works that dominate the discussion and interpretation of this problem. It is widely acknowledged that among these works Hume provides us with one of the great "classic" statements of the "compatibilist" position—the view that human freedom and moral responsibility are not threatened or undermined by determinism (and, indeed, that they require it).[1]

Hume's statement of the compatibilist position is closely identified with the compatibilist positions taken up by a number of other well-known philosophers. In one direction, for example, Hume is generally thought to have been greatly influenced by the compatibilist strategy of his predecessor Thomas Hobbes.[2] In the other direction, there are a host of philosophers in the empiricist tradition—including Mill, Russell, Schlick, and Ayer—all of whom are widely understood to be following Hume's basic lines of thought on free will.[3] Indeed, Hume has become so closely identified with this group of thinkers that the compatibilist strategy that they are taken (collectively) to pursue has been labelled the "Hobbes-Hume-Schlick doctrine", or "Hume-Mill-Schlick-Ayer" position, and so on.[4] The general point is that in the relevant literature there is near universal agreement that Hume belongs to the classical compatibilist tradition of thought and that his arguments on this subject should be interpreted in this light.[5]

3

The strategy of the classical compatibilist tradition is very familiar. It argues that because we confuse causation with force and compulsion we mistakenly conclude that freedom (and responsibility) requires the absence of causation and necessity. Moral freedom, therefore, is wrongly supposed to require the metaphysics of indeterminism. The compatibilist maintains, against this view, that causation and necessity are actually required for freedom and responsibility. An agent is responsible for an action only if it was his motives or desires that *caused* it. Uncaused action could never be attributed to any person and would be random and capricious. Moreover, rewards and punishments secure valuable social benefits only because they motivate people to act differently than they would do in their absence. In other words, they *cause* people to alter or change their conduct in desirable ways. This is the essence of the classical compatibilist position. This strategy is understood to be primarily concerned with the *logic* of the concepts in question (i.e. freedom, necessity, etc.).[6] So interpreted, this strategy involves a kind of pure conceptual or philosophical analysis that is required to clarify the framework within which any independent empirical investigation into the nature of moral life must take place.[7] It is this position which Hume is widely held to be a principal spokesman for.

The view that Hume provides one of the principal statements—if not *the* principal statement—of classical compatibilism remains current within the field of Hume scholarship. Indeed, this view of Hume has been defended and elaborated on by a number of distinguished Hume scholars over the past thirty years, right up to the present. Although their interpretations vary somewhat, these commentators are all agreed that Hume's general strategy fits squarely into the classical compatibilist tradition. (Hereafter, I will refer simply to the "classical interpretation" of Hume's strategy.) The commentators whom I primarily have in mind include influential figures, such as Flew, MacNabb, Ayer, Stroud, Mackie, and Penelhum.[8] Moreover, I am unaware of any substantial effort to challenge this general account of Hume's compatibilist arguments or intentions.[9] Clearly, then, the view that Hume is a principal spokesman of the classical compatibilist strategy that runs from Hobbes to Schlick and Ayer is not only the dominant view—it has gone almost unchallenged.

It is of some contemporary importance that Hume continues to be interpreted in this manner. The reason for this is that there is an increasing consensus among philosophers in the field that the classical compatibilist strategy has now been effectively discredited or surpassed by more recent developments in compatibilist thinking. Insofar as Hume continues to be read as holding to the classical compatibilist position, his views will inevitably be judged as of less immediate contemporary interest and significance.[10] In other words, if the classical reading of Hume's compatibilism is indeed correct and it is also true that compatibilist thinking has now advanced well beyond the confines of this general strategy, then we must conclude that Hume's thinking on this subject is now somewhat dated and passé.[11] The crucial question, therefore, is whether or not Hume has been properly interpreted by his commentators.

In this book I argue that Hume's views on this subject—although they have been very widely discussed and hugely influential—have nevertheless been seriously misrepresented. More specifically, I argue that commentators and scholars have distorted Hume's views on this matter because they have overlooked a key element in

Hume's analysis of the nature and conditions of moral responsibility. This element is moral sentiment. One of the key objectives of Hume's science of man was to discover under what circumstances people are *felt* to be responsible. To hold a person responsible is to regard that person as an object of a moral sentiment, which is a calm, indirect passion. Hume believed that "in the production and conduct of the passions, there is a certain regular mechanism, which is susceptible of as accurate a disquisition, as laws of motion, optics, hydrostatics or any part of natural philosophy" (DP, 166). Hume is concerned to *describe* the "regular mechanism" which generates the moral sentiments. This feature of Hume's discussion, I maintain, shapes his general account of the nature and conditions of moral responsibility.

Hume's discussion of the subject of free will must be interpreted within the framework of this *naturalistic* account of responsibility. In particular, it is not possible to understand the general structure and significance of Hume's effort to "reconcile" liberty and necessity until we properly appreciate how these arguments depend on Hume's description of the causal mechanism that produces our moral sentiments. Part I of this book is especially concerned with these points. I show that Hume introduces "the experimental method of reasoning" *into* the free will controversy in order to put an end to this "long disputed question" (EU, 81). His general strategy, therefore, is in important respects very different from that of other (classical) compatibilist thinkers, such as Hobbes and Schlick.

There are, I argue, striking parallels and affinities between Hume's general strategy and the views that have been advanced more recently by P. F. Strawson in his influential paper "Freedom and Resentment". What Hume and Strawson are fundamentally agreed about is that questions of moral responsibility, and how they relate to traditional problems of free will, can be properly understood and analysed only within the framework of moral sentiment. Moral sentiment, they hold, must be considered as a "given" of our human nature. As such, it constitutes the very fabric within which issues of freedom and responsibility arise. Any effort to justify or describe responsibility outside this framework is bound to mislead and perplex us. In this way, the naturalistic avenue of interpretation and criticism, far from draining Hume's discussion of its contemporary interest and significance, makes plain what precisely that interest and significance consists in.

Part II of this book builds on the naturalistic theme raised in Part I. Hume's theory of responsibility draws from—and depends on—several different aspects of his moral theory and his philosophy of mind. The nature of these commitments, and their relations with one another, are the particular concern of Part II. In this regard, I discuss a range of issues, such as Hume's views about the nature and content of moral sentiment; the relevance of character to ascriptions of responsibility; the role of intention, will, and feeling in arousing moral sentiment; the extent to which we have control over our (moral) character; and, finally, the question of the justification of punishment. Beyond this, Hume's views on the subject of responsibility are considered in relation to his wider and deeper philosophical concern with problems of religion. I will show that the naturalistic theory of responsibility is an especially important aspect of Hume's more basic anti-Christian philosophical objectives and concerns. In the final chapter, I draw some general conclusions about the strengths and weaknesses of Hume's naturalistic theory. In this context, I am especially concerned to emphasize the significance of Hume's account of the relationship between issues of freedom and issues of responsibility.

On the classical account, Hume understands the problem of responsibility simply in terms of the conditions of free action. Hume's account of the relationship between responsibility and freedom, I explain, is more complex than this. For Hume, the issue of responsibility is not reducible to the problem of free will. The scope of moral evaluation extends well beyond the sphere of intentional action. A person may be held responsible for aspects of character that are manifest neither in their will nor through their intentions. In general, it is Hume's view that we must not exaggerate the importance of voluntariness and control for moral responsibility. Hume's (complex) account of the relationship between freedom and responsibility, I maintain, constitutes a particularly important and illuminating aspect of his wider naturalistic strategy.

My discussion, as the summary account above indicates, is structured around a few basic themes. These are themes which are fundamental for a proper understanding of Hume's intentions in this sphere, but which are, nevertheless, neglected or overlooked by the classical reading.

The first theme is Hume's *naturalism*. This refers to Hume's objective to describe and explain, in empirical and scientific terms, the workings of the human passions (i.e. moral sentiments) in accounting for the nature and conditions of moral responsibility.

The second theme that I emphasize is Hume's *rejection of voluntarism*. What I mean by this is that (contrary to the classical interpretation) Hume rejects the view that responsibility is simply a matter of acting freely. Hume's position is that the relationship between freedom and responsibility is more complex than this. In particular, according to Hume it is not the case that we are responsible only for that which we control or do voluntarily.

Finally, I am also concerned to place appropriate emphasis on Hume's *secularism*, considered in relation to his views on freedom and responsibility. What Hume has to say on these matters is deeply motivated by his more fundamental philosophical objective to discredit Christian metaphysics and morals and to develop in its place a secular, scientific account of moral and political life.

A proper understanding of these features of Hume's philosophical system, I argue, is essential for any adequate appreciation and critical assessment of Hume's moral philosophy and, indeed, his philosophy as a whole. I argue that in both matters of detail and matters of general strategy the significance and interest of what Hume says on this subject is obscured by the classical interpretation. This is in no way to deny that Hume's views have serious shortcomings or difficulties. On the contrary, I am equally concerned to identify and expose (significant) shortcomings and difficulties in Hume's system. Nevertheless, whatever shortcomings may remain with Hume's position, there is a great deal more to be learned from it than is suggested by the classical reading.

Recently there has been a great deal of debate—much of it very interesting— about the nature of the history of philosophy and how it relates to the history of ideas. I take the historian of philosophy, unlike the historian of ideas, to be particularly concerned with the *critical* study of the work at hand. The history of philosophy must *begin* as a disciplined historical study, but this is not its final objective. Its final objective must be to shed light on contemporary philosophical problems.[12] In this way, unlike the history of ideas, the history of philosophy finishes firmly on a philosophical note—on a note which focusses on present philosophical concerns. Consistent with this, my primary objective in this study is not simply to clarify our understanding of Hume's thinking on freedom and responsibility. Rather, it is to clarify our own (contemporary) understanding on the issues of freedom and responsibility *by means* of a careful consideration of Hume's work.

The classical interpretation of Hume's position on the subject of freedom and responsibility presents his general strategy as simple and straightforward. I will show that this is not the case. Hume's arguments relating to these problems are both subtle and complex. In order to secure benefit from the study of Hume's work, we require a careful and detailed analysis of his philosophical principles. This requires some patience and stamina, as we follow Hume into the *labyrinth* of his system. Nevertheless, as I will show, the journey repays the philosophical effort.

However, for those readers who require only a general overview of Hume's strategy, the following shortcut may suffice: chapter 1, sections 1, 2, 4; chapter 2, section 4; chapter 3, section 1; chapter 4; and chapter 12. Readers with more time may also look at chapters 5, 9, and 10.

I will discuss and refer to secondary literature only when it is necessary for explaining the significance of the interpretive or critical issues at hand. By and large, I try to confine all such references to the notes—leaving the text free so far as possible for discussion of Hume's writings. In the body of the text, I am concerned with historical references only insofar as they shed direct light on the interpretation or criticism that I am advancing. References in the notes, along with the bibliography, should provide the reader with a fairly detailed account of the essential contemporary secondary literature.

Hume's attitude to the fate of his philosophy is of a piece with his wider attitude to life and the role of philosophy within human life. It is his view that the philosopher, no matter how subtle his reflections, will always be "lost in the man" (ESY, 179n [Sceptic]). There is no serene "temple of wisdom" where we can seat ourselves above the "rolling thunder" (ESY, 150 [Stoic]). Hume, clearly, wrote his philosophy, and accepted the reaction to it, in this general spirit. It is not unreasonable, therefore, that this study of Hume's philosophy should be written in much the same spirit.[13]

Notes

1. Penelhum, for example, says that Hume's "philosophical system contains the best-known classical statement of what is now known as compatibilism" ("Hume's Moral Psychology", 129).

2. See, e.g., Stroud, *Hume*, 153, who claims that "the general strategy of [Hume's] 'reconciling project' is not new. It is found in all essential respects in Hobbes". Hendel (*Philosophy of Hume*, 289) notes that Hume's title for the sections discussing the free will problem—"Of Liberty and Necessity"—seems to have been taken from Hobbes's essay of the same title as it appeared in Hobbes's *Tripos* (Hobbes, *English Works*, vol. 4).

3. The remarks of Glover are representative of this view. Glover says that "the philosophers of the empiricist tradition, with remarkable uniformity, have argued that the belief that determinism is incompatible with responsibility is confused and false" (*Responsibility*, 50).

In a footnote attached to this passage, he claims that "almost identical versions of this doctrine [compatibilism] are to be found in Hobbes, Hume, Mill, Russell, Schlick and Ayer".

4. The "Hobbes-Hume-Schlick" label appears in Berlin, *Four Essays*, xv; the "Hume-Mill-Schlick-Ayer" label appears in Hospers, "What Means This Freedom?" 140.

5. For an especially clear and recent statement of this well-established picture of Hume's "compatibilist commitments", as presented in the more general literature on free will, see Honderich, *Consequences of Determinism*, 88–106, and *How Free Are You?*, 95–101. Honderich says, "Hume, although he is sometimes cited as the founder of the tradition of Compatibilism, of freedom as voluntariness, does not advance greatly beyond Hobbes in fundamental conceptions" (*Consequences of Determinism*, 90–92).

6. In the context of explaining Hume's compatibilism, Penelhum says, "Compatibilism is the thesis that there is no inconsistency in holding that human actions are caused and yet are free. This is a logical thesis, normally combined with the substantive claim that our actions always *are* caused, and that they are sometimes free as well" ("Hume's Moral Psychology", 129).

7. See, e.g., Flew, *Hume's Philosophy of Belief*, 156–58, and Stroud, *Hume*, 153–54. Both Flew and Stroud, in their particularly influential discussions of Hume on this subject, emphasize the "verbal" or "conceptual" nature of Hume's concerns, as distinct from his empirical project of a "science of man".

8. Flew, *Hume's Philosophy of Belief*, chp. 7; MacNabb, *David Hume*, 199–203; Ayer, *Hume*, 75–78; Stroud, *Hume*, chp. 7; Mackie, *Ethics: Inventing Right and Wrong*, 245; Penelhum, *Hume*, 117–22, and "Hume's Moral Psychology," 129–32.

9. The only exception to this is my "On the Naturalism of Hume's 'Reconciling Project'". (See also Flew's reply to my paper and my own rejoinder to Flew.) It is worth noting that, not only has there been no book-length study of Hume's influential views on freedom and responsibility, there is also surprisingly little in the way of substantial journal literature devoted to these matters. Most of the basic literature on this subject has taken the form of book chapters or passages in larger studies of Hume's philosophy.

10. For recent references to Hume's views on freedom and responsibility that present him in this light, see, e.g., Wolf, *Freedom within Reason*, 26–35, and Double, *The Non-Reality of Free Will*, 27–31. (The newer form of compatibilism which Wolf and Double have principally in mind is the "hierarchical account" advanced by such philosophers as Frankfurt and Watson.)

11. Of course, there may still be considerable interest and value in studying the principles and development of the classical compatibilist tradition so that we may properly grasp how the contemporary debate has evolved. Accordingly, even if (as I will argue) the classical reading is mistaken, we still need a proper understanding of Hume's arguments *so interpreted*. The ongoing importance of Hume's writings on the subject of free will in this respect can hardly be denied. The extent of Hume's influence in this area can easily be gauged simply by noting the frequency with which selections of Hume on "liberty and necessity" continue to appear in introductory text books. These selections have served as the general basis on which several generations of philosophy students have been taught the fundamental principles of classical compatibilism. However, suffice it to say at this point that one of the reasons why Hume's views on this subject have been seriously misrepresented is precisely because what he has to say on the subject of "liberty and necessity" has generally been read in isolation from the other parts of his philosophical system in which it belongs.

12. For a succinct and clear statement of this account of the relationship between the history of ideas and the history of philosophy, see Williams, *Descartes: The Project of Pure Enquiry*, 9.

13. For a further statement of Hume's wider attitude to life and the place of philosophy within human life, see the last paragraph of his essay "The Sceptic" (ESY, 180).

I

THE NECESSITY
OF MORAL SENTIMENT

This affords an argument, which the advocates for liberty have urged in its full
force, against the doctrine of necessity. They reason thus: If actions be necessary, and not in our own power, and if we know it to be so, what ground can
there be for reprehension and blame, for self-condemnation and remorse? . . .
This difficulty is great, and never has been surmounted by the advocates for
necessity. They endeavour to surmount it, by reconciling feeling to philosophic
truth, in the following manner. We are so constituted, they say, that certain affections, and the actions which proceed from them, appear odious and base; and
others agreeable and lovely; that, wherever they are beheld, either in ourselves
or others, the moral sense necessarily approves of the one, and condemns the
other; that this approbation is immediate and instinctive, without any reflection
on the liberty or necessity of actions.

Kames, *Essays on the Principles of Morality and Natural Religion*

1

Logic, "Liberty", and the Metaphysics of Responsibility

Liberty, when oppos'd to necessity, not to constraint, is the same thing with chance.

Hume, *An Enquiry concerning Human Understanding*

In effect it would be very singular that all nature, all the planets, should obey eternal laws, and that there should be a little animal five foot high, who, in contempt of these laws, could act as he pleases, solely according to his caprice.

Voltaire, *The Ignorant Philosopher*

Hume's discussion of the problem of "liberty and necessity" was first presented in the *Treatise* (II, iii, 1–2) and, then, in a slightly amended form, in the first *Enquiry* (Sec. 8). It is widely held that what Hume has to say on the subject of the nature and conditions of moral responsibility is very largely limited to these important sections of his work. More specifically, Hume's concern with the problem of moral responsibility is generally interpreted in terms of his discussion of the nature of "liberty," or moral freedom, and the way in which it is related to causation and necessity. From this perspective, once we have acquired a proper grasp of Hume's arguments that show how liberty and necessity are related (i.e. that they are compatible), there is little else to learn from him about the nature and conditions of moral responsibility.[1]

This general perspective on Hume's views on responsibility suggests that Hume, like many other philosophers writing on this subject, believes that the problem of responsibility just *is* the problem of "free will and determinism". According to this approach, any adequate interpretation and discussion of moral responsibility must begin with, or develop out of, some relevant and appropriate account of the nature of moral freedom. I believe that this perspective on Hume's views on responsibility fundamentally misrepresents his approach. Nevertheless, what Hume has to say on the subject of "free will" has been enormously influential, and it is appropriate, therefore, that we begin our discussion of Hume's views on responsibility with an analysis of his specific arguments on the subject of free will.

In his discussion of liberty and necessity, Hume draws the following three conclusions:

1. Necessity, properly understood, is the constant conjunction of objects and the inference of the mind from one object to the other. Let us call the argument which seeks to establish this conclusion the 'necessity argument'.[2]

11

2. A liberty which means "a negation of necessity and causes" (T, 407) has no existence and would make morality impossible. Let us call the argument which seeks to establish this conclusion the 'antilibertarian argument'.

3. Actions that are liable to moral evaluation are not distinguished from those that are not by an *absence* of cause but rather by a *different type* of cause. Responsible or morally free actions are caused by our willings, whereas unfree actions are brought about by causes external to the agent. Let us call the argument that seeks to establish this conclusion the 'spontaneity argument'.

It will be convenient to refer to the strategy developed on the basis of all three of these arguments as Hume's 'compatibilist strategy' and also to refer to the spontaneity and antilibertarian arguments jointly as the 'liberty arguments'. These two arguments set out to differentiate two rival conceptions of moral freedom and to provide a defence of one conception and a refutation of the other. I will present the classical interpretation of these arguments and indicate, in general terms, certain difficulties that arise for them. In the chapters that follow, I argue that the nature and significance of these arguments, and the way in which they are related to the necessity argument, have been substantially misrepresented by the classical interpretation.

I

Most interpretations of Hume's compatibilist strategy place heavy emphasis on the liberty arguments and thereby suggest that Hume's views on the subject of *liberty* serve as the key to his "reconciling project" (EU, 95).[3] It is also widely held that the liberty arguments can be understood without reference to the specifics or details of the necessity argument and hence that Hume's views concerning freedom and responsibility are largely independent of *his particular understanding* of causation and necessity. Clearly, then, on this view of things, in order to understand Hume's compatibilist strategy we must begin by considering what he has to say about the nature of liberty.

Hume's views on the meaning of "liberty" vary between the *Treatise* and the *Enquiry*. In the *Treatise*, Hume claims to have proved "that liberty and chance are synonimous" (T, 412; see also T, 407–8). Accordingly, in that work he is not so much concerned to "reconcile" liberty and necessity as to deny the existence of the former. In light of this, he tends to identify 'liberty' with "liberty of indifference", an idea of liberty "which means a negation of necessity and causes", rather than with "liberty of spontaneity", a liberty "which is oppos'd to [external] violence" (T, 407). We find, then, that the young Hume readily presents himself as an adherent of the "necessitarian" position (i.e. as he understands it).

In the *Enquiry*, by contrast, Hume tries to sound a more balanced note. In the first place, he does not employ the terminology of "liberty of indifference" and "liberty of spontaneity". Instead, he provides a defence of what he terms "hypothetical liberty" (EU, 95). Hypothetical liberty, however, is essentially the same as "liberty of spontaneity". As a result of this change in his terminology, Hume's discussion in the *Enquiry* is presented as a "reconciling project" rather than a refutation of "the doctrine of liberty or chance" (T, 412).[4]

This difference between the two discussions can, nevertheless, be exaggerated. Hume makes it clear in the *Treatise* that liberty of spontaneity is "the most common sense of the word" and that it is "only that species of liberty, which it concerns us to preserve" (T, 407–8). Clearly, then, there is also a "reconciling project" implicit in the discussion of the *Treatise*. Hence Hume's change of terminology in the *Enquiry* does not affect the substance of his position.[5]

Both the spontaneity and the antilibertarian arguments are, as I have suggested, primarily concerned to identify and eliminate our confusions on the subject of liberty. The spontaneity argument, it is claimed, presents us with a viable or philosophically defensible interpretation of moral freedom. Hume maintains that liberty, properly understood, is simply "a power of acting or not acting according to the determinations of the will" (EU, 95).[6] This is liberty of spontaneity or hypothetical liberty. When we enjoy liberty of this kind, then, "if we choose to remain at rest, we may; if we choose to move, we also may". This sort of liberty is to be contrasted not with causation and necessity but rather with force or constraint. Only those who are in prison or in chains lack this sort of freedom (EU, 95; cf. T, 406–7). Hume's point is that free actions are those which are caused by our willings or choices. We hold an agent responsible because it was *his* desires or willings which were the determining *causes* of the action in question. There is, therefore, no incompatibility between, on the one hand, an action's being caused or determined and, on the other hand, an action's being a free action for which an agent is fully responsible. Morally free and responsible action requires that an agent be connected to his actions through his willings. If an action is the result of external violence or constraint, then, although it may be necessitated or caused, it is not the result of the agent's will, and hence it cannot be attributed to him. In these circumstances, the agent is forced or compelled to act, and, therefore, he is not responsible for his actions. In short, the spontaneity argument seeks to establish that free action is to be distinguished from unfree action not by the *absence* of cause (as is suggested by conceptions of liberty of indifference) but rather by a different *type* of cause.

On this interpretation, the spontaneity argument involves two important conditions—one "positive" and the other "negative". The positive condition requires that a free or responsible action must be one to which the agent is "linked" or "connected" through his willings or desires. In the absence of this requirement, the agent cannot be said to produce or bring about his actions at all. Such actions simply "happen to" or "befall" the agent; they are not *his*.

The negative condition requires that a free or responsible action be one which was not compelled or constrained by "external" forces. It is concerned to establish that in the presence of such compelling or constraining external forces, the agent cannot be said to be acting freely and, therefore, cannot be responsible for the action in question. According to the spontaneity argument, in order to determine whether or not the agent is acting freely, we must first identify the *nature of the cause of his actions*. Clearly, then, the fundamental distinction drawn by the spontaneity argument between causation and compulsion serves as the basis of the compatibilist account of the relevant "positive" and "negative" conditions of freedom and responsibility.

Hume's antilibertarian argument draws on, or develops out of, several of the basic features of the spontaneity argument. The antilibertarian argument purports to have found a fatal flaw in the libertarian position. Liberty of indifference, as we have noted, is "that which means a negation of necessity and causes". Such a libertarian view holds that it is a necessary condition of moral responsibility that the act was *not* necessitated or caused. But such a freedom, claims Hume, is nothing on which moral responsibility could rest. If one removes necessity from actions, then one thereby removes causes as well, and this "is the very same thing with chance" (T, 407; cf. EU, 96 and T, 171). It seems clear that we cannot hold someone responsible for an action which just happened, an action he contributed nothing to. Such an action would be totally random and could be as little attributed to the agent as it could be to anything or anybody else. If an agent enjoyed this sort of liberty, he would have no power to determine his actions one way or the other. His actions, being uncaused, would be outside his control. As Hume puts it, where actions "proceed not from some cause in the character and disposition of the person who performed them, they can neither redound to his honour, if good, nor infamy, if evil" (EU, 98). For the libertarian, therefore, there is a serious difficulty in giving a plausible account of the mechanism or source of responsibility.

According to the classical interpretation, these two arguments (i.e the liberty arguments) are principally concerned with the *logic* of our concepts of moral freedom and responsibility. That is to say, they involve a priori reflections about the *meanings* of the *terms* involved. They do not rely on any empirical observations regarding the nature and circumstances, or the moral psychology involved, in actual ascriptions of responsibility. Hume's arguments, on this account, are not viewed as *part* of his "science of man" but rather as an attempt to clear up verbal and conceptual confusions that may hinder this enterprise.[7] Hume is understood to be claiming that it would be *illogical* to say that an agent did not cause this action but that we will still hold him responsible for it. Therefore, it is illogical to say that either an uncaused action or an action that is caused by factors external to the agent is nevertheless an action for which the agent may be justly held responsible. It is *logically necessary*, therefore, that a responsible action is one that has been determined by the will of the agent. It is reasonable to hold an agent who has liberty of spontaneity responsible, whereas it is unreasonable to hold an agent responsible for actions that are due to indifference or external violence. This is the essence of the classical interpretation of Hume's compatibilist strategy.

The significance of the spontaneity and antilibertarian arguments, so interpreted, is generally described in terms of the well-known dilemma of determinism. One horn of this dilemma is the argument that if an action was caused or necessitated, then it could not have been done freely, and hence the agent is not responsible for it. The other horn is the argument that if the action was not caused, then it is inexplicable and random, and thus it cannot be attributed to the agent, and hence, again, the agent cannot be responsible for it. In other words, if our actions are caused, then we cannot be responsible for them; if they are not caused, we cannot be responsible for them. Whether we affirm or deny necessity and determinism, it is impossible to make any coherent sense of moral freedom and responsibility.

The antilibertarian argument constitutes one horn of this dilemma. It is on this horn of chance, compatibilists argue, that the libertarian is mortally impaled.[8] The spontaneity argument, by contrast, serves to defend the compatibilist position against those incompatibilist arguments which constitute the other horn of the dilemma (i.e. if an action is necessitated, then it must be unfree, etc.). The compatibilist strategy deploys the spontaneity argument in order to show that the horn of necessity is quite innocuous as regards our moral attitudes and practices. Indeed, given the alternative—the horn of chance—it is claimed that causation and necessity are *absolutely essential* to these attitudes and practices. It is within this general framework of the dilemma of determinism that Hume's liberty arguments have been interpreted and have acquired their contemporary significance.

The spontaneity argument, so interpreted, may be characterized as basically defensive. It is designed to show that necessity poses no threat to freedom and responsibility and that incompatibilist concerns are misplaced. The antilibertarian argument, on the other hand, is designed to show that libertarian conceptions of freedom and responsibility are both inadequate and implausible. In other words, the first argument is designed to show that responsibility can survive on the horn of necessity, and the second argument is designed to show that it cannot survive on the horn of chance. From a historical perspective, the general difficulty with this compatibilist strategy has been that the critical, destructive attack on libertarianism seems to be much more convincing and effective than the effort to defend and articulate an alternative conception of freedom and responsibility. The upshot is that the dilemma of determinism seems to be intractable.

II

Incompatibilist objections to the basic tenets of the spontaneity argument are very familiar, so I will describe them briefly. There are several objections which are distinct but nevertheless closely related.

The first and most obvious objection to the spontaneity argument is that "liberty of spontaneity" is a wholly inadequate conception of moral freedom. Kant, famously, describes this account of moral freedom as a "wretched subterfuge". Freedom of this nature, Kant claims, belongs to a clock that moves its hands by means of internal causes.[9] From the point of view of understanding and accounting for moral freedom and responsibility, the distinction between internal and external causation, he argues, is neither helpful nor relevant. If our will is itself determined by antecedent natural causes, then we are no more accountable for our actions than any other mechanical object whose movements are internally conditioned. Individuals who enjoy nothing more than a liberty of this nature are, the incompatibilist claims, little more than "robots" or "puppets" subject to the play of fate. In these circumstances, the "agent" lacks all autonomy; nothing can be said to be within his control or "up to him". This general line of criticism against the spontaneity argument relates directly to the next two criticisms.

According to incompatibilists, the issue which ought to concern us in this context is not so much whether or not we could have acted otherwise if we had chosen to do so but whether or not we could have *chosen otherwise* given the circumstances. If our choices and willings are themselves determined by antecedent natural causes, then we could never choose otherwise than we actually do.[10] Given the actual circumstances, it seems evident that we (always) *have to* act as we do. We therefore cannot be held responsible for our actions, because there are, on this account, no "genuine alternatives" or "open possibilities" available to us. In this way, given that on this account nobody (actually) could have acted otherwise, it follows that nobody is responsible for his actions. Responsibility, it is argued, requires *categorical* freedom. Hypothetical freedom alone will not suffice. This is, indeed, the crux of the standard incompatibilist attack on compatibilism.[11]

The spontaneity argument also suffers from further difficulties. More specifically, according to the spontaneity argument, the distinction between free and unfree (i.e. compelled) action should be understood in terms of the difference between internal and external causes. Critics of compatibilism argue that this—attractively simple— distinction is impossible to maintain. It seems obvious, for example, that there are cases in which an agent acts according to the determinations of his own will but is nevertheless clearly unfree. There are, in particular, circumstances in which an agent may be subject to, and act on, desires and wants that are themselves *compulsive* in nature. Desires and wants of this kind, it is claimed, limit and undermine an agent's freedom no less than external force and violence. Although it may be true that in these circumstances the agent is acting according to his own desires or willings, it is equally clear that such an agent is neither free nor responsible for his behaviour.[12] It would appear, therefore, that we are required to acknowledge that some causes "internal" to the agent may also be regarded as compelling or constraining. This concession, however, generates serious difficulties for the classical compatibilist strategy. It is no longer evident, given this concession, just which "internal" causes should be regarded as "constraining" or "compelling" and which should not. Clearly, then, as it stands, the spontaneity argument does not provide us with an adequate account of what constitutes a compelling or constraining ("external") cause. Lying behind this objection is the more fundamental concern that the spontaneity argument presupposes a wholly inadequate understanding of the nature of excusing and mitigating considerations. In light of these observations, it seems evident that the distinction between free and unfree action is far more complex than Hume's spontaneity argument suggests. We must conclude, therefore, that Hume's understanding of moral freedom and responsibility is too crude to be helpful and that it cannot account for the distinctions which we need to be able to draw in this sphere.

The spontaneity argument, as Hume presents it, is generally thought to contain the seeds of an essentially forward-looking and utilitarian account of moral responsibility. That is, Hume, following thinkers like Hobbes and Collins, points out that rewards and punishments serve to *cause* people to act in some ways and not in others and that this is clearly a matter of considerable social utility (T, 410; EU, 97–98). Hume's brief remarks on this subject have been further developed by other compatibilists with whom Hume has been closely identified. Moritz Schlick, for example, analyses responsibility in precisely these terms.[13] This sort of forward-looking, utilitarian account of responsibility has been subject to severe and telling criticism. The basic problem with this account, it is argued, is that it is entirely blind to matters of *desert* and thus lacks the required (backward-looking) retributive element demanded in this sphere. Moreover, such a theory of responsibility, critics claim, is at the same time both too wide and too narrow. It is too wide because it would appear to make children and animals responsible; it is too narrow insofar as it would appear to deny that those who are dead, or beyond the reach of the relevant forms of "treatment", can be judged responsible for their actions.[14] In short, all efforts to interpret responsibility along these lines seem to be plagued with difficulties. (It is important to note, however, that this sort of forward-looking, utilitarian account of responsibility goes beyond the core theory implied by the classical interpretation of the spontaneity argument.)

Some compatibilists maintain that these objections are all entirely misguided.[15] Contrary to this view, however, there can be little doubt that these criticisms certainly serve to weaken and discredit the account of freedom and responsibility presented by the spontaneity argument as understood on the classical account. In other words, in light of these criticisms, it seems hard to avoid the conclusion that Hume's account of freedom and responsibility, so interpreted, is both thin and flimsy and must, therefore, be firmly rejected.

III

Whatever difficulties the spontaneity argument encounters, the libertarian is also required to provide some (alternative) account of freedom and responsibility. As I have suggested, any such effort involves confronting Hume's antilibertarian argument. In reply to the various criticisms described above, compatibilists may argue that, whatever its shortcomings, the spontaneity argument seems to offer a plausible solution to the specific difficulties which are raised by the antilibertarian argument. That is, liberty of spontaneity, unlike liberty of indifference, appears to provide us with a fairly straightforward account of the mechanism and source of responsibility (i.e. agents are responsible for their actions insofar as it is their willings and desires that caused them). Libertarians believe that the way to get around the difficulties that the antilibertarian argument poses for them is to attack one or the other of the presuppositions on which Hume's argument rests.

One strategy, for example, has been to argue that actions are not amenable to *causal* explanation.[16] On this basis, it may be argued that the dilemma of determinism is entirely spurious because it is based on false assumptions about the nature of action and explanation. Another strategy has been to attack specific assumptions about the nature of causation which the spontaneity argument relies on. More specifically, such assumptions as "all causes are of the same kind" or "all causes necessitate their effects" may be rejected by libertarians who are developing this line of defence. In this way, we find that some libertarians seek a middle way through the horns of the dilemma by showing that, although actions may be caused, they are nevertheless not necessitated by antecedent conditions.[17]

Clearly, then, libertarians have developed a number of strategies in reply to the antilibertarian argument, and these strategies have the common objective of showing that if we reject the horn of necessity we will not, as the antilibertarian argument suggests, thereby impale ourselves on the horn of chance. Whatever the merits of these replies, however, it is evident that the antilibertarian argument effectively poses some serious and awkward problems for the libertarian insofar as it reveals the extent to which libertarians are required to appeal to metaphysical claims and assumptions that are themselves highly questionable.[18]

Other features of the antilibertarian argument may also be questioned. These are features which draw attention to weaknesses in the overall compatibilist position that have not, in my view, been pressed hard enough by its critics. In particular, there are certain limitations which the antilibertarian argument is subject to that reveal more basic defects in the spontaneity argument.

The success or force of the antilibertarian argument, it seems, depends very largely on a *particular interpretation* of the libertarian position. Contrary to what compatibilists generally suppose, liberty of indifference and liberty of spontaneity may *not* be incompatible with each other. What, then, is the alternative interpretation to be considered? According to the antilibertarian argument (on the classical interpretation), if actions were not caused, then it would be unreasonable to attribute them to the agent or hold the agent responsible for them. The target here is liberty of indifference interpreted, on this account, as the view that our *actions* are uncaused. However, it may be argued that this is not the only position which is available to libertarians or defenders of "free will". They may locate the requisite "break in the causal chain" elsewhere. It is important to distinguish between the following two types of liberty of indifference: a notion of liberty of indifference which suggests that *actions* are not caused or determined by antecedent conditions and a notion of liberty of indifference which suggests that our *willings* are not caused or determined by antecedent conditions (our willings being understood as the causal antecedents of action). For convenience, let us call the first liberty of indifference in acting (LIA) and the second liberty of indifference in willing (LIW). Both of these notions of liberty of indifference are vulnerable to well-known objections, but LIA is open to some objections to which the LIW is not liable.

The libertarian may seek to evade the antilibertarian argument by conceding that our actions must be caused by our antecedent willings, thereby rejecting LIA, but refuse to abandon or reject LIW. By rejecting LIA, the defender of "free will" can avoid the main thrust of the antilibertarian argument, namely, that liberty of indifference would render *actions* random and capricious and would make it impossible to attribute such actions to the agent. Those who accept LIW may, quite consistently, maintain that free action is determined by the antecedent willings of the agent and thus reject any suggestion that they licence random events at the level of *action*. Any randomness that LIW permits (assuming, as we do, that any alternative metaphysical conception of causation is excluded) occurs only at the level of the determination of the *will*.

The presence of random events at the level of *willing* will not prevent an agent from enjoying liberty of spontaneity. Such an agent may well be able to act in accordance with the determinations of her (capricious) will. Nor would it be impossible to attribute actions to such an agent, because it would be *her* (capricious) motives, desires, and so on, which caused them. Clearly, then, liberty of indifference, interpreted in terms of LIW, is compatible with, and thus need not exclude, liberty of spontaneity. It is true that the actions of an agent who enjoys LIW will be quite unpredictable, and it is also true that her future actions will not be amenable to the conditioning influences of punishments and rewards. In this way, LIW is still liable to other serious criticisms (especially if one interprets responsibility in terms of amenability to the conditioning influence of rewards and punishments). However, the actions of an agent who enjoys LIW share much with those of an agent whose will is necessitated by (external) antecedent causes. Liberty of spontaneity does not require that agents be able to determine their own wills, and it therefore makes little difference, on the face of it, whether our wills are determined by external causes or are merely capricious. In this way, it may be argued that the (classical) antilibertarian argument is not straightforwardly effective against the libertarian position when the notion of liberty of indifference is interpreted in terms of LIW rather than LIA.[19]

It is, perhaps, tempting to suggest that the significance of these observations lies with the fact that they reveal certain limitations of the antilibertarian argument and that they may, therefore, open up new avenues of defence for the libertarian position. I believe that the real interest and significance of these observations lies elsewhere. What they bring to light are certain serious inadequacies in the *spontaneity* argument. An agent who enjoys LIW may also enjoy liberty of spontaneity, and this is a point that many defenders of classical compatibilism may find rather awkward and embarrassing. It follows from the fact that liberty of spontaneity is compatible or consistent with LIW that we may reasonably hold an individual responsible for actions caused by her capricious, random willings. Clearly, then, there is, in these circumstances, as much, or as little, reason to hold an agent responsible for actions due to a capricious will as there is to hold an agent responsible for actions that are due to a will that is conditioned by antecedent external causes. Both agents may *equally* enjoy liberty of spontaneity. If we have reason to conclude that LIW constitutes an inadequate foundation for freedom and responsibility, then surely we must also conclude that there is more to freedom and responsibility than liberty of spontaneity. In short, compatibilists must either concede that agents whose actions are due to LIW are nevertheless free and responsible or else acknowledge that the spontaneity argument provides us with an inadequate and incomplete account of freedom and responsibility.[20]

IV

The interpretation of Hume's compatibilist strategy offered so far has been concerned almost entirely with the significance of the liberty arguments and has, therefore, placed heavy emphasis on Hume's distinction between two kinds of liberty. As I have already suggested, many commentators believe that it is Hume's remarks concerning the nature of liberty that serve as the key to his position on this subject. If this were true, then it would certainly be correct to say, as Barry Stroud maintains, that there is little that is new about Hume's "general strategy" and that it is "found in all essential respects in Hobbes".[21] Does Hume's "general strategy" turn very largely on his distinction between two different kinds of liberty?

Two points may be briefly noted, both of which should lead us to question this claim. First, as Stroud notes, Hume explicitly states in the *Abstract* that it is his "new definition of *necessity*" which puts the whole controversy in a "new light" (T, 661). Second, Hume explicitly acknowledges the scholastic origins of the distinction between two kinds of liberty (cf. T, 407). Given this, it would appear that Hume thought that there was something new and *substantially different* about his "reconciling project" and that it is not founded on the (long-established) distinction between two different kinds of liberty.[22] Thus, for the time being, suffice it to note that Hume supposed that his "general strategy" on this subject was in important respects quite different from that of his predecessors. It may be that those commentators who have concentrated their attention on Hume's remarks concerning the nature of 'liberty' have largely missed what Hume regarded as the distinctive features of his "general strategy".[23]

It seems quite clear that what is missing from the interpretation offered so far is that it provides us with no adequate account of the role of the necessity argument.[24] Indeed, it may be argued that without some relevant account of the significance of Hume's necessity argument in this context, we misrepresent not only Hume's views on this subject but also, more generally, the classical compatibilist tradition with which Hume is so closely identified. The mainstream of the classical compatibilist tradition has enthusiastically embraced the basic tenets of Hume's necessity argument and put them to work for the compatibilist position. From this perspective, the necessity argument is understood as an effort to present the liberty arguments in terms of the regularity theory of causation. It is claimed, moreover, that this feature of Hume's strategy greatly *strengthens* the classical compatibilist position, by removing certain *confusions* that constitute important obstacles to a proper understanding of the significance of the liberty arguments. Clearly, then, not only Hume but also many of his most prominent successors (e.g. Mill, Russell, Schlick, Ayer, et al.) believe that it is his arguments concerning the nature of necessity, rather than liberty, that constitute Hume's most lasting and notable contribution on this subject.[25] In light of this, it is obvious that we require a more detailed account of Hume's views on causation and necessity and how they are supposed to relate to the free will controversy.

The fact that some philosophers have recognized, and tried to account for, the significance of Hume's necessity argument for the compatibilist strategy in no way implies that they reject the classical interpretation of the liberty arguments. On the contrary, as I have indicated, there is virtually universal consensus that the classical interpretation of these two arguments is essentially correct and accurately represents Hume's intentions on this matter. This is a point of some importance in that it seems to imply that the liberty arguments can be understood and properly appreciated independently of the necessity argument. The basic points established by these two arguments are that liberty of spontaneity is *logically essential* to ascriptions of responsibility and that liberty of indifference is wholly incompatible with all such ascriptions. In other words, in the absence of causation and necessity, no one could reasonably be held responsible for anything. These basic points involve no direct reference to the specifics or details of Hume's necessity argument as such. It is, clearly, quite possible to argue for these fundamental points concerning the nature of liberty or moral freedom on the basis of something other than the regularity theory of causation (as, for example, Hobbes does). It would seem, therefore, that the spontaneity and antilibertarian arguments, so interpreted, are entirely independent of the necessity argument.

The upshot of these observations concerning the relations between the necessity argument, on the one hand, and the liberty arguments, on the other, is that although the necessity argument is held to be entirely *consistent* with the other two arguments, it is in no way essential to an adequate understanding or interpretation of them.[26]

Contrary to what Hume appears to suggest, therefore, some of the most basic features of his "reconciling project" (i.e. the liberty arguments) neither involve nor depend on his "new definition of necessity". This is, obviously enough, rather surprising.

In the chapters that follow I argue, first, that Hume's necessity argument is indeed *inconsistent* with the *classical* interpretation of the liberty arguments and, second, that when these two arguments are properly interpreted (i.e. along different lines from that suggested on the classical account), it becomes clear that the necessity argument is in fact essential to a proper understanding and appreciation of Hume's intentions regarding them. In other words, I will be concerned to show that the classical interpretation of the liberty arguments entirely misrepresents the nature and character of Hume's compatibilist strategy and, in particular, that it misrepresents and misunderstands how these arguments are related to Hume's necessity argument.

Notes

1. See, e.g., Stroud, *Hume*, 153.

2. This formulation of the conclusion of the necessity argument requires some explanation. Being a *conjunction* of constant conjunction and the inference of the mind, this formulation accords with Hume's remarks at the beginning of his discussion of "liberty and necessity": "Here then are two particulars, which we are to consider essential to necessity, viz. the constant union *and* the inference of the mind; and wherever we discover these we must acknowledge a necessity" (T, 400; my emphasis). However, clearly this formulation does vary from the *disjunctive* formulation of the "two definitions" passage: "I define necessity two ways. . . . I place it *either* in the constant union and conjunction of like objects, *or* in the inference of the mind from one to the other" (T, 409; my emphasis). How is this difference to be accounted for? I believe that in the context of Hume's discussion of free will it is of little significance. In the *Enquiry*, Hume completes his account of the "two definitions" by remarking that both these senses of necessity "are at bottom the same" (EU, 97). Evidently, Hume takes the view that whenever we discover a constant conjunction in the objects (i.e. as represented by our perceptions), then we will also find an inference of the mind. This psychological fact about the human mind perhaps explains why Hume regards the two senses of necessity as "at bottom the same" and also why he feels free to slip between the disjunctive and conjunctive formulations of necessity in this context. (This general matter is discussed at length in chp. 2.)

3. For example, O'Connor, *Free Will*, 72–73. O'Connor notes that an "early statement" of the compatibilist or soft determinist position can be found in Hobbes's *Leviathan*. He claims, rightly, that Hobbes's "main point" is that "free action is not to be contrasted with action that is caused but with action that is compelled". He goes on to say that "this approach was developed in subtle detail by David Hume". Such an interpretation clearly takes the liberty of indifference/liberty of spontaneity distinction to be the key to Hume's "reconciling project". O'Conner's remarks are, I believe, entirely representative of most philosophers' understanding of Hume's position on this issue. (See also, e.g., Stroud, *Hume*, 144–46.)

4. On this, see Flew, *Hume's Philosophy of Belief*, 140–42.

5. It should also be noted that in the *Enquiry* Hume sometimes identifies "liberty" with liberty of indifference, contrary to what we would expect in this context. See, e.g., EU, 94n: "The prevalence of the doctrine of liberty . . ."; and EU, 99: "No contingency anywhere in the universe; no indifference; no liberty". In neither work, therefore, is the term "liberty" employed in a wholly uniform manner.

6. Clearly, Hume's account of "liberty" or freedom is very similar to that offered by some of his predecessors—most notably Hobbes, Locke, and Anthony Collins.

7. See, e.g., Stroud, *Hume*, 153–54, and Flew, *Hume's Philosophy of Belief*, 156–58. Flew says, "Since he conceived of his *Inquiries* as contributions to descriptive moral science, real problems were those which he could think of as belonging to 'an attempt to introduce the experimental method of reasoning into moral subjects' and, in particular, to the development of a would be Newtonian science of man. The reconciliation of liberty and necessity fails to rate, because he cannot see it as either factual or explanatory".

8. Of course, not all those who hold that libertarian "free will" cannot support ascriptions of responsibility need also be compatibilists. On the contrary, some critics of libertarianism may also be incompatibilists. They maintain that whether or not our actions are necessitated, we cannot be responsible for them, and, hence, they regard the dilemma of determinism as intractable.

9. Kant, *Critique of Practical Reason*, 189–90. (Kant's metaphor of the workings of a clock for compatibilist freedom was quite common throughout the eighteenth century.)

10. Reid expresses the difficulty as follows: "If the physical laws of nature make [man's] obedience to the moral laws to be impossible, then he is, in the literal sense, *born under one law, bound unto another*, which contradicts every notion of a righteous government of the world" (*Active Powers*, 337 [Essay IV, chp. 9]).

11. The literature on this subject is vast. Stroud suggests that this is the most serious difficulty that confronts Hume's "reconciling project" and that Hume does little to address or account for the problem (*Hume*, 148–53). An influential compatibilist effort to evade this difficulty, by way of providing a conditional account of "could have done otherwise", can be found in Moore, *Ethics*, chp. 6. The standard statement of the Kantian-libertarian view on this matter can be found in Campbell, "Is 'Freewill' a Pseudo-Problem?" A great deal of the contemporary "free will" debate has been concerned with this general issue.

12. See, e.g., Ayer, "Freedom and Necessity", 20. Ayer—an apparent follower of Hume on this subject—acknowledges that the actions of a kleptomaniac are psychologically compelled.

13. Schlick, "When Is a Man Responsible?" 60.

14. For criticisms of this nature, see, for example, Bradley, *Ethical Studies*, esp. 26–33; Campbell, "Is 'Freewill' a Pseudo-Problem?" 113–17; Berlin, *Four Essays*, xv.

15. Consider, for example, the following remarks from Davidson, "Freedom to Act", 63: "There are broadsides from those who believe they can see, or even prove, that freedom is inconsistent with the assumption that actions are causally determined, at least if the causes can be traced back to events outside the agent. . . . I know of none that is more than superficially plausible. Hobbes, Locke, Hume, Moore, Schlick, Ayer, Stevenson, and a host of others have done what can be done, or ought ever to have been needed, to remove the confusions that can make determinism seem to frustrate freedom".

16. One variant of this particular strategy has been to argue that the "rational explanation" of action is sui generis and does not conform to the empiricist "covering law" model of explanation. See, e.g., Dray, "Historical Explanation of Actions Reconsidered", 87: "The incompatibility of representing actions. . .".

17. See, e.g., Richard Taylor, "Determinism and the Theory of Agency", 227–28. Taylor argues that if we are to "salvage moral responsibility", we require a theory of agency which "involves an extraordinary conception of causation, according to which something that is not an event can nevertheless bring about an event". Obviously, on this theory, actions are not caused by antecedent conditions. Thus the theory of agency also "involves the conception of a self or person (i.e. an agent) that is not merely a congeries or series of states or events". A slightly different strategy is pursued by Sorabji, *Necessity, Cause and Blame*. Sorabji suggests that morally free (i.e. responsible) actions may be caused by antecedent causes, such as our motives and desires, but argues that these causes need not be determining or necessitating causes. (I criticize this strategy in "Sorabji and the Dilemma of Determinism".) Of re-

lated interest, see Wiggins, "Towards a Reasonable Libertarianism", 50–56, and Van Inwagen, *An Essay on Free Will*, 138–50. Sorabji, Wiggins, and Van Inwagen base their discussions on Anscombe, "Causality and Determination"—an influential attack on Humean theories of causation.

18. Some libertarians frankly acknowledge this point. See, e.g., Van Inwagen, *An Essay on Free Will*, 150: "I must choose between . . .".

19. It is worth pointing out that many libertarians do in fact defend some version of LIA rather than LIW. That is, traditional libertarians (e.g. Kantians) usually argue that our *actions* are (somehow) determined by our (metaphysical) "self". This version of libertarianism is, I suggest, particularly vulnerable to Hume's antilibertarian argument.

20. We might think of an individual who enjoys LIW as being akin to an extreme case of multiple personality—although such people act according to their own will, we can never tell what that will is going to be. From another perspective, such a person may be regarded as having no discernable personality or character at all. There is considerable evidence that Hume would be very reluctant to accept the suggestion that an agent who enjoys LIW should be regarded as a free and responsible agent. For example, in the *Treatise* (T, 404), Hume points out that the actions of "mad-men" seem on the face of it to be entirely "irregular" and unpredictable. Few people, however, believe that these individuals are free or responsible. In other words, according to Hume, indifference of this sort seems to be incompatible with freedom and responsibility properly understood. Someone who enjoys LIW might well be regarded as "mad" insofar as his behaviour would, indeed, be wholly irregular and unpredictable. Nevertheless, as I have shown, it is not obvious that such "mad-men" never enjoy liberty of spontaneity.

21. Stroud, *Hume*, 153. Even as it stands this claim is rather ungenerous insofar as it gives little recognition to Hume's specific effort to develop and articulate the antilibertarian argument.

22. The liberty of indifference/liberty of spontaneity distinction was well-established in the free will literature of the early eighteenth century. For an especially notable example of this, see Bayle, *Dictionary*, art. "Rorarius", note F; see also King, *Origin of Evil*, chp. 5, sec. 1, and Leibniz, *Theodicy*, Pt. 3, esp. secs. 288–320.

23. As I will explain in more detail in the following three chapters, Hume thought that Hobbes's strategy failed because it did not touch on the fundamental difficulties associated with our idea of "necessity". It is for this reason that Hume was certain that his "new definition of necessity" would put an end to the dispute.

24. Many Hume scholars are aware that we are liable to misrepresent Hume's position on this subject if we ignore or downplay the relevance which his views on the nature of necessity have for his compatibilist strategy. Penelhum, for example, notes that it is not Hume's "attempt to use the concept of necessity in the analysis of human actions, but his criticism of the doctrine of liberty that has been most influential" (*Hume*, 120). See also Flew, *Hume's Philosophy of Belief*, 142.

25. See, e.g., Schlick's remarks in praise of Hume in "When Is a Man Responsible?" 54.

26. From the perspective of the classical account, therefore, any interpretation of Hume's compatibilist arguments that overlooks the significance of the necessity argument must be rejected, not because it misrepresents the other two arguments but only because it gives us an *incomplete* picture of Hume's overall position on free will.

2

Minding the Matter of Necessity:
A Paradox Regarding Causation

I am sensible, that of all the paradoxes, which I have had, or shall hereafter have occasion to advance in the course of this treatise, the present one is the most violent.

Hume, *A Treatise of Human Nature*

He may well admit this doctrine to be a violent paradox, because in reality, it contradicts our natural feelings, and wages war with the common sense of mankind.

Kames, *Essays on the Principles of Morality and Natural Religion*

The details of Hume's views on causation and necessity are notoriously enigmatic, and scholarly interpretations of his position vary greatly.[1] Clearly, an understanding of his views cannot be taken for granted.[2]

In the *Abstract*, Hume makes the following remarks concerning necessity and the free will problem:

> Our author [Hume] pretends, that this reasoning puts the whole controversy in a new light, by giving a new definition of necessity. And, indeed, the most zealous advocates for free-will must allow this union and inference with regard to human actions. They will only deny, that this makes the whole of necessity. But then they must shew, that we have an idea of *something else in the actions of matter*; which, according to the foregoing reasoning, is impossible. (T, 661; my emphasis)

These remarks of Hume's are both important and illuminating. First, they plainly indicate that Hume believed that a proper understanding of the nature of necessity is essential if we are to resolve the free will controversy. Second, they are also indicative of Hume's belief that it is because of our experience of the "actions of *matter*" that we are naturally reluctant to accept that necessity is nothing but "union and inference". In this chapter, I am principally concerned to explain the latter feature of Hume's system—an aspect of his thought which, although of central importance to an understanding of his views, has nevertheless been almost entirely overlooked by commentators. This failure to appreciate Hume's specific concern with causation as it appears in matter or bodies explains, in some measure, the confusion regarding his position on free will.

In my presentation and analysis of Hume's views on causation and necessity, I emphasize, for reasons which become apparent, the significance of the *development* of Hume's thought on this subject. I begin, accordingly, by focussing attention on Hume's discussion in Book I of the *Treatise* and then move on to consider his later views as presented in the *Abstract*, the Appendix (Bk. III), and the first *Enquiry*. Throughout this chapter, however, it is my particular objective to establish and clarify Hume's original intentions in his discussion of causation in Book I of the *Treatise*. I show that Hume's views on ontology, as presented in Part iv of that Book, shed light on his views on causation as presented in Part iii. Further, I argue that Hume's views on ontology account for the original motivation behind his two definitions of cause. This relationship between Hume's ontology and his account of causation explains something that has baffled Hume scholars for some time, namely, why Hume's discussion of causation in the *Treatise* (I, iii, 14) has such a paradoxical air about it. I show that it is because it rests on an ontology of "double existence"—an ontology which Hume describes as the "monstrous offspring of two principles, which are contrary to each other, which are both at once embraced by the mind, and which are unable mutually to destroy each other" (T, 215). Finally, I argue that these observations, concerning the relationship between "double ontology" and the two modes of causation and necessity, explain why Hume believes that it is our experience of the "actions of *matter*" that lead to such confusion and perplexity on this subject. According to Hume, if we can identify and eliminate *this* source of confusion and perplexity in our thinking, then we can also position ourselves to overcome the free will problem which has been with us for so long.

My interpretation centres on the following two claims:

1. When Hume wrote Section 14, "Of the idea of necessary connexion", he was *primarily* concerned to attack the view that the origin of our idea of necessity was to be discovered in the operations of matter or bodies. Of the suggested sources from which our idea of necessity could be thought to originate, this is the source which, initially, interested Hume the most. It is, therefore, of great importance that we interpret Hume's remarks in light of this fact.

2. Hume offers the first definition of cause as an account of causation as it exists in the material world "independent of our thought and reasoning". He offers the second definition as an account of causation as we find it in our perceptions. In this context, I will argue that necessity constitutes "an essential part" of *both* of Hume's definitions of cause.

I

In *Letter from a Gentleman*, Hume replies to several criticisms and objections raised against the doctrines of the *Treatise*. Two of these objections concern the "atheistic" implications of Hume's views on causation. It is objected, in particular, that Hume casts doubt on the principle that "the Deity is the prime Mover of the Universe, who first created Matter, and gave its original Impulse, and likewise supports its Existence, and successively bestows on it its Motions" (LG, 12). In reply to this, Hume makes some brief remarks about the history of the debate concerning our idea of "force or power" (i.e. necessity):

When men considered the several Effects and Operations of Nature, they were led to examine into the Force or Power by which they were performed . . . all the ancient Philosophers agreed, that there was *a real Force in Matter. . . . No one, until Des Cartes and Malebranche, ever entertained an Opinion that Matter had no Force.* . . . These Philosophers last-mentioned substituted the Notion of occasional Causes . . . [but this opinion] never gained great Credit, especially in England, where it was considered as too much contrary to received popular Opinions, and too little supported by Philosophical Arguments, ever to be admitted as any Thing but a mere Hypothesis. (LG, 27–28; my emphasis)

These remarks indicate that Hume believed there was a close connexion between our supposition that there is a "real force in matter" and the question concerning the origin of our idea of necessity. In what way does Hume believe that these issues are related? An examination of the relevant passages of the *Treatise* will clarify Hume's position.

In Section 14, Hume returns to the question he raised in Section 2 (T, 77): From what impression does our idea of necessary connexion originate? Hume is faced with the difficulty that given his theory of meaning if no such impression can be found, then this term must be meaningless. Hume comes to consider three possible sources of our idea of necessity before presenting his own account: "the known qualities of matter" (T, 157–59); "the deity" (T, 159–60); and "the will" (T, 632–33—this being appended to T, 161).

The most obvious differences between the section entitled "Of the idea of necessary connexion" in the *Treatise* and its counterpart in the first *Enquiry* is that the former is mostly concerned with the first suggested source of our idea of necessity, whereas the latter places the most emphasis on the third source. In the *Treatise*, Hume is primarily concerned to refute the claim that our idea has its source in the "known qualities of matter", whereas in the *Enquiry* he is more concerned to refute the claim that its origin is to be found by reflecting on our willings. This change of emphasis is not without significance and is of some importance in coming to an understanding of Hume's views on causation as he originally put them forward in Book I of the *Treatise*.[3]

It was only *after* Hume wrote and published Books I and II (January 1739) that he came to discuss the third possible source of our idea of necessity. The view that our idea of necessity or power is derived from our reflection on our willings is to be found in Locke's *Essay*:

Bodies, by our Senses, do not afford us so clear and distinct an Idea of active Power, as we have from reflection on the Operations of our Minds. . . . The Idea of the beginning of motion, we have only from reflection on what passes in our selves, where we find by Experience, that barely by willing it, barely by a thought of the Mind, we can move the parts of our Bodies, which were before at rest. (*Essay*, 235 [II, xxi, 4])

This suggestion of Locke's was first expressly considered by Hume in the *Abstract* (published in March 1740), where he deals with it tersely: "Now our minds afford us no more notion of energy than matter does. When we consider our will or volition *a priori*, abstracting from experience, we should never be able to infer any effect from it. And when we take the assistance of experience, it only shows us objects contiguous, successive and constantly conjoined" (T, 656–57). This argument is somewhat expanded in the Appendix to the *Treatise* (published with Book III in November 1740). Here again he argues "that the will being here consider'd as a cause, has no more discoverable connexion with its effects, than any material cause has with its proper effects" (T, 632). By the time the first *Enquiry* was published, eight years later (April 1748), Locke's suggestion had come to preoccupy Hume (see EU, VII, i). However, even up to the time of writing the Appendix, Hume retained his original view that the most natural and plausible place to look for the origin of our idea of necessity is in external objects or matter: "No *internal impression has an apparent energy, more than external objects have.* Since, therefore, *matter* is confess'd by philosophers to operate by an unknown force, we shou'd in vain hope to attain an idea of force by consulting our own minds" (T, 633; my emphasis).

Further evidence of Hume's primary concern in Book I with matter considered as a source of our idea of necessity can be found in his discussion of liberty and necessity in Book II. In that discussion, Hume regards his opponents as taking the view that, although there can be little doubt that necessity exists in the material world, it does not exist in the realm of our thought and action. Accordingly, Hume begins his discussion by describing necessity as it exists in the operations of bodies. Hume suggests that his opponents may "refuse to call [constant union and inference of the mind] necessity" because they assume that "there is something else *in the operations of matter*" (T, 410; my emphasis; see also T, 661, as cited above, which makes much the same point). Hume goes on to point out to his opponents that they should be careful not to take him to be ascribing "to the will that unintelligible necessity, *which is supposed to lie in matter*" (T, 410; my emphasis). I believe there can be little doubt that it is this "unintelligible necessity which is supposed to lie in matter" which serves as Hume's prime target in Book I.[4]

Hume notes in the *Abstract* that he confines most of his remarks "to the relation of cause and effect, as discovered in the motions and operations of matter" (T, 655). This reflects the emphasis that we find in Book I. Although he believes that "the same reasoning extends to the operations of mind" and that the causal relation remains the same between both internal and external objects, his attention was, at that time, firmly fixed on the case of matter.[5]

Why was Hume initially preoccupied with the case of matter? Why did he fail to consider Locke's suggestion in Book I? It has already been pointed out that he was impressed by the fact that most philosophers, including many of his contemporaries, believed there was "a real force in matter". Obviously, this was a deeply entrenched, traditional supposition which had to be swept away if his own (alternative) account was to be accepted. More important, Hume also thought it was quite plausible to suggest that our experience of the material world is the source of our idea of necessity. Evidence that he took this view is to be found in an objection he raises against his own position:

> What! the efficacy of causes lie in the determination of the mind! As if causes did
> not operate entirely independent of the mind, and would not continue their opera-

tion, even tho' there was no mind existent to contemplate them, or reason concerning them. *Thought may very well depend on causes for its operation, but not causes on thought.* This is to reverse the order of nature, and to make that secondary, which is really primary. (T, 167; my emphasis)[6]

Hume held that we naturally suppose that there exists an independent, external world of bodies. These bodies are taken to exist quite independently of mind and are also supposed to operate on one another independently of our thoughts about them (cf. T, 195–97). In this way, it seems quite *natural* to suppose that the efficacy of causes lies in matter. The two suppositions are connected.[7]

There is also some evidence that Hume misunderstood Locke's position insofar as Hume misrepresents Locke's views about the origin of our idea of necessary connexion. That is, it seems that Hume initially took Locke to be as much of a rationalist with regard to the origin of our idea of necessity as he rightly took him to be with regard to the causal maxim (cf. T, 81 with *Essay*, 620 [IV, x, 3]). Locke suggests that we get the idea of necessity (or power, to use his term) in two ways:

> Power also is another of those simple Ideas, which we receive from Sensation and Reflection. For observing in our selves, that we can, at pleasure, move several parts of our Bodies, which were at rest; the effects also, that natural Bodies are able to produce in one another, occurring every moment to our Senses, *we both these ways get the Idea of Power.* (*Essay*, 131 [II, vii, 8])

The order in which Locke places these two sources of our idea of power is not without significance. As I have already noted, Locke is committed to the view that the first source is of greater importance, because "bodies, by our senses, do not afford us so clear and distinct an idea of *active* power, as we have from reflection on the operations of our minds". Despite this, in Book I Hume discusses only the second and less important of Locke's two suggestions.

> I believe the most general and most popular explication of this matter [the origin of our idea of necessity], is to say [here Hume adds the footnote: "See Mr. Locke; chapter of power."], that there are several new productions in *matter*, such as the motions and variations of *body*, and concluding that there must somewhere be a power capable of producing them, we *arrive at last by this reasoning at the idea of power and efficacy.* (T, 157; my emphasis)

This passage provides further evidence of Hume's primary concern in Book I with the suggestion that our idea of necessity originates with our observations of the operations of matter. Against this suggestion of Locke's, Hume argues that no reasoning can give rise to any original idea (a point which he notes in the *Enquiry* that Locke would accept: EU, 64n).

Nowhere in Book I does Hume even mention Locke's first and more important suggestion. That is to say, of the two proposed solutions to this problem which Locke put forward, Hume, in Book I, attacks the one Locke clearly regards as being of the least importance. Evidently, Hume came to realize, shortly after Books I and II were published, that he had misrepresented Locke's position and that Locke's alternative account of the origin of our idea of necessity (i.e. reflection on our willings) raised difficulties for his own views which he would need to address.[8]

II

Let us now try to reconstruct Hume's problem in the *Treatise* (I, iii, 14) as he originally saw it when he wrote that passage. Given that in this section he does not discuss Locke's suggestion, his view of the problem must centre on two points. First, Hume accepted the negative conclusion of the "Cartesians" that to all appearances matter "is endowed with no efficacy" and therefore cannot be the source of our idea of necessity. Second, he rejected the "occasionalist" claim of Malebranche that God is "the prime mover of the universe". Against this suggestion, Hume points out that we have "no idea of power or efficacy in any object", because in "neither body nor spirit" are we able to discover a single instance of it.

Hume here seems to be in agreement with Locke's remarks:

> If we are at this loss in respect to the Powers, and Operations of Bodies, I think it is easy to conclude, *we are much more in the dark in reference to Spirits*; whereof we naturally have no Ideas, but what we draw from that of our own, by reflecting on the Operations of our own Souls within us, as far as they can come within our Observation. (*Essay*, 548 [IV, iii, 17])

In other words, looking to "spirits" (i.e. spirits other than ourselves), such as God, for the origin of our idea of necessary connexion is *even less* likely to be of any help to us.[9] Hume's rather disparaging remarks in his subsequent writings concerning the attempts of occasionalists to resolve the problem they generated by robbing matter of its power and efficacy make it clear that he never thought that their "hypothesis" was even a starter.[10]

In this way, the problem which Hume sets himself to resolve is this: having failed to find the origin of our idea of necessity in those sources in which we expected to find it, it *seems* as if this expression is meaningless.

> Thus upon the whole we may infer, that when we talk of any being, whether of a superior or inferior nature, as endow'd with a power or force . . . when we speak of a necessary connexion betwixt objects, and *suppose, that this connexion depends upon an efficacy or energy, with which these objects are endow'd; in all those expressions, so apply'd, we have really no distinct meaning*, and make use only of common words, without any clear and determinate ideas. But . . . 'tis more probable, that *these expressions do here lose their true meaning by being wrong applied, than that they never have any meaning.* (T, 162; my emphasis)

Hume's point is not that these expressions are in fact meaningless but only that they are meaningless when applied to "objects" (keeping in mind that the "objects" which concern Hume the most are physical objects or bodies). It was Hume's view that these expressions should, properly speaking, be applied only to our perceptions. As we shall see, the fact that these terms are wrongly applied in these ways is, for Hume, connected with the fact that we have sought the origin of our idea of necessity in the wrong place—that is, in the operations of matter.

Near the end of Part ii of Book I, Hume states that his "intention never was to penetrate into the nature of bodies, or explain the secret cause of their operations". He continues:

For besides that this belongs not to my present purpose, I am afraid, that *such an enterprise is beyond the reach of human understanding*, and that we can never pretend to know body otherwise than by those external properties, which discover themselves to the senses. . . . I content myself with knowing perfectly the manner in which objects affect my senses, and their connections with each other, as far as experience informs me of them. This suffices for the conduct of life; and this also suffices for my philosophy, *which pretends only to explain the nature and causes of our perceptions, or our impressions and ideas*. (T, 64; my emphasis)[11]

However, despite this disclaimer of any interest in the nature of bodies and their operations, Hume also takes the view that our imagination makes it impossible for us to "reject the notion of an independent and continued existence" (T, 214). Hume is also aware that this natural belief in the existence of body is bound to conflict with his sceptical principles.

In his discussion of our natural tendency to believe in the existence of body, Hume distinguishes between "objects" and "perceptions"; "perceptions" are those existents that are interrupted, perishing and dependent on the mind, and "objects" or "bodies" are those existents that are independent, continuing and external to the mind.[12] "The vulgar", Hume says, "confound perceptions and objects" (T, 193) and "can never assent to the opinion of a double existence and representation" (T, 202). They "take their perceptions to be their only objects and suppose, that the very being, which is intimately present to mind, is the real body or material existence" (T, 206). Philosophers cannot accept this view of things. They have devised the hypothesis of "the double existence of perceptions and objects; which pleases our reason in allowing, that our dependent perceptions are interrupted and different; and at the same time is agreeable to the imagination, in attributing a continu'd existence to something else, which we all call *objects*" (T, 215). In this way, the conflicting principles of the imagination and reason create a double ontology. Hume believes that this hypothesis of double existence is only "a palliative remedy, and that it contains all the difficulties of the vulgar system, with some others, that are peculiar to itself" (T, 211). However, as neither nature nor reason will "quit the field" (T, 215), we are left with this "philosophical hypothesis". This is a "malady" which philosophy can never cure. "Carelessness and inattention alone can afford us the remedy" (T, 218). Although Hume stops short of abandoning the commonsense belief in the existence of the material world, he nevertheless argues that we cannot infer the existence of a material world on the basis of our perceptions, and even if we could do so, we "should never have any reason to infer that our objects resemble our perceptions" (T, 216).

In short, the ontology of double existence permits Hume to embrace a position which is consistent with his "mitigated scepticism". On the one hand, he argues that we never penetrate the nature and operations of the material world of bodies, that we have no reason to believe that there exists such a world, and that we have even less reason to believe that it resembles the world of our perceptions. On the other hand, Hume accepts that it is an inescapable fact about human nature that we suppose that there exists such a world of bodies and that they operate "independent of our thought and reasoning".

How this ontology of double existence sheds light on Hume's discussion of causation and, in particular, how it helps to account for the motivation behind Hume's two definitions of cause can best be appreciated by considering his arguments concerning "the relation of cause and effect, as discovered in the motions and operations of matter" in some detail.

The following three arguments form the core of Hume's position concerning the causal relation as we discover it in physical objects or bodies:

1. There are no intelligible or a priori discoverable connexions between bodies themselves.

2. After repeated *experience* of one sort of object (i.e. body) being conjoined with another object, for example, bodies resembling X being constantly conjoined with bodies resembling Y, we find that our *perceptions* of Xs and Ys become connected. That is to say, our experience of constant conjunction generates connexions among our ideas (i.e. generates connexions *in our mind*).

3. This "connexion" is the product of a natural relation. It is an association which holds only between our perceptions, and it cannot, therefore, be attributed to the objects (i.e. bodies) themselves. Nevertheless, insofar as we suppose bodies to be represented by our perceptions, the philosophical relations which exist between these perceptions may be attributed to the bodies themselves.

Hume argues that our idea of necessity does not arise directly from our observation of physical objects or bodies. That is to say, he holds that there is no necessity observed in bodies themselves. Constant conjunction is all that we observe of causation as it is in these objects. Hume holds that it is not the bodies that are the source of our idea of necessity but rather our perceptions of them. We must "change the point of view, from the objects to the perceptions" (T, 169) if we are to discover the source of this idea. Hume has already stated that his procedure has been "like those, who being in search of anything that lies concealed from them, and not finding it in the place they expected, beat about all the neighbouring fields" (T, 77–78). The "neighbouring field" where he has found the origin of our idea is that of our perceptions. The traditional reluctance of philosophers to change their perspective from bodies to perceptions has prevented both ancient and modern philosophers from arriving at the true source of our idea of necessity.

> [These philosophers] have sufficient force of genius to free them from the vulgar error, that there is a natural and perceivable connexion betwixt the several sensible qualities and actions of matter; but not sufficient to keep them from *ever seeking for this connexion in matter*, or causes. . . . At present they seem to be in a very lamentable condition. . . . For what can be imagined more tormenting, than to seek with eagerness, what for ever flies us; *and seek for it in a place where it is impossible it can ever exist*? (T, 223; my emphasis)

Accordingly, the change of perspective from bodies to perceptions is, for the Hume of Book I, fundamental to discovering the actual source of our idea of necessity. The reason for this is quite straightforward. The connexion which we think of as holding between cause and effect turns out to be the same as that which holds between our perceptions whereby one idea naturally introduces the other. That is, the necessary connexion turns out to be an association between our perceptions. Thus, in one move Hume can account for both the failure of philosophers to find the origin of this idea in matter and for our natural tendency to believe that bodies themselves are necessarily connected.[13] Hume argues that, as "the idea of necessity is a new original idea", constant conjunction "must either discover or produce something new, which is the source of that idea" (T, 163). We feel that a cause produces or determines its effect and is not simply followed by it because of "that propensity, which custom produces, to pass from an object to the idea of its usual attendant. This therefore is the essence of necessity. Upon the whole, *necessity is something, that exists in the mind, not in objects; nor is it possible for us to form the most distant idea of it, considered as a quality in bodies*" (T,165–66; my emphasis). This very important passage offers further evidence of Hume's primary concern, in Book I, with body or matter considered as a source of our idea of necessity. Apart from the explicit reference to bodies emphasized above, it seems clear that Hume is arguing that necessity exists *in the mind as opposed to bodies*. Because mental objects (i.e. perceptions) must, obviously, "exist in the mind", Hume's remark that "necessity exists in the mind, not in objects" would lose its significance if he were referring to mental objects. He is, rather, drawing a contrast between his view, that necessity exists in the mind, and the view that he is attacking, that necessity exists in matter or bodies. Clearly, the "objects" to which Hume refers must be physical objects or bodies.

Hume completes this passage as follows: "Either we have no idea of necessity, or *necessity is nothing but that determination of the thought* to pass from causes to effects and from effects to causes, according to their experienced union" (T, 166; my emphasis). The "determination of the thought" is what we have the internal impression of, and *this* is the origin of our idea of necessity. This impression would not arise were it not for associations among our perceptions, associations which constitute the only "connexions" we will discover among things. We are "led astray by a false philosophy", Hume suggests, "when we transfer the determination of the thought to *external objects*, and suppose any real intelligible connexion between them; that being a quality which can *only belong to the mind that considers them*" (T, 168; my emphasis—note that Hume mentions this "false philosophy" again at T, 222–23).

I have already pointed out that Hume held that it was impossible for us to abandon our belief in the independent and continuing existence of bodies—that is, the material world. The question naturally arises as to what relations and connexions hold among bodies themselves, as distinct from our perceptions of them. The gist of Hume's answer to this question seems to be that although we may attribute philosophical relations to physical objects, we cannot attribute those connexions which are produced by natural relations to them. For example, Hume states explicitly (T, 168) that physical objects may "bear to each other the relations of contiguity and succession; that like objects may be observ'd in several instances to have like relations; and that all this is independent of, and antecedent to the operations of the understanding". But, as we have seen, he will not allow that the product of natural relations, that is, those "connexions" which hold between our perceptions of these objects, may also be "transferred" to these bodies (although he notes that we have a natural tendency to do this [cf. T, 167] because we "confound perceptions and objects"). A natural relation is a *"quality, by which two ideas are connected together in the imagination*, and the one naturally introduces the other after the manner above explained" (T, 13—as explained at I, i, 4, in terms of "the connexion or association of ideas"). These effects of natural relations (viz. the generation of "connexions" among our ideas) must, obviously, be confined to our perceptions. However, we find philosophical relations wherever there are qualities "which make *objects admit of comparison*" (T,14; my emphasis). There is no reason, therefore, to suppose that such relations do not exist in the material world among bodies (assuming, that is, that we also suppose that our perceptions represent these objects).

III

Let us briefly digress from our primary concern, Hume's discussion of the origin of our idea of necessary connexion in Book I, in order to consider whether or not Hume's reasoning concerning "the relation of cause and effect, as discovered in the motions and operations of matter . . . extends to the operations of mind" (T, 655). In light of what has already been said in the first part of this chapter, it should be clear that the first two of Hume's arguments outlined above suffice to refute Locke's suggestion regarding the will (the will being the specific mental object which Hume comes to consider). First, as we have noted, Hume argues that "we learn the influence of our will from experience alone". That is to say, there are no intelligible or a priori discoverable connexions between the will and its effects. From the idea of the cause, we cannot by any sort of reasoning demonstrate what its effect will be. Second, experience teaches us "how one event constantly follows another, without instructing us in the secret connexion, which binds them together, and renders them inseparable" (EU, 66). Hume is anxious to establish, as he was when considering the operations of matter, that our experience of the constant conjunction of our willings and their consequent effects does not create any change in our conception of these objects (i.e. does not involve a change in "the parts or composition" of these ideas; cf. T, 95):

> And even after we have experience of these effects [of the will], 'tis custom alone, not reason, which determines us to make it the standard of our future judgments. When the cause is presented, the mind, from habit, immediately passes to the conception and belief of the usual effect. This belief is something different from the conception. It does not, however, join any new idea to it. It only makes it felt differently, and renders it stronger and more lively. (T, 655–56)

In short, it is evident that Hume's first two arguments "extend" to the case of the will and can, therefore, be used to refute Locke's suggestion that our idea of necessity originates with our reflecting on our volitions. Further, these arguments apply not only to the case of our will considered as a cause but also to mental objects or perceptions in general. There are no intelligible or a priori discoverable connexions among any objects, including perceptions. Nor does our experience of the constant conjunction of perceptions produce or discover any further metaphysical tie or bond between them. After experiencing the constant union of a given perception with another object, these two objects, like our ideas of physical objects in these circumstances, become connected *in our thought*. Here again, therefore, the reasoning seems to be on the same footing as we found with material bodies.

Hume's third argument—that is, that "the determination of the thought" cannot be transferred to the "external objects"—is not required for his refutation of Locke's suggestion. Rather, it is designed to undercut the supposition which is fundamental to the "false philosophy", namely, the supposition that there exist connexions among the bodies themselves, "independent of our thought and reasoning". Because we naturally tend to "confound perceptions and objects", we are liable to suppose that there exist some intrinsic connexions among the external objects which correspond to "the determination of the thought" or "connexions among our ideas". This tendency in our thinking is seriously in error, and it is a source of considerable support for the "false philosophy". In this way, it suffices for Hume's purposes that his first two arguments "extend" to the case of the operations of mind, thus refuting Locke's suggestion concerning the will, and that the third holds in the case of the operations of matter, thus refuting the "false philosophy".

It should be noted, however, that the third argument does not in fact "extend" to the case of the operations of mind. Any perception, viewed as a mental object, can be considered as a cause of another perception. Initially, as with physical objects, there is no connexion of *any sort* between the two. That is to say, when we first experience a mental object resembling an x, say x_1, we may find that it is conjoined with an object resembling a y, say y_1. This is all that we will find relating them. There is, in other words, no connexion whatsoever between x_1 and y_1. However, after experiencing the constant conjunction of Xs and Ys, we will eventually find that there exists a *felt connexion* between x_n and y_n. Now, in the case of physical objects or bodies, we noted that this "determination of the thought" or "felt connexion" holds only among our perceptions of these bodies and not among the objects themselves. But in the case of mental objects or perceptions, they are the objects themselves—there is no representation involved. That is to say, there is no gulf between mental objects and our perceptions of them. Hence, these felt connexions can, obviously, be attributed to the mental objects themselves. In this way, it seems clear that Hume's argument that "the determination of the thought" should not be transferred to "external objects" cannot be "extended" to the case of the operations of the mind.

Does the fact that "felt connexions" can, on Hume's principles, be attributed to the operations of the mind in any way undermine Hume's claim that "the same reasoning extends to the operations of the mind"? I think not. Hume's point is, I suggest, that all the *relevant* reasoning extends to the operations of mind. Felt connexions are clearly not conceived of as "connexions" in the "loose" or "popular" sense.[14] Felt connexions do not impinge on Hume's principle that all objects, including our perceptions, are entirely distinct. Nor do connexions of this nature disclose any tie or bond between cause and effect which render them "inseparable". Most important, felt connexions, unlike connexions as commonly conceived, do not make this relation "an object of reasoning". The inference from the cause to the effect rests entirely on custom or habit rather than reason. Thus, in all these important respects (i.e. all relevant respects), it seems clear that Hume is justified in claiming that "the same reasoning extends to the operations of mind".

IV

Let us return to Hume's concerns in Book I and examine what he has to say about causation as it exists in nature "independent of our thought and reasoning" (i.e. in the material world). Hume says that such objects "bear to each other the relations of contiguity and succession" and "that like objects may be observed in several instances to have like relations" (T, 168). This passage is almost immediately followed by Hume's "two definitions" of cause. I believe that it is significant that this account of causation as it exists in bodies or the material world comes very close to giving Hume's first definition of cause, which I call definition C_1: "[A cause is an] object precedent and contiguous to another, and where all the objects resembling the former are plac'd in like relations of precedency and contiguity to those objects, that resemble the latter". I suggest that Hume is here concerned to define the cause as it exists in nature, independent of our thought and reasoning. Accordingly, because he is considering bodies, he makes no mention of perceptions, that is, impressions and ideas, nor of the effects of natural relations (i.e. those "connexions" which relate only perceptions).

By contrast, his second definition is concerned with cause as it exists in our perceptions (i.e. mind). When we change the point of view from the objects (i.e. material objects) to perceptions, Hume says, "the *impression is to be considered as the cause, and the lively idea as the effect*; and their necessary connexion is that new determination, which we feel to pass from the idea of one to that of the other" (T, 169; my emphasis). Thus we have Hume's second definition of cause as it exists in our thought or perceptions, definition C_2: "A cause is an object precedent and contiguous to another, and so united with it, that *the idea of the one* determines the mind to form *the idea of the other*, and the *impression* of the one to form a more *lively idea of the other*" (my emphasis). It is by considering causation as we find it in our perceptions that we discover that (internal) impression of the necessary connexion which our examination of matter failed to reveal.

Hume's two definitions of cause reflect the fact that he embraces the ontology of double existence of perceptions and bodies. The criticism of his position which he considers prior to offering his two definitions (i.e. "As if causes did not operate entirely independent of mind. . ." [T, 167–69]) makes clear the relevance of his views on ontology, as developed in Part iv, to his discussion of causation. Given that people ordinarily "confound" perceptions and bodies, it is understandable that they arrive at the mistaken conclusion that material bodies are necessarily connected. They attribute those connexions which exist in their imagination, that is, those associations which connect their perceptions, to the bodies themselves. However, as Hume points out, even philosophers—who distinguish between bodies and our perceptions of them—continue to assume that the necessary connexions hold among bodies and thereby adhere to the "false philosophy" which he seeks to dispose of.

Hume seeks to establish that necessary connexions, like secondary qualities (T, 226–27) and moral qualities (T, 469), can be said to exist only in the mind that considers these material objects. Thus, what Hume has to say can be assimilated to other central doctrines in the *Treatise*. Necessary connexions, like colours, smells, virtue, and vice, exist in the mind and not in objects themselves, and we must check our inclination to attribute these features to the objects.[15]

Hume offers two definitions of necessity which are, as with his two definitions of cause, founded on his ontology of double existence: "I define necessity two ways, comfortable to the two definitions of cause, of which it makes an essential part. I place it either in the *constant union of like objects, or in the inference of the mind from the one to the other*" (T, 409; my emphasis—cf. EU, 97).

Let us call "the constant union of like objects" definition N_1 and "the inference of the mind from one [object] to the other" definition N_2. N_1, like C_1, is a definition offered in terms of philosophical relations and makes no reference to our perceptions. N_2 refers to "the inference of the mind" and is, consequently, dependent on an ontology of perceptions rather than external objects. It is dependent on an ontology of perceptions because the inference of the mind must be an association between *ideas*. On Hume's account, inferred "objects" must be capable of "enlivening" and of possessing the phenomenological property of vivacity; clearly, these are properties which only ideas (as opposed to bodies) are capable of possessing. Here again, we find the change in point of view which reflects the ontology of double existence.

Given that N_1 and N_2 follow the ontological distinction which we found between C_1 and C_2, how are C_1 and N_1 and C_2 and N_2 related? Specifically, does necessity make an essential part of *both* Hume's definitions of cause, as his remarks would seem to suggest? When Hume examines material bodies, all he can discover are the relations of contiguity, priority, and constant conjunction—he cannot find any relation of necessary connexion. Consider the following "part" of definition C_1: "and where all the objects resembling the former are plac'd in like relations of precedency and contiguity to those objects, that resemble the latter". This is simply all that we find of the relation of necessary connexion if we (mistakenly) look for it in material bodies—that is, constant conjunction. It is, therefore, not surprising that this "part" of C_1 is simply N_1 reworded. N_1, as we have noted, confines itself to an ontology of objects and philosophical relations. Now consider the following "part" of C_2: "and so united with it, that the idea of the one determines the mind to form the idea of the other". This is simply the relation of necessary connexion as we find it in our perceptions—that is, the inference of the mind, or N_2. It is obvious that necessity does, as Hume suggests, form an essential part of *both* definitions of cause.

We are now in a position to clarify in what way N_1 and N_2 form an essential part of C_1 and C_2, respectively. First, Hume takes the view that a cause is an "object", and, as such, it may be viewed as either a body or a perception. The alternative perspective reflects the natural alternative we find in the ontology of double existence. Second, this "object" bears certain relations to another "object" (i.e. its effect). These relations include the philosophical relations of contiguity and priority, which both bodies and perceptions share. Third, it is also "essential" that these objects be related by a necessary connexion. When we mistakenly seek this relation in bodies, all we discover is the relation of constant conjunction. This is all that exists of necessity independent of our thought and reasoning. However, when we change our point of view and consider these "objects" as perceptions, then the necessary connexion turns out to be a determination or inference in our thought.

As we have already noted, Hume states that "either we have no idea of necessity, or *necessity is nothing but that determination of the thought* to pass from causes to effects and from effects to causes, according to their experienc'd union" (T, 166). This claim, although it might accord with definition N_2, makes it difficult to understand why Hume offers definition N_1 at all. Further, in some contexts (e.g. T, 162), Hume clearly suggests that necessity should not be ascribed to objects and does not exist in objects. Why, then, does he offer us an account of necessity as it exists independent of our thought and reason? He does this, I believe, because he is committed to the view that we naturally believe in an independent, material world—however much that belief may lack rational foundations. It is understandable, given this view of things, that he offers some account of causation and necessity as they exist in that material world, independent of mind. Just as Hume refuses to join Berkeley in abandoning our belief in matter (cf. EU, 155n), so, too, he refuses to abandon the "common sense" view (as expressed at T, 167–69) that causation and necessity also exist independent of our thought and reasoning.

If we try to define cause as it exists independent of mind, then we must also define necessity, which makes an "essential part" of cause, as it exists independent of the mind. From this perspective, the only account of necessity that one can offer is, as we have seen, constant conjunction, or N_1. It is in this way that the ontology of double existence yields Hume's definitions C_1 and N_1 as an account of "the operations of nature" as they exist independent of mind. It must be noted, however, that Hume also maintains, somewhat paradoxically, that any such account is quite "beyond the reach of human understanding". I suggest, therefore, that these definitions, C_1 and N_1, should be viewed as "palliative remedies" which Hume offers so as to "set [us] at ease as much as possible", given our inescapable "malady" of believing in a world we can know nothing of. This is entirely in keeping with both the spirit and letter of Hume's philosophy.[16]

V

Let us briefly note some of the more important and illuminating aspects of the interpretation argued for in this chapter.

1. On this interpretation, it is possible to explain *why* Hume claims that "the mind has a great propensity to spread itself on external objects" (T, 167; cf. T, 222–23 and 266–67). The mind has a tendency to "spread itself on external objects"—and hence to "transfer the determination of the thought to external objects"—because the mind tends to "confound perceptions and objects" (T, 193).

2. On this interpretation, we can explain why Hume believes that we are inclined to *suppose* that the source of our idea of necessity is to be discovered in the operations of matter. According to Hume, we naturally suppose there is a world of objects that exist and operate on one another "independent of our thought and reason". Consequently, we naturally suppose there must be some intrinsic necessity or power in these objects independent of our thought and reason. (How else could these bodies operate on one another?)

3. On this interpretation, we can explain why Hume suggests that we are reluctant to accept that there is nothing more to necessity as it exists in the objects themselves than mere constant conjunction. We tend to suppose there must be some intrinsic connexions among the objects themselves because we have a natural tendency to attribute those connexions which we feel among our perceptions (i.e. in the mind) to the objects themselves. (See point [1] above.) In other words, because we confound perceptions and objects, we tend to suppose that necessity inheres in the objects themselves.

4. On this interpretation, we can explain why Hume suggests that we must "change the point of view from the objects to the perceptions" (T, 169). When we consider causation as it exists in objects (i.e. bodies), we cannot discover the source of our idea of necessity. However, when we change our perspective to our perceptions, we discover that the source of our idea of necessity is an association of ideas. These "felt connexions" among our perceptions cannot be attributed to the objects themselves (although we are, as has been noted, naturally inclined to do this).

5. On this interpretation, we can account for the force of Hume's criticism of his own position (at T, 167: "What! the efficacy of causes lie in the determination of mind! . . ."). In this passage, Hume acknowledges that his account of the origin and nature of our idea of necessity deeply conflicts with our natural belief that bodies exist and operate on one another independent of the mind. That is to say, as has been noted, Hume recognizes that we naturally *suppose* that there exists some necessity in the objects themselves.

An appreciation of the significance of these points is essential for a proper understanding of Hume's position. The fact that Hume's views on ontology consistently and strikingly shed light on these aspects of his discussion provides strong support for the interpretation offered in this chapter. Previous interpretations have almost entirely failed to note the significance of these points. Any adequate interpretation of Hume's views on causation must cohere with the details of the relevant passages in Book I; and must also be able to account for the original starting point and subsequent development of Hume's discussion. In this way, it seems clear that the strengths of this interpretation reveal the weaknesses of its rivals.[17]

In conclusion, if Hume's views on causation have a paradoxical air about them, that is because they rest on an ontology of "double existence" which Hume describes as "the monstrous offspring of two principles, which are contrary to each other, which are both at once embrac'd by the mind, and which are unable mutually to destroy each other" (T, 215). In this way, the dualism which we find in Hume's account of causation simply reflects the dualism of the ontology of double existence. On the one hand, in order to set our imagination at ease and to take into consideration our natural belief in the material world, Hume offers an account of causation as it exists in matter independent of mind (as at T, 168). Hence, he offers us the first definition of cause. This account of causation indicates his respect for the fact that we cannot abandon or escape from our natural beliefs. On the other hand, in order to set our reason at ease, Hume also points out that we cannot infer that there exists a material world, that we have no reason to believe that our perceptions represent such a world, and that any attempt to "penetrate into the nature of bodies" is beyond the reach of human understanding and liable to produce scepticism and uncertainty. All that we require for "the conduct of life" and for an understanding of Hume's philosophy is knowledge of the nature and operations of our perceptions. Hume, accordingly, is primarily concerned with "the universe of the imagination" and therefore with the nature of causation as we find it there. Thus, he offers us his second definition of cause. By viewing the problem in this light, Hume seeks to establish that "the cement of the universe" (i.e. the universe of the imagination) is the association of our ideas. As his concluding remarks in the *Abstract* make clear, this is what Hume set out to prove in Book I of the *Treatise*.

Notes

1. Discussion in the secondary literature concerning this issue has centred on such questions as whether or not Hume supported the regularity view of causation; whether or not he really intended to offer two *definitions* of our notion of cause; which, if either, of these two definitions is primary; and what part the idea of necessity plays in these definitions. In this context, I do not directly discuss the various interpretations that have been put forward in the secondary literature. For a discussion that contains a fairly detailed account of much of the relevant secondary literature, see Beauchamp and Rosenberg, *Hume and the Problem of Causation*, chp. 1. (See also note 17.)

2. Beauchamp and Rosenberg begin their book *Hume and the Problem of Causation* by claiming that "virtually all parties to the current disputes about causation consider Hume's account a live option" (p. vii). Similar sentiments are expressed by Mackie in *Cement of the Universe* (see, e.g., p. 3). It seems evident, therefore, that a clear understanding of Hume's views on causation will be of interest not only to Hume scholars, narrowly conceived, but also to all those philosophers engaged in the current debate about the nature of causation. It is worth noting, however, that Beauchamp, Rosenberg, and Mackie take Hume to be a supporter of the "regularity theory" of causation, and they take this to be a plausible and defensible position to maintain. For a very different interpretation of Hume's position and of the relative merits of the "regularity theory", see Galen Strawson, *The Secret Connexion*, esp. viii–ix.

3. Flew has pointed out that the *Enquiry* has often been viewed as merely a "popularized version of Book I" (*Hume's Philosophy of Belief*, 1). Although there is, as Flew notes, some truth in this view, it nevertheless leads philosophers into missing many important differences in Hume's concerns and arguments.

4. In his discussion "Of the ancient philosophy" (I, iv, 3), Hume refers to the supposition that there is some power, efficacy, etc., which we can discover and attribute to the operations of matter as a "false philosophy" (T, 222–23). In this, he may well have been influenced by Malebranche's discussion of "the most dangerous error of the ancients" (*The Search After Truth*, VI, ii, 3—Hume in fact refers to this section at T, 159n). Malebranche states:

> There are therefore no forces, powers, or true causes in the material, sensible world; and it is not necessary to admit the existence of forms, faculties, and real qualities for producing effects that bodies do not produce and for sharing with God the force and power essential to Him. (*Search*, 449)

In his *Elucidations*, Malebranche returns to this theme:

> Feeling himself a sinner, man hides, flees the light, fears encountering God and prefers to imagine *in bodies surrounding him* a blind nature or power that he can master and without remorse use towards his bizarre and disordered intentions. . . . there are many people who through a principle different from that of the pagan philosophers follow their opinion on *nature* and secondary causes. (*Search*, 657; first emphasis is mine)

Malebranche's discussion of "the most dangerous error of the philosophy of the ancients" seems closely related to Hume's discussion of the "false philosophy" of the ancients. Further, in his *Elucidations*, Malebranche, like Hume in Book I of the *Treatise*, is *primarily* concerned with the question of whether or not matter possesses some force or power. Hume, clearly, shares Malebranche's conclusion that we discover no such power, force, etc., in these objects. It should also be pointed out that Malebranche, unlike Hume in Book I of the *Treatise*, does consider, in *The Search After Truth*, the *Elucidations*, and the *Dialogues*, the suggestion that we derive our idea of power by reflecting on our willings. (See, e.g., *Search*,

448, 449–50, 668–71, and 679.) Given Hume's obvious familiarity with Malebranche's writings, it seems certain that, despite his failure to discuss this suggestion in the context of Book I, he must nevertheless, at the time of writing Book I, have been aware of Malebranche's comments on it. Not surprisingly, Hume's subsequent discussion in the *Abstract*, the Appendix, and the first *Enquiry* follows Malebranche's general line of criticism.

5. Hume's example of billiard balls in the *Treatise* (T, 164), the only example he uses in I, iii, 14, is a paradigm case of causation as it exists in bodies or the operations of matter, and, as such, it is indicative of Hume's primary interest. The example is even more prominent in the *Abstract* and is used again in the *Enquiry* (EU, secs. 4, 5, and 7), in those contexts in which he is concerned with causation as it exists in external objects. (It should be noted that Keynes and Sraffa incorrectly imply that this example does not appear in the *Treatise*; see their introduction to the *Abstract*, xxix.) Significantly, Malebranche repeatedly uses the example of colliding balls (*Search*, 448, 451, 659, and 660, and *dialogue* 7, Sec. 11), and Locke uses the specific example of billiard balls at *Essay*, 235 (II, xxi, 4).

6. Cf. T, 410: "I change therefore . . ." In this context, Hume makes very clear that he holds unorthodox views about the nature of the material world and changes the "receiv'd systems" in respect of it.

7. Hume's early preoccupation with the question of whether matter possesses any power, force, or activity is perfectly intelligible in its historical context. In this regard, there are two particularly important points to be noted: this issue was of enormous contemporary importance because of the impact of Newton's natural philosophy, and it was laden with theological ramifications which Hume would certainly have been very well aware of (the criticisms and replies in LG cited above are plainly indicative of this).

8. It seems very likely that these difficulties would have been pointed out to Hume by one of those who read the *Treatise* shortly after it was published. By far the most likely candidate for this role is Lord Kames (i.e. Henry Home). Kames—who was an intimate friend and early mentor of Hume's—read and discussed Hume's work when Hume returned to Scotland in early 1739 (i.e. shortly after the first two books of the *Treatise* were published). Kames had a deep and long-standing interest in the subject of causation and was, in particular, much impressed by Locke's views on "power." (Relevant material regarding these facts can be found in Mossner, *Life of Hume*, 118–19; and Ross, *Kames*, 60–66, 76–77, 174–75.)

In his *Essays on the Principles of Morality and Natural Religion* (1751), Kames devotes a whole essay to the "Idea of Power". His discussion includes a sustained attack on Hume's views on this subject (282–92). Kames interprets Hume as denying that there are any powers or forces in the material world or bodies. This is a view which Kames asserts conflicts with humankind's "natural feelings and sentiments". Against Hume, Kames argues that both our experience of our own will and our observations of the operations of bodies immediately give rise to the *feeling* that these objects are necessarily connected and that the one (i.e. the cause) produced the other (i.e. the effect). (Cf. Kames, *Essays*, 279–80.) Given the intimate relations which Hume and Kames enjoyed, and their closely overlapping concerns on this subject, I suggest that Kames's discussion should be given careful consideration by those who are interested in interpreting Hume's views.

9. Clearly, however, Hume differed from Locke insofar as he did not believe that reflecting on our own case would be any more enlightening. (Note that Hume uses a rather Lockean argument to deal with Malebranche's "hypothesis" of occasionalism, and he uses, in his subsequent writings, Malebranche's general line of attack against Locke's suggestion concerning the will.)

10. At the time of publishing the *Treatise*, Hume made some effort to be "discreet" when expressing his views on religion. However, Hume clearly thought that, philosophically speaking, any appeals to "the deity" were fraught with difficulties. In *A Letter from a Gentleman*,

Hume describes occasionalism as a doctrine that was considered by most English philosophers (e.g. Locke, Cudworth, and Clarke) as "too little supported by philosophical arguments [to] ever be considered as any thing but a mere hypothesis" (LG, 28). In the *Enquiry*, Hume suggests that "we are got into a fairy land, long ere we have reached the last steps of [this] theory" (EU, 72).

11. To this passage Hume appends the following remarks: "As long as we confine our speculations to *the appearances* of objects to our senses, without entering into disquisitions concerning their real nature and operations, we are safe from all difficulties, and can never be embarrass'd by any question. . . . If we carry our enquiry beyond the appearances of objects to the senses, I am afraid, that most of our conclusions will be full of scepticism and uncertainty" (T, 638–39).

12. In Part iii, Hume uses the term "object" to include mental as well as physical objects (i.e. bodies), and it would seem, therefore, that there is a sudden change in the meaning of this term. However, it should be kept in mind that in Part iii Hume was primarily concerned with physical objects. Once this emphasis is noted, then it should be apparent that his usage of the term "object" in Part iv is not as out of keeping with his usage of that term in Part iii as appears at first glance.

13. We have a natural tendency to believe this because we have a natural tendency to "confound perceptions and objects" (T, 193; see also T, 223: " 'Tis natural for men . . .").

14. On Hume's view, "real connexions" (cf. T, 168) depend on the *nature* of the objects (i.e. their "parts or composition") rather than on the *manner* in which they are conceived by the mind.

15. Of course, the *sense* in which Hume thinks that virtue and vice "are not qualities in objects, but perceptions in the mind" (T, 469) requires careful interpretation. However, this is not our present concern. (For more on this, see chp. 4, sec. 2, and chp. 6, sec. 2, in this volume.)

16. Clearly, for Hume, neither C_1 nor N_1 are philosophically defensible—but then, strictly speaking, no account of external objects and their operations will be. The most that we can do, by way of concession to the principles of the imagination, is describe external objects *as they are represented by our perceptions*. In this respect, neither C_1 nor N_1 commits Hume to the existence of (unintelligible) metaphysical powers or forces in the external, material world. Indeed, "forces" and "powers" of this (metaphysical) nature cannot even be conceived of as represented by our perceptions. Regularities, by contrast, can be represented and conceived of as existing independent of the mind.

17. In recent years, several commentators have argued—primarily on the basis of Hume's discussion in the first *Enquiry*—that Hume should be interpreted as a "causal realist". (See, e.g., John Wright, *The Sceptical Realism of David Hume*, 123–86, and Galen Strawson, *The Secret Connexion*, passim.) The "realist" interpretation presents Hume as claiming that within the realm of bodies or external objects (i.e. those objects that are represented by our perceptions) there exist "secret powers" and forces which account for the regularities that we actually observe among our perceptions. Hume, it is said, is committed to the existence of such metaphysical powers or forces even though he also maintains that we neither know nor comprehend the nature of these "secret powers" or underlying metaphysical forces. I will not respond to these claims in any detail. Suffice it to say that my own alternative interpretation provides a rather different account of Hume's basic strategy and concerns on this subject. The following four points, however, may be briefly noted. First, Hume is clearly committed to the view that we *naturally suppose* that there are "powers" and "forces" in bodies beyond mere regularity (i.e. for the reasons which I have already explained in detail). This natural supposition is shown to be groundless, lacking any specific content, and wholly explicable in terms of the workings of our perceptions. Second, Hume also appears to allow, in some con-

texts, that there *might* be some (incomprehensible and unknowable) "secret powers" in external objects (for all that we know and understand of such of objects). Third, Hume is especially concerned to argue that whether or not such unknowable and incomprehensible "secret powers" in fact exist in the objects, we have every reason to avoid conflating this "unintelligible" account of necessity (T, 410; and EU, 92–93) with the intelligible and coherent account of necessity which he is particularly concerned to provide us with. Fourth, Hume's philosophy is concerned "only to explain the nature and causes of our perceptions", and this suffices not only for his philosophy but also "for the conduct of life" (T, 64 and 632). It is within this framework that Hume sets out to explain why we *mistakenly suppose* that we have some (further) *idea* of necessity beyond that of constant conjunction and inference. Given these general points, I suggest that Hume's (apparent) concern with the *possible* existence of (noumenal) "secret powers" is very largely irrelevant to the workings of his system. Any interpretation which suggests otherwise, I would argue, wholly misrepresents Hume's fundamental intentions on this subject.

In regard to this general issue, see Kames's discussion of Hume's position. Kames, as I have indicated, plainly interprets Hume as denying that there is anything more to causation in the material world than mere regularity (*Essays*, 282–86). He also notes, however, that Hume's language in his "philosophical essays" (i.e. the first *Enquiry*) is sometimes infelicitous insofar as talk of "secret powers" is at odds with Hume's sceptical thesis and intent regarding such "powers". Kames, indeed, cites those passages that contain talk of "secret powers" as evidence *against* Hume's revisionary (and sceptical) thesis.

3

Causation, Compulsion, and Compatibilism

Let no one, therefore, put an invidious construction on my words, by saying simply, that I assert the necessity of human actions, and place them on the same footing with the operations of senseless matter. I do not ascribe to the will that unintelligible necessity, which is suppos'd to lie in matter.

Hume, *A Treatise of Human Nature*

'Tis difficult for us to persuade ourselves we were govern'd by necessity, and that 'twas utterly impossible for us to have acted otherwise; the idea of necessity seeming to imply something of force, and violence, and constraint, of which we are not sensible.

Hume, *A Treatise of Human Nature*

In chapter 1, I was primarily concerned to present and analyse the classical interpretation of Hume's liberty arguments (i.e. the spontaneity and antilibertarian arguments). It is, I noted, the very essence of the classical interpretation to present Hume as claiming that liberty of spontaneity is *logically* or *conceptually* essential to responsibility and that liberty of indifference is, by contrast, logically or conceptually incompatible with ascriptions of responsibility. This account of the liberty arguments constitutes the core of the classical interpretation of Hume's overall compatibilist strategy. The question remains, however, what role or significance the necessity argument has for the overall compatibilist strategy as Hume presents it. Many of Hume's successors in the classical compatibilist tradition have, as I have indicated, sought to explain and articulate the significance of the necessity argument in a way that is *consistent* with the classical interpretation of the liberty arguments. To this extent, there is an established classical interpretation of the role and significance of the necessity argument for Hume's compatibilist strategy.

In this chapter, I am primarily concerned with the classical account of Hume's necessity argument. In this regard, there are two basic points which I am particularly concerned to establish.

First, the significance of the necessity argument for the free will problem is, for Hume, bound up much more intimately with the details of his discussion of the problem of necessity than the classical account suggests. More specifically, Hume maintains that the major obstacle to resolving the free will controversy lies with our natural tendency to suppose that we have some idea of necessity as it exists in the material world beyond that of constant conjunction (and the accompanying inference of the mind with respect to these objects). Much of what Hume says about the "verbal" nature of the free will controversy has to be understood in light of these points.

Second, according to the classical interpretation, the importance of Hume's necessity argument is that it provides us with a description of causation that avoids all suggestion that what is caused is somehow compelled or constrained. In this way, it is argued that Hume's regularity theory of causation serves to strengthen the (classical) compatibilist position and frees it of difficulties which metaphysical (i.e. nonregularity) conceptions of causation would otherwise present for it. Contrary to these claims, I argue that not only does the necessity argument fail to strengthen the classical compatibilist strategy, it in fact threatens to undermine it altogether. These difficulties, I conclude, bring the adequacy of the classical interpretation of Hume's compatibilist strategy into some question.

I

In the *Abstract*, Hume, we have noted, claims to have put the free will controversy "in a new light by giving a new *definition* of necessity" (T, 661). This remark accords with his statement in the first *Enquiry* "that a few intelligible definitions would immediately . . . put an end to the whole controversy" (EU, 81). The terminological aspect of this dispute is repeatedly and strongly emphasized throughout his discussion in the *Enquiry* (cf. EU, VIII). The fact that this controversy has been "kept on foot" since ancient times and "remains still undecided" indicates, Hume suggests, "that there is some ambiguity in the expression, and that the disputants affix different ideas to the terms employed in the controversy" (EU, 80). In another passage, Hume states that "the whole controversy has *hitherto* turned merely upon words" (EU, 81; my emphasis); in yet another passage, he states that the dispute has been "*hitherto* merely verbal" (EU, 95; my emphasis). Clearly, these remarks, all from the *Enquiry*, lend considerable support to Antony Flew's view that Hume regarded this controversy as "spurious" and "unreal".[1] On the basis of these remarks, some scholars have concluded that Hume's attitude toward this controversy was somewhat cavalier. However, I believe that few commentators have really understood properly why Hume believes that this "verbal" dispute is so intractable nor even what, precisely, he takes the major "verbal" obstacle to be. On the basis of our analysis of Hume's account of causation and necessity, as presented in the previous chapter, I think that we can now shed some further light on Hume's views on the "verbal" nature of the free will dispute.

It is important to begin by noting that the "verbal" aspect of this dispute is not emphasized in the *Treatise* in the way that it is in the *Enquiry*. However, Hume does make clear in the *Treatise* what he takes the "verbal" aspect of the dispute to be. At the end of II, ii, 1, he states, "I dare be positive no one will ever endeavour to refute these reasonings otherwise than by altering my definitions. . . . If any one alters the definitions, I cannot pretend to argue with him, 'till I know the meaning he assigns to these terms [viz. 'cause', 'effect', 'necessity', 'liberty', and 'chance']" (T, 407). Hume's subsequent remarks make it very clear that it is the meaning of the term 'necessity' which he believes has been the major stumbling block: "The only particular in which any one can differ from me, is either, that perhaps he will refuse to call this [constant conjunction and inference of the mind] necessity. But as long as the meaning is understood, I hope the word can do no harm. Or that he will maintain there is something else *in the operations of matter*" (T, 409–10; my emphasis). This is restated in the *Abstract*: "the most zealous advocates for free will must allow this union and inference with regard to human actions. They will only deny, that this makes the whole of necessity. But then they must show, that we have an idea of something else *in the actions of matter*; which according to the foregoing reasoning, is impossible" (T, 661; my emphasis). Finally, in the *Enquiry* the point is made even more clearly:

> Necessity, according to the sense in which it is here taken, has never yet been rejected ... by any philosopher. It may only, perhaps, be pretended that the mind can perceive, *in the operations of matter*, some farther connexion between the cause and effect ... as long as we will rashly suppose, that we have some farther idea of necessity and causation *in the operations of external objects*; at the same time, that we can find nothing farther in the voluntary actions of the mind; *there is no possibility of bringing the question to any determinate issue, while we proceed upon so erroneous a supposition.* (EU, 92–93; my emphasis; cf. EU, 97)

It would appear, then, that Hume believes that the crucial first step in resolving this dispute is to become clear about the nature of necessity as we discover it in the "actions of matter". This is hardly surprising given that the first step of his own discussion, in both the *Treatise* (T, 399–400) and the *Enquiry* (EU, 82), is a clarification of our idea of necessity as it exists in the operations of matter.

It is still not clear, however, in exactly what way Hume thinks that this issue is related to the "verbal" nature of the free will controversy. An understanding of this feature of Hume's discussion will, I suggest, reveal that Hume regarded the "verbal" difficulty about the nature of necessity to be anything but a superficial problem. Hume's position on this issue can be summarized as follows. First, he considers it of vital importance, if we are to resolve this dispute, that we recognize that there are "two particulars which we are to consider as essential to necessity, viz. the constant union and inference of the mind" (T, 400). (Whether or not we choose to use the term 'necessity' is, however, immaterial.) Second, no one in actual practice doubts that there is constant conjunction and inference in the moral realm (i.e. the realm of our thoughts and actions). Third, there is, however, a widespread and natural reluctance to accept that this is all that there is to our idea of necessity. Fourth, this reluctance to accept that necessity is simply constant conjunction and inference of the mind is a consequence of the fact that "men still entertain a strong propensity to believe that they penetrate farther into the powers of nature" (i.e. the operations of matter; cf. EU, 92). This "supposition" is *the major obstacle* in resolving this dispute. This last point, on which all the rest of his argument hinges, is now perfectly intelligible in light of our reinterpretation of Hume's views on causation and necessity.

What is the source of this "strong propensity" to suppose that there is "something else" to our idea of necessity in the material world beyond mere union and inference"? There are, as we have noted, two closely related explanations for this tendency in our thinking. First, we naturally suppose that there exists a material world of bodies and that they operate on one another "independent of our thought and reasoning". Accordingly, we naturally (and mistakenly) suppose that we can discover some power or agency in these objects and that this is the source of our idea of necessity. Second, in ordinary life we "confound perceptions and objects" and thereby naturally "transfer" those connexions which we "feel" between our perceptions to the objects (i.e. bodies) themselves. We consequently suppose that these connexions exist among these objects "independent of our thought and reasoning". In this way, as a result of these "strong propensities" of the human mind, we are very reluctant to take the crucial first step in resolving the free will controversy—that is, accepting that necessity is simply "union and inference". It would appear, therefore, that according to Hume this "verbal" dispute is deeply rooted in our difficulties in recognizing the true source of our idea of necessity. Clearly, then, there is much more to Hume's account of these difficulties than a simple juggling with definitions.[2]

The following remarks, which I quote at length from the *Treatise*, may help us to understand why Hume came to suggest (in the *Enquiry*) that the "liberty and necessity" controversy should be regarded as "merely verbal".

> I may be mistaken in asserting, that we have no idea of any other connexion in the actions of body. . . . But sure I am, I ascribe nothing to the actions of the mind, but what must readily be allow'd of. Let no one, therefore, put an invidious construction on my words, by saying simply, that I assert the necessity of human actions, and place them on the same footing with the operations of senseless matter. *I do not ascribe to the will that unintelligible necessity, which is suppos'd to lie in matter.* But I ascribe to matter, that intelligible quality, call it necessity or not, which the most rigorous orthodoxy does or must allow to belong to the will. *I change, therefore, nothing in the receiv'd systems, with regard to the will, but only with regard to material objects.* (T, 410; my emphasis; cf. EU, 97)

Hume's point would seem to be that it is only his views concerning material objects which may be deemed "unorthodox". No one, he claims, can reasonably dispute that our willings and actions are subject to necessity *as he understands this term* (i.e. constant conjunction and inference). To deny, on the one hand, that our willings and actions are "necessary" but, on the other hand, accept in practice, if not explicitly, that we discover regularity and make inferences in the moral realm is to reduce this issue to one of whether or not constant conjunction should be *termed* 'necessity'. A disagreement of this nature, Hume argues, while it may be a substantial issue within the context of "natural philosophy and metaphysics" (because it suggests that we have no further idea of necessity in the operations of matter), is "merely verbal" in the context of the free will controversy. In this way, Hume is demanding that his "free will" opponents recognize that it is his amended conception of causation and necessity in the material world which is contentious or unorthodox rather than the substance of what he has to say about the will and our actions.

Hume's suggestion that the free will issue is "merely verbal" is one feature of his discussion in the *Enquiry* which is particularly unsatisfactory. (There is no similar suggestion made in the *Treatise*.) Indeed, his remarks to this effect tend to conceal the nature and complexity of his own intentions on this issue. Hume's motive for stressing the verbal aspect of this dispute can, however, be accounted for. That is, as we have seen, Hume anticipated, in the *Treatise* and the *Abstract*, that his opponents may reject his solution to this dispute simply because they reject his account of "necessity". Given the nature of the introductory remarks in the *Enquiry*, it seems very likely that Hume's worries on this score were realized, and so he consequently decided to express himself in stronger language in order to fend off this line of criticism. Beyond this, as we have also pointed out, Hume got himself enmeshed in some "verbal" difficulties as regards what he meant by the term 'liberty' in the *Treatise* and the *Enquiry*. According to Hume, this further "verbal obstacle" concerning the nature of "liberty" can itself be accounted for, in some measure, in terms of our general confusion about the nature of causation and necessity. It is to this issue that I now turn.

II

All that we can discover of causation as it exists "in the objects", according to Hume, is constant conjunction. Beyond this regularity, we discover no further "tie" or "bond" between cause and effect. Nor can we discover any "power", "force", or "agency" in *any* cause. Hume's successors in the classical compatibilist tradition—however they may differ over points of detail—have generally accepted these basic tenets of Hume's "regularity theory" and have, following Hume, built it into their compatibilist position. On this view of things, Hume is understood to have been concerned to reconstruct the liberty arguments by placing them on the foundation of the regularity theory of causation.

What is the significance of Hume's regularity theory of causation for the classical compatibilist position? Hume's successors have interpreted the significance of Hume's views in this regard largely in terms of his suggestion that causation or necessity seems "to imply something of force, and violence, and constraint, of which we are not sensible" (T, 407). Obviously, this suggestion is intimately related to Hume's claim that he does not "ascribe to the will that unintelligible necessity, which is suppos'd to lie in matter". That is, the idea of necessity seems to imply some sort of compulsion or constraint, Hume suggests, because we erroneously believe that we have some idea of necessity beyond that of constant conjunction and inference. Hume, naturally, accepts that his position would appear rather "invidious" if it committed him to the view that all our actions were somehow compelled. In this way, Hume seems to suggest that traditional "metaphysical" theories of causation have encouraged a fundamental confusion between the notion of an event's being caused and that of an event's being compelled. On the basis of such an erroneous conception of causation, many philosophers have arrived at the equally mistaken conclusion that there must be an incompatibility between determinism and freedom. The regularity theory of causation, it is argued, identifies and removes the source of this confusion in the free will dispute by way of challenging the deep-seated assumption that there is something more to causation than mere constant conjunction or regular succession.

The significance of Hume's necessity argument for the accompanying liberty arguments seems clear in light of this. It may be accounted for in terms of the "positive" and "negative" conditions for freedom and responsibility established by the spontaneity argument (see chp. 1, sec. 1). Free, responsible action, it is claimed, must be *both* uncompelled and caused (i.e. by the agent's willings). Traditional, metaphysical theories of causation, however, confuse or conflate causation and compulsion and thus generate an ineradicable conflict between the positive and negative requirements of freedom and responsibility. It is, therefore, the great merit of Hume's regularity theory that it shows how the positive and negative requirements of freedom and responsibility can be reconciled and how the ("pseudo") conflict generated by traditional theories of causation can be overcome.

These observations regarding the significance of Hume's necessity argument with respect to our tendency to confuse causation and compulsion suggest that our tendency to slide from the idea of liberty of spontaneity to that of liberty of indifference can itself be accounted for primarily in terms of our troubles regarding the issue of causation. That is to say, it seems that it is confusion about the nature of causation that encourages us to embrace a false conception of liberty. We correctly apprehend that liberty (i.e. liberty of spontaneity) is "opposed" to compulsion and constraint. We then, mistakenly, suppose that causation and necessity imply some sort of compulsion and constraint. This leads us to assume that liberty requires the absence of necessity and causation. In other words, we assume that liberty of indifference is required to secure the negative condition demanded for liberty of spontaneity (i.e. the absence of compulsion and constraint). Within this framework, the confusion between two kinds of liberty is perfectly explicable. Commentators like Stroud, who have placed heavy emphasis on Hume's distinction between two kinds of liberty and very little on the relevance of his views on necessity, have, in consequence, failed to recognize the extent to which the problem regarding liberty can be accounted for, given Hume's remarks, in terms of confusion about the nature of necessity. Stroud repeatedly criticizes Hume for failing to *explain* why people are disposed to accept "the doctrine of liberty" (i.e. liberty of indifference) and why they find it so "attractive".[3] In reply to such criticism, it must be said that whatever the *merits* of Hume's explanation, it cannot be said that he provides us with *no* explanation for these features of our thinking. Criticism of this nature suggests that Stroud has failed to come to grips with the significance of the necessity argument in this context. Whatever Hume's intentions may have been, he was certainly anxious to explain the apparent attractiveness of "liberty of indifference" in terms of our confusion about causation and compulsion.

So interpreted, Hume's necessity argument is understood to strengthen the compatibilist strategy by exposing and eliminating a source of potential confusion. Hume's successors in the classical compatibilist tradition, however they may vary in the particular way in which they articulate the "regularity theory" of causation, are nevertheless agreed on the fundamental strategy described above. We find, therefore, that Hume's effort to reconstruct the compatibilist strategy on the foundation of the regularity theory of causation has, over the past two centuries, become an integral part of the classical compatibilist strategy.

Compatibilists have made Hume's point regarding the distinction between causation and compulsion in a variety of ways, and we can trace the argument back through the centuries. Ayer, for example, notes that the word 'determinism' tends to suggest that "one event is somehow in the power of another, whereas the truth is merely that they are *factually correlated*" ("Freedom and Necessity", 22; my emphasis). One source of this confusion, says Ayer, "is the survival of an animistic conception of causality, in which all causal relationships are modelled on the example of one person's exercising authority over another" (ibid.). In a similar vein, Schlick suggests that because we confuse "descriptive" laws of nature with "prescriptive" laws of society, we mistakenly confuse natural necessity with compulsion ("When Is a Man Responsible?" secs. 2, 3, 4, and 7). It is this confusion which encourages us to identify freedom with indeterminism and to regard it as being opposed to causality. Russell argues the same point as follows:

> The subjective sense of freedom, sometimes alleged against determinism, has no bearing on the question whatever. The view that it has a bearing rests upon the belief that causes compel their effects, or that nature enforces obedience to its laws as governments do. These are mere anthropomorphic superstitions, due to the assimilation of causes with volitions and natural laws with human edicts. . . . It is one of the demerits of the traditional theory of causality that it has created an artificial opposition between determinism and the freedom of which we are introspectively conscious. ("On the Notion of Cause", 206)

According to Russell, a volition "operates" when there is "some law in virtue of which a similar volition in rather similar circumstances will usually *be followed by* what it wills" (ibid., 192; my emphasis).

The above remarks, it may be noted, leave us with the firm impression that were the causal relation to involve some stronger "bond" or "union" than that of mere "uniformity of sequence", then causes would indeed (somehow) compel or constrain their effects. This view of the matter is stated more explicitly by Mill. Mill suggests that people are reluctant to accept that "there is nothing in causation but invariable, certain, and unconditional sequence". He continues,

> There are few to whom mere constancy of succession appears a sufficiently stringent bond of union for so peculiar a relation as that of cause and effect. Even if the reason repudiates, the imagination retains, the feeling of some more intimate connection, of some peculiar tie or mysterious constraint exercised by the antecedent over the consequent. Now this it is which, considered as applying to the human will, conflicts with our consciousness and revolts our feelings. We are certain that in the case of our volitions, there is not this mysterious constraint. We know that we are not compelled, as by a magical spell, to obey any particular motive. (*A System of Logic*, VI, ii, 2)

On the basis of these remarks, Mill proceeds to argue that a stronger conception of causation than that of mere regularity may lead us into full-blown fatalism. That is to say, traditional theories of causation seem to imply that a cause has some "irresistible" power over its effect. This leads to the fatalistic conclusion that there is "no use in struggling against it" (*Logic*, VI, ii, 3). The event in question "will happen however we may strive to prevent it". Mill, like others in the classical tradition, maintains that an understanding of causation in terms of regularity enables us to steer clear of these pitfalls.

Clearly, then, Hume's suggestion that metaphysical or nonregularity conceptions of causation lead us to confuse causation and compulsion has become a salient and established feature of the classical compatibilist strategy. What are we to make of this aspect of their position? Considered as an attempt to *strengthen* the liberty arguments, it must be deemed a failure. It suffers from two closely related shortcomings. First, this line of reasoning gives credence to the view that if there were some stronger "bond" or "tie" between cause and effect beyond that of mere regularity, then causes would (somehow) compel or constrain their effects. A close examination of the spontaneity argument, however, reveals that this assumption is itself confused. The distinction which is fundamental to the compatibilist position is that between those actions which have external causes (i.e. compelled or constrained actions) and those which have causes internal to the agent.[4] This crucial distinction between actions that originate from the agent and those that do not is not compromised by "metaphysical" (i.e. nonregularity) views of causation. (Hobbes, for example, consistently adheres to a metaphysical account of causation without undermining his compatibilist position.) What is relevant to whether an action was compelled or not is the nature of the *cause*, not the nature of the *causal relation*. Nothing about the metaphysical conception of cause when applied to human action need suggest that we do not act according to our will and could not act otherwise *if* we so willed. Clearly, therefore, proponents of the line of reasoning under consideration are mistaken when they suggest that metaphysical theories of causation would pose a threat to the (classical) compatibilist strategy. To concede this point to the incompatibilist is to be confused about the very force or significance of the spontaneity argument itself.

This brings us to the second and closely related shortcoming of the argument concerning compulsion and metaphysical conceptions of causation. The argument presented suggests that our (supposed) tendency to confuse causation and compulsion has its source in mistaken views regarding the nature of the causal relation. This, quite simply, makes the wrong point against the incompatibilist. The point at issue, as I have noted, concerns the nature of the cause, not the nature of the causal relation. If incompatibilists are confused about *this* issue, then so, too, are those compatibilists who have put forward this particular rejoinder to them. Confusion about the significance of the caused/compelled distinction cannot be eliminated by trying to describe "noncompelling" causal relations in terms of regularity or constant conjunctions. Causal relations, as such, are neither compelling nor noncompelling. It is the nature of the *cause* (i.e. the object) which determines whether or not a given action was compelled. In this way, it seems clear that the argument presented is fundamentally misconceived. It involves, ironically enough, a failure to grasp the significance of the spontaneity argument. We must conclude, therefore, that it is not obvious that this effort to strengthen the compatibilist position by means of the regularity theory of causation succeeds. On the contrary, as it stands, it seems clear that traditional theories of causation pose no threat to the distinctions that are essential to the liberty arguments and that the regularity theory, therefore, has no claim to be especially congenial to the compatibilist position.

III

We have shown that Hume's necessity argument is motivated, at least in part, by an effort to explain why we confuse causation and compulsion (and hence find liberty of indifference an attractive doctrine). It is this aspect of Hume's necessity argument that has, historically speaking, been most influential. I have argued that it is fundamentally misguided.[5] Whatever the faults of this aspect of Hume's strategy, however, it is important to note that in respect of his concern with the nature of the causal relation, there are certain affinities with the traditional libertarian strategy. That is, from one point of view, we may describe Hume as endeavouring to show that the dilemma of determinism, as it is usually conceived, misconstrues our alternatives. Hume is arguing that a middle path may be travelled between, on the one hand, a confused and unintelligible conception of necessity and, on the other, an erroneous belief in the existence of chance. This strategy may be illustrated in the following way:

(A) Chance　　　　　　(B) Humean Necessity　　　　(C) Metaphysical Necessity

　　No regular　　　　　　Regular succession　　　　　"Compelling"
　　succession or　　　　　and inference　　　　　　　powers in objects
　　inference

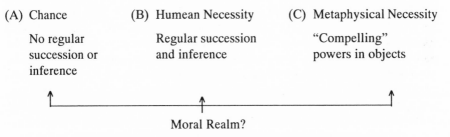

Moral Realm?

Humean Necessity and the Dilemma of Determinism

In light of the above diagram, it appears evident that one aspect of Hume's strategy is to reveal that the dilemma of determinism, presented as an alternative between horns A and C, is a *false* dilemma. What has encouraged philosophers to misconstrue the problem in this way has been their confusion about the nature of necessity as we discover it in the natural realm. According to Hume, our experience of both the natural and the moral realms makes it plain that the only genuine alternative is the middle path of Humean necessity; therefore, in this respect, our actions and willings are on the same footing as the operations of bodies. It is important to recognize and appreciate this aspect of Hume's strategy. Apart from anything else, it should make us wary of those interpretations which present Hume as placing himself firmly, and without qualification, on the horn of necessity.[6]

The distinction that is crucial to the spontaneity argument between free and compelled action, it has been noted, concerns the type of cause, rather than the nature of the causal relation. Given this, it may be asked why the compatibilist should slide away from concern with the former (i.e. the nature of the causal object) to the latter (i.e. the nature of the causal relation)? Indeed, in light of my criticisms, it may be said that compatibilists are altogether mistaken in concerning themselves in any way with the nature of the causal relation (this being, it is said, the basic source of incompatibilist confusion on this subject). I think that this more extended line of criticism fails to recognize the complexity of the objectives which the compatibilist is pursuing. The issue which is relevant to the free/*compelled* distinction is, as I have shown, that regarding *types* of cause (i.e. the nature of the causal object). In itself, however, this will not enable us to distinguish between caused and *random* behaviour or action. In regard to *this* distinction, we must turn our attention to the nature of the causal *relation*. In other words, if we are to distinguish "actions" (or items of behaviour) that are "random" from those that are "caused" (and attributable to the agent), then we evidently require some *interpretation* of the causal relation. That is, we must be able to say what it is for an action to be "caused" (rather than random or capricious). The compatibilist, as I have described the position, is concerned to argue not only that necessity is *consistent* with freedom and responsibility (as claimed by the spontaneity argument), but that it is actually *essential* to, or *required* for, freedom and responsibility. It is this further, stronger claim that requires that the compatibilist provide some relevant or appropriate account of the nature of the causal relation. Without any such account, it remains open for the libertarian to simply maintain (as I indicated in chp. 1) that what is caused need not be necessitated—and hence, contrary to what the compatibilist seeks to establish, necessity is *not* essential to freedom and responsibility. This specific issue can be debated independently of the related but separate matter of whether or not a distinction between *types* of causes serves to show that necessity is *consistent* with freedom and responsibility. Obviously, someone *might* take the view that necessity is consistent with freedom and responsibility (for the reasons established by the spontaneity argument) but also claim that it is *not essential* to freedom and responsibility (e.g. because an action may be caused without being necessitated).[7]

Within the framework of Hume's discussion, the claim that necessity is an essential part of causation (and that when we "remove" necessity we thereby also "remove" causes) is very largely an unargued for assumption (e.g. T, 77, 87, 171, and 407; and EU, 97). Much the same is true of most of Hume's successors in the classical compatibilist tradition.[8] Granted, however, that the compatibilist is concerned to show that necessity is not just compatible with freedom and responsibility but is actually essential to it (i.e. required for it), compatibilists cannot avoid taking up the issue of the causal relation and committing themselves to some such general interpretation of it.

These features of the compatibilist strategy bring to light certain tensions or strains between the objectives of the spontaneity and the antilibertarian arguments. Things would certainly be simpler, from the perspective of the spontaneity argument, if it were argued that all that is relevant to the question of freedom and responsibility is the type of cause (i.e. the nature of the object) that produced the action. Incompatibilists argue, against this view, that if the causal relation involves necessitation, then freedom and responsibility are threatened. In taking up the antilibertarian argument and arguing that necessity is essential to the causal relation (and hence to freedom and responsibility), compatibilists are required to acknowledge, with their critics, that the *interpretation* of the causal relation is indeed directly relevant to the question of freedom and responsibility. To this extent, the "simple solution" offered by the spontaneity argument is denied compatibilists because of their (further) concern to establish the stronger claim that necessity is essential to freedom and responsibility. Only by limiting their objectives to the weak thesis that necessity is not *incompatible* with freedom and responsibility, could compatibilists continue to maintain that the distinction between types of causes serves on its own to establish their position. Clearly, however, their objectives extend beyond this, and hence they must provide some relevant account of the causal relation, in terms of which it can be shown that when we remove necessity we also, thereby, remove causes.

When we examine Hume's effort to reinterpret the causal relation and explain its relevance to the free will dispute, it becomes apparent that there is a deep ambivalence in the classical compatibilist strategy in respect of this issue. That is, the compatibilist, on the one hand, seems to argue that were we to remove "necessity" from the causal relation, we would threaten the "connexion" between agent and action on the basis of which attributions of responsibility are founded. On the other hand, compatibilists also argue (in light of Hume's remarks) that we must remove "metaphysical" necessity from our conception of the causal relation so as to rid it of all suggestion of compulsion and constraint. In this way, we find that the compatibilist strategy has sought to find an account of the causal relation which has to be "weak" enough to avoid implying compulsion and "strong" enough to show that necessity is indeed essential to freedom and responsibility. The regularity theory of causation, evidently, is thought to allow the (classical) compatibilist to travel this middle path. However, it may be argued, against this view, that the regularity theory in fact constitutes something of an Achilles' heel for the compatibilist position. That is, the regularity theory, we may argue, not only fails to strengthen the compatibilist position, as I have already suggested, but—what is even more disconcerting—eats away at the metaphysical underpinnings of the compatibilist position. These underpinnings are the "connexions" that must hold between agent and action in order to ascribe responsibility at all. In order to understand these difficulties, we must consider, again, the relations between the liberty arguments and the necessity argument.

IV

I have suggested that one of the most notable strengths of the classical compatibilist position—particularly when compared to the libertarian alternative—is that it seems able to provide a fairly straightforward and plausible account of the mechanism and source of responsibility. That is, agents are deemed responsible for their actions insofar as it is their willings and desires that caused or determined them. Without this causal link or connexion between agent and action, the action could not be attributed to the agent. It is the causal activity of the agent's own will which links or connects him to those actions which we hold him responsible for. In other words, the existence of a causal connexion between agent and action is, on the classical compatibilist view, essential to the "positive" requirement of responsibility. Clearly, then, the causal relation—understood in terms of some sort of link or connexion between cause and effect—is a crucial and indispensable component of the metaphysical foundations of compatibilism as it is generally understood. Hume's remarks plainly suggest that his analysis of the causal relation is not only consistent with the other basic theses of the compatibilist strategy but it further advances and fortifies them. However, on almost *any* interpretation, Hume's necessity argument seems to generate awkward and difficult problems for the classical compatibilist strategy as it is generally understood.

It is a fundamental contention of the necessity argument that "the efficacy of causes" lies "in the determination of the mind" (i.e. the mind of the observer).

(Remember, too, that Hume claims "that the terms of efficacy, agency, power, force, energy, necessity, connexion and productive quality, are all nearly synonimous" [T, 157; cf. EU, 96].) Thus, as we have noted, Hume argues that we do not perceive any power or agency in any objects. Nor do we perceive any connexions between objects other than those "felt connexions" which arise as a result of the subjective operations of our mind (i.e. the principles of association). Further, these felt connexions hold only among our perceptions and cannot be attributed to the (represented) objects themselves. In this way, the necessity argument firmly commits Hume to the view that, so far as we can judge, objects in the external world—such as the thoughts and actions of other people—remain entirely loose and separate and are "conjoined but never connected" (except insofar as they are connected in *our mind*). The essence of Hume's necessity argument is to be found in the claim that we remain entirely ignorant of any powers or connexions existing among the objects, independent of thought and reasoning.

So interpreted, the necessity argument strikes at the very heart of the liberty arguments and renders them most unsatisfactory. Hume is understood to have objected to libertarianism on the ground that if the agent could not be said to have caused his actions, then he could hardly be said to be responsible for them. Now this criticism makes sense if by "caused" we have in mind the non-Humean notion of a cause as a power which necessitates or brings about its effect. The agent would be regarded as responsible for his action because it was his powers that brought about the action and he determined his actions. If the agent did not cause his actions—in the sense of having the power to bring about and determine them—then he cannot be said to be responsible. Accordingly, being responsible for our actions requires that our actions be the *product* of our own powers.[9]

When the notion of causation we employ is Hume's weakened version, this argument becomes less plausible. Hume denies that any cause, of itself, can be known to determine its effect or even could be said to have the power to bring it about. All that we observe between cause and effect, in both the natural and moral realms, is their regular succession. On the basis of experience, we come to feel connexions *in our mind* (i.e. among our perceptions). Thus, the power of the cause and its connexion with its effect is nothing but an association of ideas which has been generated in the mind of the observer. When we observe a constant conjunction between an agent's motives and his actions, this creates *in us a feeling* that he determined or produced his actions.[10] However, there is nothing in the objects themselves which corresponds with this feeling of determination and connexion; the objects themselves remain entirely loose and unconnected. This is equally true in the case of the first person. Even in our own case we do not discover any power or energy in our will, nor any connexions between our willings and our actions (cf. EU, 64–69). Therefore, insofar as the antilibertarian argument depends on a notion of agents' having some intrinsic power to produce, determine, or bring about their actions, the necessity argument suggests that it is flawed. There are no (known) powers in any objects; there are only constant conjunctions between them.

Nor does Hume's account of liberty of spontaneity seem very plausible given the necessity argument. A mere constant conjunction between the agent's motives and his actions will not suffice to establish his responsibility. That is, such constant conjunctions do not, according to the necessity argument, establish that an agent produced his actions (although they may make observers feel that the agent produced his actions). For the purposes of the liberty arguments, if we are to reasonably hold an agent responsible, then we require evidence that there exists some intrinsic connexion between the agent's will and his actions, some intrinsic power by which the agent produces or brings about his actions. The necessity argument is committed to the view that there is, in fact, no such evidence to be found. Thus, Hume's account of liberty of spontaneity seems vulnerable to the very same objections which the antilibertarian argument raised against the libertarian position. That is, given the necessity argument, we still have no reason to believe that such agents produce or bring about their actions, although our subjective experience may make us feel that they do.[11]

In short, the liberty arguments presuppose that any adequate theory of responsibility must establish that agents produce or determine their actions and are, thereby, connected with their deeds. The necessity argument suggests that there exist only constant conjunctions between these objects (i.e. willings and actions) and that these constant conjunctions do not reveal or uncover any power or agency in any cause, nor any connexions between cause and effect. Further, insofar as we may suppose that these causes do possess some power or agency and are, thereby, connected with their effects, this is only because the mind fails to distinguish between an (acquired) association of ideas and a perceived power or connexion in the objects themselves. Hence, according to Hume, the fact that we suppose that the objects themselves possess a power or efficacy by which they are connected with their effects is entirely due to the influence of experience or "custom" on the human mind; there are no corresponding features in the objects themselves. In this way, Hume's account of necessity appears to undermine the plausibility of the antilibertarian argument and leave the spontaneity argument open to serious objection.[12] In light of these difficulties, one of two things must be true of Hume's "reconciling project". Either what he took to be its greatest source of strength, the necessity argument, generates awkward and serious difficulties for this project, *or* his liberty arguments have been misunderstood. I will show that it is indeed the case that Hume's liberty arguments have been misunderstood.

Notes

1. Flew, *Hume's Philosophy of Belief*, 157. In this context, Flew argues that it is a mistake to suppose that conceptual issues (i.e. problems concerning meaning, implication, and consistency) are "merely verbal" in any pejorative sense. He says, "Hume's dismissal of the whole issue as 'merely verbal' . . . is surely one of the primary sources of the still fashionable careless talk about pseudo-problems" (p. 157). Flew's emphasis on the "verbal" or "conceptual" nature of Hume's intentions in this sphere clearly reflects, in some measure, the dominant methodology of analytic philosophers of a generation or so ago. (It is not so clear, however, that Stroud's similar approach can be explained in these terms [cf. Stroud's remarks in *Hume*, 153–54]. Stroud is well aware of the anachronisms involved in reading Hume as a modern "analytic philosopher" [see *Hume*, chp. 10, esp. pp. 220–24].)

2. When it is understood that by 'necessity' we *mean* only regularity and inference, then, Hume argues, experience and observation establish that necessity does in fact hold in the moral

realm no less than in the natural. In other words, by clarifying our terminology and freeing ourselves of the (natural) confusions associated with this term, we make it possible for *observation* to settle this issue.

3. Stroud, *Hume*, 145: "Hume . . . offers no explanation at all of exactly how our intense concern with 'the liberty of spontaneity' leads us to confuse it with the absence of causality". See also p.148: "I have already mentioned . . ." and p. 153: "Once again, we might be . . .". In a footnote, Stroud points out that others, such as Schlick and Ayer, have been concerned with our tendency to confuse causation and compulsion—but Hume's remarks on this score are entirely ignored.

4. Schlick provides a very concise account of this basic distinction: "Freedom means the opposite of compulsion; a man is *free* if he does not act under *compulsion*, and he is compelled or unfree when he is hindered from without in the realization of his natural desires. Hence . . . a man will be considered quite free and responsible if no such external compulsion is exerted upon him" ("When Is a Man Responsible?" 59). I have already indicated, however, that this sharp divide is very difficult to maintain (see chp. 1, sec. 2).

5. Given the importance of these claims for the classical compatibilist position, it seems clear, in light of these criticisms, that this strategy loses a significant part of its original appeal (i.e. the suggested diagnosis of why we naturally confuse the two kinds of liberty is plainly flawed).

6. Norman Kemp Smith, for example, suggests that "Hume adheres, without qualification, to the necessitarian standpoint" (*Philosophy of David Hume*, 433). Even allowing for the more "necessitarian" flavour of the *Treatise*, this remark is rather misleading.

7. The point that I am concerned to establish can perhaps be expressed more simply as follows. The compatibilist strategy demands that we be able to draw two different distinctions: free/compelled and caused/random. The first distinction is crucial to the spontaneity argument, the second to the antilibertarian argument. The first distinction depends on discriminating between *types* of cause (i.e. causal objects, such as our willings). The second distinction is based on some interpretation of the nature of the causal relation (e.g. in terms of necessity and regularity).

8. "[Hume] assumed that *necessary connection* is an essential part of the idea of the relation of cause and effect, and he sought for its nature. . . . The twist that Hume gave to the topic thus suggested a connection of the notion of causality with that of deterministic laws. . . . The well-known philosophers who have lived after Hume may have aimed at following him and developing some of his ideas, or they may have put up a resistance; but in no case, so far as I know, has the resistance called in question the equation of causality with necessitation" (Anscombe, "Causality and Determination", 65). I note in passing that Anscombe, surprisingly, does not cite Hume's Scottish contemporary, and one of his most notable critics, Thomas Reid. Reid criticizes, in considerable detail, the view that what is caused must be necessitated by antecedent events or circumstances. See especially, his *Active Powers*, Essay IV, chp. 9.

9. Hume also denies the existence of powers understood as possessed but unexercised *abilities* (see T, 171 and 311–13). However, this notion of power is distinct from the notion of the force or energy in a cause which determines its effect. It is this second notion which we are concerned with.

10. See, e.g., T, 408: "The necessity of any action, whether of matter or of the mind, *is not properly a quality in the agent, but in any thinking or intelligent being, who may consider the action*, and consists in the determination of his thought to infer its existence from some preceding objects" (my emphasis). See also T, 266: "And how must we be disappointed . . .".

11. Not surprisingly, Malebranche runs into similar difficulties on this issue. Having

claimed that "all the volitions of minds are only occasional causes" and not the "true causes" of our actions, it would appear that even sinful acts are brought about "only through the force and efficacy of the will of God" (see, especially, *Elucidations*, XV, proof 6 and reply). This, of course, creates some awkward theological problems for Malebranche. He is certainly anxious to avoid suggesting that God commits acts of sin! Obviously, Hume's theory does not run into the theological difficulties which Malebranche's occasionalism encounters. However, Hume's theory does seem liable to the same sort of objections which Malebranche realized could be raised against his own position. Namely, given that Hume accepts Malebranche's doctrine that there is no discoverable power or agency in any object, including our will, and that our willings and actions remain entirely unconnected, it may be suggested that we cannot be held responsible for bringing about actions which we do not produce. On this, see Hume's remarks at T, 249.

12. These general observations on Hume's strategy, I suggest, reveal serious flaws in the classical compatibilist position—a position that has been erected to a great extent on the basis of Hume's arguments. In more general terms, the regularity theory of causation presents fundamental problems for the (classical) compatibilist strategy, and these problems have gone largely unnoticed. In response to the line of criticism advanced, some defenders of the classical compatibilist strategy might argue that—whatever particular difficulties *Hume* may run into in this regard—there is more to be said for the general position than I suggest. More specifically, it may be argued that the criticism offered depends on the "sceptical" view that there are no causal "connexions", "ties", or "bonds" of *any sort* between cause and effect. There is, however, an alternative "revisionary" view which maintains that regularity or constant conjunction is *constitutive* of the causal connexion. On this interpretation, free agents do possess the power to produce or bring about their actions, but this relationship between an agent's willings and actions must be understood in terms of regularity or a uniform sequence of events. There exists no *further* bond or union between agent and action. This revisionary account, it may be suggested, removes the danger which the sceptical account of the causal relation (e.g. as per Hume's account) presents for the compatibilist strategy. In my view, however, this "revisionary" approach encounters its own difficulties. For further discussion of this issue, see my "Causation, Compulsion and Compatibilism".

4

The Naturalism of Hume's "Reconciling Project"

Most of those who have written about the emotions and human conduct seem to be dealing not with natural phenomena that follow the common law of Nature but with phenomena outside Nature. They appear to go so far as to conceive man in Nature as a kingdom within a kingdom. They believe that he disturbs rather than follows Nature's order.

Spinoza, *Ethics*

'Tis only upon the principles of necessity, that a person acquires any merit or demerit from his actions, however the common opinion may incline to the contrary.

Hume, *A Treatise of Human Nature*

My suggestion that the necessity argument undermines the liberty arguments sharply conflicts with Hume's view which was, plainly, quite the reverse. In this chapter, I show that Hume's liberty arguments have been largely misunderstood and misrepresented. I argue that, on Hume's view, regarding a person as responsible "is more properly felt than judg'd of". To hold a person responsible is to regard them as the object of a certain kind of *passion*—namely, a moral sentiment. In the absence of any appropriate passion of this nature, no one would, as a matter of fact, be regarded as responsible. One of the objectives of Hume's science of man was to discover under what circumstances people are *felt* to be responsible for their actions. Hume believed that "in the production and conduct of the passions, there is a certain regular mechanism, which is susceptible of as accurate a disquisition, as the laws of motion, optics, hydrostatics, or any part of natural philosophy" (DP, 166). Hume's liberty arguments, I will show, can be properly understood only within the framework of his account of the "regular mechanism" which generates the moral sentiments. When Hume's arguments are interpreted within this naturalistic framework, the necessity argument does not undermine the liberty arguments properly understood. On the contrary, as Hume's remarks suggest, the necessity argument is indeed essential to his overall (naturalistic) compatibilist strategy.

I

Much of Hume's writing on the subject of liberty and necessity is concerned to establish that our *actual experience shows* that the moral realm, like the natural realm, is subject to necessity. As we have noted, Hume takes it that "two circumstances form the whole of that necessity, which we ascribe to matter" (EU, 82). These two circumstances are the constant conjunction of like objects and the inference of the mind from one object to another. If we allow that "these two circumstances take place in the voluntary actions of men and in the operations of mind" (EU, 83), then we must accept that the moral realm is governed by necessity. Hume proceeds to show, first, that there is constant conjunction in the moral realm and, second, that given the very nature of society and morality, we *must* make inferences in the moral realm.

Hume believes that the question of whether or not there is constant conjunction in the moral realm is amenable to empirical resolution. It is just a matter of fact that there is constant conjunction in the moral realm as well as the natural realm. Hume admits that there are apparent irregularities and uncertainties in *both* the natural and moral realms, but these can be attributed to "imperfect knowledge" and can be accounted for by contrary causes (T, 403–4; EU, 86–88).[1]

> Thus it appears, not only that the conjunction between motives and voluntary actions is as regular and uniform as that between the cause and effect in any part of nature; but also that this regular conjunction has been universally acknowledged among mankind, and has never been the subject of dispute, either in philosophy or common life. (EU, 88)

Accordingly, Hume proceeds to try to show that this "regular conjunction" between motive and action allows for inference in the moral realm by "*determining* us to infer the existence of one from that of another" (T, 404). I believe that Hume's arguments here are based on two incontestable facts about mankind: "that men *always* seek society" (T, 402) and that men regard other people as objects of praise or blame— that is, they hold them responsible.

These two arguments establishing that people *must* make inferences in the moral realm are closely related. For people to live in society, they must be able to infer the actions of others from their character, and—in the opposite direction but parallel to this—for people to regard one another as responsible, they must be able to infer character from actions.

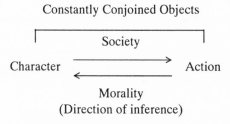

Constantly Conjoined Objects

Society

Character ⟶ Action

Morality
(Direction of inference)

Hume proceeds to demonstrate that we draw inferences concerning motives and actions even though "it may seem superfluous to prove" this. We observe that men always seek society.

> The mutual dependence of men is so great in all societies that scarce any human action is entirely complete in itself, or is performed without some reference to the actions of others, which are requisite to make it answer fully the intention of the

agent. . . . In all those conclusions [expectations concerning the actions of others] they take their measures from past experience, in the same manner as in their reasonings concerning external objects; and firmly believe that men, as well as all the elements, are to continue, in their operations, the same that they have ever found them. . . . In short, this experimental inference and reasoning concerning the actions of others enters so much into human life that no man, while awake, is ever a moment without employing it. (EU, 89)

Hume points out that inferences based on both moral and natural evidence often "link together and form only one chain of argument". The prisoner, for example, infers the impossibility of escape as much from the character ("obstinacy") of the jailer as the nature of the walls and bars around him (T, 406; EU, 90). Our inferences in the moral realm seem no less certain than those in the natural realm. "Moral evidence is", Hume says, "nothing but a conclusion concerning the actions of men, deriv'd from the consideration of their motives, temper and situation" (T, 404).[2] This sort of reasoning "runs thro' politics, war, commerce, oeconomy, and indeed mixes itself so entirely in human life, that 'tis impossible to act or subsist a moment without recourse to it" (T, 405). Hume takes it as an empirical fact that men make such inferences about the actions of others and that society would not be possible if they did not or could not make such inferences. Accordingly, it is a matter of fact that the moral realm is not subject to liberty of indifference (i.e. the absence of regularity and inference), for otherwise society would be impossible.

It seems quite clear that if no one were regarded as responsible, then morality would collapse. Hume believed that his doctrine of necessity was "not only consistent with morality, but [is] absolutely essential to its support" (EU, 97). In the midst of arguing that men need to be able to infer the actions of others to operate in, and speculate about, society, Hume makes the following remark: "Where would be the foundations of *morals* if particular characters had no certain or determinate power to produce particular sentiments, and if these sentiments had no constant operations on actions?" (EU, 90). Clearly Hume believes that if character did not, via certain sentiments or motives, determine action, the foundations of morals would be threatened. In another passage, he says, "The mind of man is so formed by nature that, upon the appearance of certain characters, dispositions, and actions, it immediately feels the sentiment of approbation and blame; nor are there any emotions more essential to its frame and constitution" (EU, 102). According to Hume, then, approbation and blame are sentiments, and the fact that they can be generated is of great importance. The significance of these passages is, I shall argue, that without inference, no sentiment of approbation or blame would be generated.

II

The reverse of inferring actions from character is inferring character from actions. We do not, Hume believed, know anyone's character immediately. We know a character only by inferring it from the sentiments which it has the "power to produce". Nor do we know anyone's passions or sentiments immediately. A passion "is at first known only by its effects, and by those external signs, in the countenance and conversation, which convey an idea of it" (T, 317). From the external signs, "we *infer* the passion" (T, 576). As has already been noted, inference requires regular succession between one object and another—in this case, character and action, via the passions. To be aware of any other person's character as an object, we must infer it from those external signs of which it is a cause.[3]

Why should inference to character have any importance or significance for morality? In order to appreciate this feature of Hume's system, we must describe the production of the moral sentiments and how it relates to the "regular mechanism" of the indirect passions. According to Hume, approval and disapproval are "nothing but a fainter and more imperceptible love or hatred" (T, 614). That is to say, approbation and blame are, for Hume, calm forms of love and hate.[4] To hold someone responsible is to regard the person as an object of approval or disapproval and is, thus, a particular way, or specific mode, of loving or hating that person. Hume says, "The constant and universal object of hatred or anger is a person or creature endow'd with thought and consciousness; and when any criminal or injurious actions excite that passion, 'tis only by their relation to the person or connexion with him." He continues, "and where [actions] proceed not from some cause in the characters and disposition of the person, who perform'd them . . . 'tis impossible he can, upon its account, become the object of punishment or vengeance" (T, 411). Evidently, it is only a person or a thinking being who is an object of hatred and anger.[5] Once it is appreciated that in Hume's view our moral sentiments are nothing more than "a fainter and more imperceptible love or hatred", then it is clear why they must take a person or thinking being as their object. In his discussion of the indirect passions of love and hatred, Hume says,

> One of these suppositions, viz. that *the cause of love or hatred must be related to a person or thinking being, in order to produce these passions,* is not only provable, but too evident to be contested. Virtue and vice, when consider'd in the abstract . . . excite no degree of love or hatred, esteem or contempt towards those, who have no relation to them. (T, 331)

In order to understand the conditions under which it is possible for us to ascribe responsibility, we must first describe, in more detail, the general features of the mechanism of the indirect passions (of which the moral sentiments are the most notable subset).

Hume describes love and hatred as "indirect passions". The first two parts of Book II of the *Treatise* is devoted to an analysis of the nature and causes of these passions. Like the direct passions (e.g. desire, joy, fear, and grief) the indirect passions arise from pleasure and pain, but this involves "the conjunction of other qualities" (T, 276). There are several different indirect passions. Hume, however, is primarily concerned with two pairs of indirect passions: pride/humility and love/hate. As with all other passions, there is no "definition" available for the passions themselves. They are distinguished by feeling alone (T, 277, 329, 472, 590, 606–7). We can, nevertheless, describe both the causes and the effects of these passions, or the circumstances which give rise to them and the "objects" that they take. Pride and humility are distinguished from love and hatred in that the natural object of the former pair is oneself, whereas that of the latter pair is some other person. The idea of oneself or some other person, then, is the *natural* effect of these passions, and hence it is to these objects that the indirect passions inevitably "direct" our view (T, 277f). Pride and humility and love and hate may also be discriminated in terms of their (distinct) pleasurable or painful feelings. The former in each pair being pleasant, the latter painful. What all these passions share, however, is the same "regular mechanism" by which they are generated.

All indirect passions, Hume claims, are "plac'd betwixt two ideas, of which the one produces it, and the other is produc'd by it. The first idea, therefore, represents the cause, the second the object of the passion" (T, 278). The objects of these passions, as I have noted, are fixed by an "original property" of human nature (T, 280, 286). We simply observe what objects these feelings are (naturally) directed toward. Hume's analysis of the *cause* of these passions, however, is more complex. In accounting for the causes, we must distinguish between the *quality* in the cause by means of which it "operates on the passion" and the *subject* in which that quality inheres. In other words, there are two aspects to the cause to be considered: some quality of the object and the subject in which that quality inheres.[6]

In order to give rise to an indirect passion, what is required is a double association of both impressions and ideas (T, 286). The specific features and relations of the subject and quality making up the cause will determine exactly what associations are generated by it. First, all associations of impressions depend on a resemblance of feeling. The cause of the passion, depending on its quality or qualities, must give rise to an *independent* pleasure or pain in ourselves or others (e.g. we find that the beautiful house is pleasing to ourselves and others independently of any love or pride which it may also give rise to). In these circumstances, the cause of the passion naturally introduces those indirect passions which resemble its pleasant or painful effects. (For example, when we think of a beautiful house this leads us to feel its pleasurable effects on ourselves and other people, and then, by association of impressions— because pride and love are themselves pleasurable—we naturally feel either pride or love.) Second, an association of ideas is also required to produce the indirect passions. This association depends on the way in which the cause of the passions is related to ourselves or others. If the subject in which the pleasant or painful quality inheres is related to ourselves (i.e. by way of causation, contiguity, or resemblance), then the mind naturally moves to the idea of the self. If, on the other hand, the subject is related to some other person, then the mind naturally moves to the idea of another. In this way, the cause of the passion must both produce an independent pleasure and pain (in order to give rise to the required association of impressions) and be related to our self or some other person (in order to produce the required association of ideas). If either of these features is lacking—and they can be weakened by degrees—then no indirect passion will be produced.[7]

Hume notes that the causes of the indirect passions vary greatly in number and kind (T, 281). Different and varied as they may be, however, they must be "either parts of ourselves, or something nearly related to us" (T, 285). Hume distinguishes four broad categories of objects or features of ourselves which give rise to the indirect passions: our wealth, external goods, or property; our immediate relatives or those people who are closely related to us on another basis; our bodily qualities or attributes; and, most important, our qualities of mind, or character traits (T, 279, 294f; DP, 146–53). Those character traits or mental qualities which produce an independent pleasure in ourselves or others also, in consequence of this, give rise to pride or love. Character traits or qualities of mind of this nature are virtues. Similarly, those mental qualities or character traits which produce pain, also, in consequence of this, produce humility or hate, and, as such, they are deemed to be vices.[8] Well into Book III, Hume summarizes his account:

> We have already observ'd, that moral distinctions depend entirely on certain peculiar sentiments of pain and pleasure, and that whatever mental quality in ourselves or others gives us a satisfaction, by the survey or reflection, is of course virtuous; as every thing of this nature, that gives uneasiness, is vicious. Now since every quality in ourselves or others, which gives pleasure, always creates pride or love; as every one, that produces uneasiness, excites humility or hatred: It follows, that these two particulars are to be consider'd as equivalent, with regard to our mental qualities, *virtue* and the power of producing love or pride, *vice* and the power of producing humility or hatred. In every case, therefore, we must judge of the one by the other; and may pronounce any *quality* of the mind virtuous, which causes love or pride; and any one vicious, which causes hatred or humility. (T, 574–75; cf. T, 473; DP, 146–47, 155–56)

Clearly, then, virtue and vice, by means of the general mechanism of the indirect passions, give rise to that "faint and imperceptible" form of love and hatred which constitutes the moral sentiments. It is, in other words, this "regular mechanism" which is, on Hume's account, essential to all ascriptions of responsibility.

Hume repeatedly claims, in a variety of contexts, that it is only qualities of mind or character which give rise to the moral sentiments. An action which in no way reflects or reveals anything of the nature of the mind or character of the agent will, he argues, never produce a moral sentiment in us. This point is made clearly in the passage at T, 411, cited above (i.e. "The constant and universal object of hatred and anger . . ."). Another important passage in Book III elaborates further on this matter:

> 'Tis evident, that when we praise any actions, we regard only the motives that produced them, and consider the actions as signs or indications of certain principles in the mind and temper. The external performance has no merit. We must look within to find the moral quality. This we cannot do directly; and therefore fix our attention on actions, as on external signs. But these actions are still considered as signs; and the ultimate object of our praise and approbation is the motive, that produc'd them. (T, 477)[9]

All this simply reinforces the essential points Hume established early on in book II in his discussion of "Pride and Humility" (i.e. Bk. II, Pt i): In respect of the peculiar form of love and hatred which constitutes the moral sentiments, the cause is always some quality of mind or character (i.e. some virtue or vice) which is itself a fixed and durable part of the person who is the object of these sentiments. In the absence of any such appropriate or relevant cause, no such sentiment would be aroused in us.

Within the framework of this account of the "regular mechanism" through which our moral sentiments are generated, it is quite obvious why inference to character is so essential to morality. In order to know anyone else's character, we require inference—from their actions to their character. Without knowledge of anyone's character, no sentiment of approbation or blame would be aroused in us. Therefore, without inference, no would be an object of praise or blame—that is to say, no one would be regarded as responsible for her actions. Accordingly, praising and blaming would be *psychologically impossible* if there were no inferences from action to character. Without this necessity, morality would become a psychological impossibility. It is also clear that external violence, like liberty of indifference, makes it impossible to regard someone as an object of praise or blame. This is because in such circumstances, we could not make any inference from action to the agent's character. Because the action is caused by external forces, we are led *away* from the agent's character.

> liberty [of spontaneity] . . . is also essential to morality, and . . . no human actions, where it is wanting, are susceptible to any moral qualities, or can be the objects either of approbation or dislike. For as actions are objects of our moral sentiment, so far only as they are indications of the internal character, passions, and affections; it is impossible that they can give rise either to praise or blame, where they proceed not from these principles, but are derived altogether from external violence. (EU, 99)

Only when an action is, or is believed to be, determined by the will of the agent is that agent regarded as an object of praise or blame—that is a matter of psychological fact for Hume. Actions that are either uncaused or caused by factors external to the agent cannot render the agent responsible, not because it would be illogical to hold the person responsible but because it would be psychologically impossible to hold her responsible.

The salient features of Hume's naturalistic compatibilism can be summarized under the following points:

1. Approval and disapproval are essential to morality.
2. Only character traits or mental qualities arouse our moral sentiments of approval or disapproval.
3. Knowledge of a person's character traits or mental qualities requires inference.
4. A person or thinking being is held responsible if we regard her as an object of a moral sentiment.
5. Regarding an agent as responsible is, therefore, a matter of feeling not judgment.
6. Without inference to character (i.e. necessity), no such feeling could, as a matter of psychological fact, be aroused in us, and therefore no one could be regarded as responsible.
7. Therefore, it is an empirical psychological fact that without necessity, morality would be *impossible*.

III

It follows from the naturalistic interpretation of Hume's position that holding someone responsible is primarily a matter of feeling rather than reasoning.[10] One knows an agent is responsible only if one is aware of that person's causing a certain sentiment of approbation or blame. Nor is this sentiment itself amenable to rational justification. Hume held that "a passion must be accompany'd by some false judgment, in order to its being unreasonable; and even then 'tis not the passion, properly speaking, which is unreasonable, but the judgment" (T, 416). Therefore, the fact that we do or do not hold an agent responsible under given circumstances cannot be deemed reasonable or unreasonable. Only if we are mistaken about those circumstances can our sentiments be said to be unreasonable. It is simply a psychological fact about human nature that under the circumstances specified an agent is felt to be responsible.

It may be suggested that some of Hume's terminology does not lend itself to the interpretation I offer here. Hume speaks, for example, of "proper objects of hatred and vengeance" and of "just proofs" of criminal mentality. If we assume that propriety and justice are determined by reason and not feeling, then it will seem that Hume is saying something other than the naturalistic interpretation suggests. However, it is clear from Hume's discussion that propriety and justice in this context are determined by feeling. It is the natural operations of the mind, not reason, that determine the "proper object" of a sentiment. Similarly, a proof of culpability is "just" insofar as it is founded neither on false belief nor in conflict with our moral sentiments. Proofs of criminality would "cease to be just proofs" if the character of the agent involved did not in fact arouse a sentiment of disapproval in us. However, when such sentiments are aroused and based on true belief, then they are just. Without necessity, no disapproval would ever be felt, and hence there would be no "just proof" of a criminal nature.[11]

Hume's discussion of liberty and necessity can on this reinterpretation be shown to be closely connected with his discussions of the passions and moral evaluations. These connexions are not apparent in the *Enquiries*, where no lengthy or detailed discussion of the passions appears. This may in part account for misinterpretations of Hume's argument. However, as has been argued above, the necessity argument is also of great importance to any adequate understanding of what Hume has to say about liberty and necessity.[12] The presentation in the *Treatise* rather obscures these connexions in Hume's argument—there being a gap of over two hundred pages between his discussion of the idea of necessary connexion and that of liberty and necessity. This quite serious flaw is remedied by the first *Enquiry* but only at the cost of leaving the reader somewhat puzzled as to why Hume put his discussion of "liberty and necessity" in Book II of the *Treatise* in the first place.[13] The naturalistic interpretation, however, shows that the discussion of the passions is also most relevant to a clear understanding of the discussion of liberty and necessity, and, therefore, the latter discussion is not, as Kemp Smith suggests, simply a "lengthy digression" in the context of Book II of the *Treatise*.[14]

I have referred to this interpretation of Hume's compatibilist strategy as being "naturalistic". In what sense are Hume's arguments "naturalistic"? There are, I think, two quite different senses of "naturalism" which can appropriately be applied to Hume's discussion of liberty and necessity. The first and most important sense is that it involves applying the experimental method of reasoning to this "long disputed question". As we have seen, Hume is concerned to *describe* the circumstances under which people are felt to be responsible (i.e. describe the "regular mechanism" which generates the moral sentiments). In this way, Hume's compatibilist strategy must be understood *within* the general context of his effort to "introduce the experimental method of reasoning into moral subjects".[15] This aspect of Hume's "general strategy" goes completely unnoticed on the classical interpretation.

The second sense in which Hume's reconciling project may be said to be naturalistic is that it stresses the role of *feeling*, as opposed to reason, in resolving this dispute. An appreciation of this sort of naturalism in Hume's philosophy is, as Kemp Smith has argued, of great importance if we are to get a balanced and complete picture of Hume's philosophy.[16] On the one hand, Hume is clearly anxious to show the limitations of human reason and is, in particular, anxious to show that reason is incapable of resolving the various philosophical problems which he comes to consider in the course of the *Treatise*. There is, on the other hand, a "positive", nonsceptical aspect to Hume's teaching which argues that it is feeling, not reason, which is our guide in human life and that therefore these philosophical "problems" are of little consequence as regards how we think and act.[17]

It seems clear, then, that according to Hume people will, in the relevant circumstances, inevitably feel one another to be responsible. There is, on this account, no reason why it is people and not other beings that arouse our moral sentiments and become the objects of praise and blame. Nor is there any reason for why people arouse our moral sentiments in some circumstances and not in others. Obviously, Hume takes the view that reason cannot "justify" these aspects of human nature. In this way, it is evident that Hume seeks to *circumscribe* the role of reason in the context of justifying ascriptions of responsibility.[18] Accordingly, it maybe said that Hume takes the view that the disputants in the free will controversy tend "to over-intellectualize the facts".[19] In this way, to the extent that Hume's arguments stress the limitations of human reason and the importance of feeling in the context of the free will dispute, we may say that it is "naturalistic" in this secondary sense. Here again we find that the classical interpretation completely ignores this aspect of Hume's strategy and, thus, inevitably, misrepresents the very nature of Hume's position on this issue.[20]

The most obvious strength of the naturalistic interpretation of Hume's compatibilist strategy is that it provides us with a set of arguments that are coherent and consistent with each other—something that the classical interpretation fails to do. More specifically, I have argued that the classical interpretation leads to two problems regarding the relationship between the necessity argument and the liberty arguments. First, as I showed in chapter 1, on the classical interpretation, the liberty arguments are in no way dependent on, or intimately connected with, the specifics of Hume's necessity argument—contrary to what Hume's remarks plainly suggest. Second, and more important, Hume's necessity argument, as I indicated in chapter 3, tends to undermine and discredit the liberty arguments as interpreted on the classical account. The naturalistic interpretation avoids both these problems. On the classical interpretation, the liberty arguments demand that the agent must—independently of the feelings of observers—produce or determine her actions if he is to be justly regarded as responsible. The necessity argument suggests that no agent, so considered, produces or determines her actions. Hume's naturalistic position demands only that there be a constant conjunction between an agent's motives and actions and that this conjunction enables us to infer character from action. In these circumstances, we will *feel* that the agent produced or determined her actions.[21] More important, we will *feel* the person to be the object of a moral sentiment, and this is the same as regarding her as responsible. Clearly, then, the necessity argument is essential to Hume's compatibilist strategy when it is interpreted along naturalistic lines. This is consistent with Hume's remarks concerning the relevance of the necessity argument to his compatibilist position.

The fundamental points of contrast between the naturalistic and classical interpretations of Hume's "reconciling strategy" can be appreciated, in more general terms, on the basis of their very different accounts of why and how both "freedom" and "necessity" are essential to responsibility. From the point of view of the classical account, the dependency is fundamentally conceptual or logical. Necessity is essential to responsibility because we require a "connexion" between agent and action; agents (logically) must produce or bring about their actions if they are to be justly held responsible for them. Similarly, liberty of spontaneity is (logically) essential to responsibility, on this account, because agents can be responsible for their actions only when their actions are determined or produced by their willings and desires. Liberty of indifference eliminates all such causal connexions between agent and action, and, hence, it is logically or conceptually inconsistent with responsibility.

The naturalistic interpretation, clearly, pursues very different avenues of thought. Necessity is psychologically essential to ascriptions of responsibility, because in the absence of the relevant regularities and inferences, the regular mechanism which produces our moral sentiments would simply fail to function. Similarly, liberty of spontaneity is (psychologically) essential to responsibility because it is only in these circumstances (i.e. in which we discover constant conjunctions between motives and actions) that it is possible for us to draw the specific kinds of inferences required to generate the moral sentiments.[22] If conduct is produced by external violence, no moral sentiment is aroused and, thus, we do not (as a matter of fact) hold the person responsible. On the naturalistic interpretation, Hume's concern with the nature and significance of moral freedom and how, specifically, it relates to ascriptions of responsibility must be understood primarily in terms of what he has to say about the role of moral sentiment in this sphere. I maintain, therefore, that any account of Hume's position which ignores these features of his discussion fundamentally misrepresents not only his general account of responsibility but also his overall effort to resolve the "free will dispute" by means of his alternative definition of necessity.

In summary, Hume's compatibilist position has generally been misrepresented. The claims made by the liberty arguments are psychological and not logical in force. The "compatibilism" or "soft determinism" for which Hume argues is grounded in an empirical science of human nature, not in the logic of our conception of responsibility. For Hume, it is a contingent fact about human nature that our moral sentiments are aroused by the mental qualities or characters of people. No reasoning could *justify* the fact that we regard persons rather than any other objects as liable to praise or blame. The most that we can do is observe and describe those circumstances in which the moral sentiments are generated. Beyond this, we must accept "that we can give no reason for our most general and refined principles, besides our experience of their reality" (T, xxii).

Hume may well have said of our tendency to hold people responsible what he said elsewhere in the *Treatise* about our tendency to believe in the existence of body: "Nature . . . has doubtless esteem'd it an affair of too great importance to be trusted to our uncertain reasonings and speculations" (T, 187). Nature has made the minds of all people "similar in their feelings and operations" (T, 575). This claim is fundamental to his view that nature rather than reason supplies the common basis on which our moral evaluations are made and thereby insulates morality from sceptical arguments. Human beings cannot escape the fact of their accountability to their own kind, because all people "must yield to the current of nature" (T, 269).[23]

Notes

1. Hume also endeavours to account for the "false sensation, or seeming experience which we have, or may have, of liberty or indifference, in many of our actions" (EU, 94n; cf. T, 408). This "looseness" in our mind does not occur in *reflecting* on human actions but only in *performing* the actions. Even when we have such a feeling of indifference, Hume claims, a spectator can still infer our actions. (On this matter, compare Kames's discussion of our experience of a *conflict* between the *feelings* which we naturally have in support of both liberty (i.e. "chance or contingency") and necessity [*Essays*, esp. 156–62, 183–87, 201–4, 382, 392].)

2. As it stands, this statement is misleading. If my interpretation is correct, the inference can be drawn in the opposite direction as well. However, the point is made in the context of Hume's discussion of necessity in society.

3. Clearly, any such inference must be based on regularities which we experience in our own case—hence the importance of our shared or common human nature and emotional life (T, 280–81, 318, 401–3, 575; EU, 83).

4. In this I follow Árdal, *Passion and Value*, esp. chp. 6. Árdal makes a number of points throughout his study that are, I believe, essential to a proper interpretation of Hume's philosophy. The interpretation offered here is in accord with Árdal's claim that Hume's discussion of the passions, in Book II, is of "vital importance for the correct interpretation of Hume's views about the evaluations of human character" (p. 1). Árdal's more specific claim, that approbation and blame are calm forms of love and hate, is more controversial. An effective defence of this interpretation, against alternative readings, is presented in Árdal's "Hume's Account of Moral Evaluation".

5. Hume claims, of course, that animals, along with man, are capable of love and hate. He points out, however, that in the case of animals, the objects of their love and hate extend beyond animals of their own species and "comprehends almost every sensible and thinking being" (T, 397). In this sense, the objects of *human* love and hate (i.e. human love and hate in general) would seem to be more confined. See, e.g., T, 329–31, 411. In respect of the particular mode of love and hate which constitutes the moral sentiments, and is produced by our perception of the virtuous or vicious mental qualities of others, Hume notes that "animals have little or no sense of virtue and vice" and thus are largely incapable of moral sentiment (T, 326).

6. In several different places (T, 279, 289, 330), Hume uses the example of a house or a palace to explain his analysis of the cause of our indirect passions. In this case, we must distinguish the quality (e.g. the beauty of the house) from the subject in which that beauty inheres (i.e. the house itself).

7. In respect of the house, for example, the mechanism will vary as follows. If the house is beautiful, it will naturally give rise to the pleasurable sentiments of love or pride. It will give rise to pride if related to oneself, to love if related to someone else. Were the house ugly or uncomfortable, however, it would be painful to those who see it or live in it, and, hence, it would naturally produce hate or humility—depending on whether it was related to oneself or someone else. It should be noted that what really matters here is that it is our *beliefs* about the object, rather than the object itself (e.g. the house), which explains how our passions are in fact generated. Hume, as many commentators have pointed out, does not properly appreciate this in his account of the generation of the indirect passions.

8. Hume, of course, believes that qualities of mind or character give rise to moral sentiments in a variety of ways. Indeed, this is the focus of a great deal of his philosophical attention. See, e.g., T, 588–91, 606f; EM, secs. 5–9.

9. A further relevant passage appears at the beginning of Part iii of Book III: "If any *action* be either virtuous or vicious, 'tis only as a sign of some quality or character" (T, 575). I discuss the significance of the passages cited in this regard (i.e. T, 411, 477, 575) in more detail in chp. 7.

10. Hume believed that calm passions, such as the moral sentiments, are frequently "confounded with reason" (T, 417). In this way, judgments which do not accord with our moral sentiments may be deemed "unreasonable" in this "popular" or nonphilosophical sense of the term. It is, however, consistent with Hume's views to regard passions and actions as *indirectly* reasonable or unreasonable insofar as they may be based on false beliefs. For Hume's account of the relationship between reason and sentiment, see, in particular, the first section of the second *Enquiry*. (This issue is discussed in further detail in chp. 6 of this volume.)

11. It is worth noting the following three points regarding the nature and role of sympathy in Hume's moral philosophy. First, without the principle of sympathy, no moral sentiment would be generated in us. For a moral sentiment to be aroused in us, we must feel *in ourselves* the pleasure or pain which the character of another would cause in himself or others. That pleasure or pain is communicated to us by the principle of sympathy. By association, that pleasure or pain leads to a sentiment of praise or blame. Second, it is a precondition of sympathy that we are able to infer the passions or sentiments of others from their external signs. Without this inference to the internal experience of others, we could have no shared or common feeling for anyone other than ourselves. Accordingly, without inference or necessity, sympathy would have no influence on us. Given that according to Hume sympathy plays a crucial role in morality, this is a point of some importance. Third, in general, without sympathy our moral concern would never reach beyond ourselves, and, hence, no recognizable, other-regarding moral life could develop or take root without it.

12. The importance of *inference* to Hume's reconciling project should perhaps be stressed. Many commentators, because they interpret Hume as adhering to a straightforward "regularity" view of causation, tend to ignore the specific role which inference plays in Hume's argument.

13. Hendel suggests that Hume used his discussion of "liberty and necessity" as a "preface" to "Of the Will and Direct Passions" (i.e. Pt. iii of Bk. II) and that Spinoza may have been his model in this respect. "It was in the manner of Spinoza, who opened the Third Part of his *Ethic, On the Origin and Nature of the Affects*, with a fine statement of his reasons for including man among the phenomena of nature and not exempting his life and conduct from natural law, merely because he enjoyed the consciousness of voluntary action" (*Philosophy of David Hume*, 288–89). Hendel's conjecture seems very plausible to me.

14. Kemp Smith, *The Philosophy of David Hume*, 161. After completing the first and second *Enquiries* (1748 and 1751, respectively), Hume wrote the *Dissertation on the Passions* (1757), which summarizes much of the material discussed in Book II of the *Treatise*. This *Dissertation* was printed in the edition of 1777, between the two *Enquiries*. From this fact alone, it should be clear that Hume did not come to consider the substance of his discussion of the passions in Book II as either uninteresting in its own right or irrelevant to the other themes that he considers in the *Enquiries*. It is not surprising to find that some proponents of the classical interpretation of Hume's compatibilism have also dismissed Hume's discussion of the passions on the grounds that it is both irrelevant to the rest of his philosophical system and also uninteresting from a contemporary philosophical perspective. See, e.g., Flew's remarks in *David Hume*, 122.

After the failure of the *Treatise*, Hume was, as Mossner puts it, "frustrated by the fact that the work was ignored by those minds that were in any way competent to deal with it and misunderstood by those who were not" (Mossner, "Philosophy and Biography", 30). Hume believed that the manner of presentation rather than the substance of the *Treatise* was the source of its debacle. In the *Abstract*, Hume acknowledges that many readers may be put off by the length of the *Treatise*. He also claims that his discussion of the passions, although not difficult to understand, could nevertheless "not be rendered intelligible without a long discourse". Because a lengthy discussion would be likely to diminish interest in his other philosophical views, it is not surprising that no detailed account of the passions is presented in the *Enquiry*. (See, too, Hume's rather scathing remarks about his contemporaries' reaction to his "abstruse philosophy", at T, 456 and LET, I, 26.)

15. This aspect of Hume's philosophy is interestingly discussed in Stroud's *Hume*, passim, esp. chp. 10. Stroud argues (p. 222) that "of all the ingredients of lasting significance in Hume's philosophy . . . this naturalistic attitude is of the greatest importance and interest".

16. Kemp Smith, "The Naturalism of Hume", and developed in greater detail in *The Philosophy of David Hume*.

17. Of course, this aspect of Hume's philosophy can be overstated. Clearly, Hume held, quite consistently with his view that there are severe limitations to the role and power of reason, that reason nevertheless has an important, indeed vital, role to play in human affairs. On this, see esp. Baier, *A Progress of Sentiments*, chp. 7.

18. I use the term "circumscribe" here in order to stress that reason has, according to Hume, an *indirect* role to play in the context of justifying ascriptions of responsibility.

19. The phrase is P. F. Strawson's, FR, 23.

20. It is evident that this aspect of Hume's general strategy (i.e. concerning the role of *feeling* in this sphere) has deep roots in the moral-sense tradition that includes such philosophers as Shaftesbury, Hutcheson, and Butler. Common to their moral philosophies is the idea that the characters and actions of our fellow human beings inevitably become objects of our thought and, thereby, unavoidably, give rise to sentiments of approval and disapproval in the human mind. However, it is important to note that the other aspect of Hume's naturalism— his *causal* analysis of the workings of human passion—does not have its source in the works of the moral-sense tradition. On the contrary, Hume's scientific description of the "mechanism" of the human passions has its roots in the approach suggested by (necessitarian) writers, such as Hobbes and, especially, Spinoza. Clearly, then, although Hobbes and Hume diverge in respect of the role of moral feeling, Hume in fact follows Hobbes (and Spinoza) in respect of his mechanistic *approach* to the working of human passions (including moral sentiment).

21. This is, clearly, all that Hume believes that we *mean* when we say an agent "produces" or "determines" his actions (e.g. as when he defines liberty as "a *power* of acting or not acting, according to the *determination* of the will" [EU, 95; my emphasis].)

22. It is important to emphasize the point that liberty of spontaneity is required for responsibility insofar as we are dealing with *action*, considered as a "sign" of character. Further, in chapter 8, I will show that for Hume there are some other "signs" of moral character, apart from action, which do not require liberty of spontaneity in order for our moral sentiments to be aroused (although necessity is still required).

23. Cf. Hume's remarks at, e.g., T, 296: "The most probable hypothesis . . ."; T, 474: "These sentiments are so rooted . . ."; T, 574–75: "We have already . . ."; T, 619: "It requires but . . ."; EM, 273: "But the sentiments . . ."; EM, 292–93: "No satisfactory . . ."; EM, 322: "Every one may employ . . ."; ESY, 140: "When by my will alone . . ."; ESY, 166n [Sceptic]: "The case is the same . . ."; DP, 146–47: "The most probable system . . .".

5

Hume's Naturalism and Strawson's Reconciling Project

> Every one may employ terms in what sense he pleases: but this in the mean time must be allowed, that sentiments are every day experienced of blame and praise which have objects beyond the dominion of the will or choice, and of which it behoves us, if not as moralists, as speculative philosophers at least, to give some satisfactory theory and explication.
>
> Hume, *An Enquiry concerning the Principles of Morals*

> It is a pity that talk of the moral sentiments has fallen out of favour. The phrase would be quite a good name for that network of human attitudes in acknowledging the character of which we find, I suggest, the only possibility of reconciling these disputants to each other and the facts.
>
> P. F. Strawson, "Freedom and Resentment"

If asked to pass quick judgment on Hume's "reconciling project", as it has been reinterpreted in the previous chapter, many contemporary philosophers would probably be inclined to say that it appears to be, quite simply, anachronistic, eighteenth-century psychology.[1] So considered, it is of little or no relevance to contemporary issues. Indeed, some philosophers may take the view that the philosophical interest—if not the philosophical substance—of Hume's compatibilism has been entirely removed. Surely, any attempt to *describe* the circumstances in which certain sentiments are aroused in us is hopelessly irrelevant to our present-day concerns and based wholly on assumptions that have long since been rejected. In particular, we can hardly take seriously an enterprise that asks us to understand the complex issue of moral responsibility in terms of *feelings*.

In this chapter, I show that it would be a mistake to dismiss Hume's objectives in this way. The best way to reveal the immediate philosophical interest of Hume's naturalistic approach is to note the striking affinities between Hume's and Strawson's position on this subject. The comparison with Strawson will also serve the purpose of showing the philosophical significance of the difference between the classical and naturalistic interpretations of Hume. Whereas the classical interpretation presents Hume as a (prime) target of criticism for Strawson, the naturalistic account, as I will explain, presents Hume as a particularly notable proponent of the lines of thought that Strawson seeks to advance in this area.

71

I

Strawson's "Freedom and Resentment" must surely rank as one of the most important and influential papers on free will written in the second half of the twentieth
century.[2] The argument of this paper is presented as a bold effort to "reconcile" the
traditional disputants in the free will problem (FR, 59–60). Strawson labels the principal opponents 'optimists' and 'pessimists'. Optimists take what is essentially the
traditional compatibilist position. They hold that the concept of moral responsibility, and associated practices such as punishing and blaming, "in no way lose their
raison d'etre if the thesis of determinism is true"—indeed, they may even require
the truth of this thesis (FR, 59). The optimist, Strawson says, typically draws attention to "the efficacy of the practices of punishment, and of moral condemnation and
approval, in regulating behaviour in socially desirable ways" (FR, 60; cf. FR, 76).
In other words, the optimist embraces and defends an essentially forward-looking,
utilitarian conception of responsibility (FR, 79). The only optimist Strawson cites
is Nowell-Smith, but the general position described is shared by several other mid-
century, empiricist-minded compatibilists—most notably, Schlick.[3]

The pessimist takes a libertarian position and finds the optimist's account of freedom and responsibility wholly inadequate. The optimist construes moral freedom as
simply the absence of constraint or compulsion (i.e. "negative freedom" or liberty of
spontaneity) and notes that this sort of freedom is compatible with determinism. By
contrast, the pessimist insists that we require the sort of freedom that implies the falsity
of determinism: We require, that is, some kind of "contra-causal" or "metaphysical"
freedom (FR, 79; cf. FR, 60).[4] Without this (metaphysical) freedom, the pessimist
claims, there is no adequate foundation for *moral* responsibility (FR, 76–77). Justified punishment, blame, and condemnation require that the person who is the object
of these practices or judgments really *deserves* it (FR, 61). The optimist's narrow
concern with matters of social utility, therefore, "leaves out something that is vital"
to our conception of moral responsibility and the justification of the practices associated with it. This gap is to be filled, according to the pessimist, with the general
metaphysical thesis of indeterminism.

Strawson rejects both optimist and pessimist accounts, but he hopes to bring them
together through "a formal withdrawal on one side in return for a substantial concession on the other" (FR, 60). Strawson agrees with the pessimist that something is
missing in the optimist's account. It is a mistake, however, to think that this gap can
be filled by "the obscure and panicky metaphysics of libertarianism" (FR, 80). On
the contrary, optimist and pessimist alike are missing or overlooking what is really
essential to moral responsibility; a proper recognition of the role that "reactive attitudes and feelings" play in this sphere. It is, says Strawson, "a pity that talk of the
moral sentiments has fallen out of favour. The phrase would be quite a good name
for that network of human attitudes in acknowledging the character and place of which
we find, I suggest, the only possibility of reconciling these disputants to each other
and the facts" (FR, 79). Strawson proposes, therefore, that we fill the "lacuna" in the
optimist's account by making appropriate reference to the essential role that the moral
sentiments play in the sphere of responsibility. In return, however, we require that
the pessimist "surrender his metaphysics" (FR, 78).

Strawson argues that both optimist and pessimist make a similar mistake:

> Both seek, in different ways, to over-intellectualize the facts. Inside the general structure or web of human attitudes and feelings of which I have been speaking, there is endless room for modification, redirection, criticism, and justification. But questions of justification are internal to the structure or relate to modifications internal to it. The existence of the general framework of attitudes itself is something we are given with the fact of human society. As a whole, it neither calls for, nor permits, an external 'rational' justification. Pessimist and optimist alike show themselves, in different ways, unable to accept this. (FR, 78–79)

Strawson has expanded on these points in his more recent work *Skepticism and Naturalism*. In this context, he draws explicitly on Hume's naturalism. He observes that all efforts to supply a justifying ground for our moral attitudes and judgments by way of "defending the reality of some special condition of freedom or spontaneity or self-determination" have not been "notably successful" (SN, 32). All such attempts, he maintains, are misguided.

> They are misguided also for the reasons for which counter-arguments to other forms of skepticism have been seen to be misguided; i.e. because the arguments they are directed against are totally inefficacious. We can no more be reasoned out of our proneness to personal and moral reactive attitudes in general than we can be reasoned out of our belief in the existence of body.... What we have, in our inescapable commitment to these attitudes and feelings, is a natural fact, something as deeply rooted in our natures as our existence as social beings. (SN, 32–33)

Strawson observes that Thomas Reid drew "an explicit parallel between our natural commitment to belief in external things and our natural proneness to moral or quasi-moral response" (SN, 33). In this respect, says Strawson, "we see Reid aligning himself with Hume the naturalist against Hume the skeptic" (SN, 33).

Earlier in *Skepticism and Naturalism*, Strawson suggests that we might "speak of two Humes: Hume the skeptic and Hume the naturalist; where Hume's naturalism ... appears as something like a refuge from his skepticism" (SN, 12).[5] He continues,

> According to Hume the naturalist, skeptical doubts are not to be met by argument. They are simply to be neglected (except, perhaps, insofar as they supply a harmless amusement, a mild diversion to the intellect). They are to be neglected because they are *idle*; powerless against the force of nature, of our naturally implanted disposition to belief. This does not mean that Reason has no part to play in relation to our beliefs concerning matters of fact and existence. It has a part to play, though a subordinate one: as Nature's lieutenant rather than Nature's commander. (SN, 13–14)

In this passage, Strawson is concerned with our "natural disposition to belief". However, neither here nor elsewhere does he give us any indication of the exact place or role of naturalism in Hume's writings on the subject of free will. It is left unclear, therefore, where, according to Strawson, Hume stands in relation to the naturalistic arguments that Strawson has advanced on the issue of freedom and responsibility. More specifically, it is not clear whether Strawson views Hume as one of the optimists whom he seeks to refute or as a naturalistic ally from whom he is drawing his own arguments and strategy.[6]

If we read Hume along the lines of the classical interpretation, then his position on these issues looks as if it accords very closely with the typical optimist strategy associated with such thinkers as Schlick. The classical interpretation, however, entirely overlooks the role of moral sentiment in Hume's reconciling strategy. It emphasizes the relevance of the (supposed) confusion between causation and compulsion in order to explain the more fundamental confusion about the nature of liberty (i.e. why philosophers tend to confuse liberty of spontaneity with liberty of indifference). With these features of Hume's position established, the classical interpretation points to Hume's remarks concerning the social utility of rewards and punishments and the way in which they depend on the principles of necessity. From this perspective, Hume's discussion of freedom and necessity clearly constitutes a "classic" statement of the optimist's position. So interpreted, Hume must be read as a thinker, like Schlick, who has "over-intellectualized the facts" on the basis of a "one-eyed-utilitarianism", one who has ignored "that complicated web of attitudes and feelings" which Strawson seeks to draw our attention to. In this way, we are encouraged to view Hume as a prime target of Strawson's attack on the optimist position.

The naturalistic interpretation, by contrast, makes it plain that any such view of Hume's approach and general strategy is deeply mistaken. Hume, no less than Strawson, is especially concerned to draw our attention to the facts about human nature that are relevant to a proper understanding of the nature and conditions of moral responsibility. More specifically, Hume argues that we cannot properly account for moral responsibility unless we acknowledge and describe the role that moral sentiment plays in this sphere. Indeed, unlike Strawson, Hume is much more concerned with the detailed mechanism whereby our moral sentiments are aroused, and thus he is particularly concerned to explain the relevance of spontaneity, indifference, and necessity to the functioning of moral sentiment. To this extent, therefore, Hume's naturalistic approach is more tightly woven into his account of the nature of necessity and moral freedom. In sum, when we compare Hume's arguments with Strawson's important and influential discussion, it becomes immediately apparent that there is considerable contemporary significance to the contrast between the classical and naturalistic interpretations of Hume's reconciling strategy.

II

I have argued, contrary to the classical interpretation, that Hume is no less opposed to the optimist's (forward-looking) strategy than Strawson—indeed, he is so on the basis of very similar considerations. This said, however, Hume might well accept the suggestion made by Strawson that "if we *radically* modify the view of the optimist, his view is the right one" (FR, 80).[7] Most important, it is clear that on the crucial issue of compatibilism, both Hume and Strawson side with the optimist against the pessimist. The truth of the thesis of determinism, they hold, would in no way undermine the basis of our commitment to the attitudes and practices associated with moral responsibility. It is equally clear, on the other hand, that there are several important respects in which Hume and Strawson stand closer to the pessimist's position than to that of the optimist. For example, both thinkers acknowledge that our moral evaluations of people are essentially *retrospective*. Our moral sentiments toward others will be determined by what we believe about their qualities of character, as revealed through their past conduct and behaviour. Similarly, both Hume and Strawson are agreed (with the pessimist) that the practices of condemnation and punishment cannot be justified in terms of social utility alone. According to their accounts, our moral sentiments play a key role within the framework of these practices. In particular, the notion of desert must be understood in terms of our moral sentiments and not in terms of social utility.[8] In these various and fundamental ways, therefore, the naturalistic character of Hume's reconciling strategy places him in a very similar situation in relation to optimist and pessimist as we find Strawson.

The targets of Strawson's naturalistic strategy extend beyond the positions of the optimist and the pessimist. Strawson's naturalism is also intended to refute or discredit the position of the moral sceptic—a position closely related to pessimism. Strawson takes the "moral sceptic" to be someone who holds that all the attitudes and practices associated with moral responsibility are "inherently confused", whether the thesis of determinism is true or false (FR, 59). The moral sceptic takes the view, therefore, that our moral sentiments are never justified and that they must be entirely suspended or withdrawn. Clearly the pessimist is a moral sceptic to the extent that he holds that if determinism is true, then our moral sentiments lack any adequate justification and must be abandoned altogether. Strawson maintains that sceptical positions of this kind are largely a product of the mistaken supposition (made by both optimist and pessimist) that responsibility requires some general rational justification.

What, then, is the connexion between the search for an external rational justification for the framework of responsibility and the scepticism that Strawson seeks to discredit and refute? Given that we suppose that we require some general (external) rationale for responsibility, we may find either that we are unable to identify any adequate or plausible rationale of this nature, or we may find that the conditions we believe necessary for a justification of this sort do not in fact hold. In these circumstances, we are led to the conclusion that the whole framework of responsibility lacks any adequate support or foundation and thus must be abandoned altogether. What is wrong with this line of reasoning, Strawson claims, is the initial supposition that responsibility requires some general rationale (e.g. of the sort that the optimist and the pessimist seek to provide it with).

Our moral sentiments are neither capable of, nor require, rational foundations of this kind. It is incorrect, therefore, to suppose that they have no acceptable place or role to play in human life and society because rational foundations of this kind cannot be supplied for them. The fact of the matter is, Strawson maintains, that our commitment to the whole framework of moral sentiment is immune to the undermining influence of sceptical arguments. Reason can neither support nor challenge our natural human propensity to sentiments of this nature. To suppose otherwise is to "over-intellectualize" these facts.

The central thrust of Strawson's reply to the moral sceptic is that reactive attitudes and feelings are (in some sense) a "given" of human nature and an inescapable feature of human life. This strong naturalistic rejoinder requires careful interpretation and analysis. The strength of Strawson's claim in this respect is made plain by the associated claim that even if we had some "theoretical ground" for abandoning the whole framework of moral sentiment, we are, nevertheless, psychologically incapable of doing so (FR, 68; cf. FR, 74). What Strawson is especially concerned to establish is that we are incapable of adopting the "objective attitude" toward everybody all of the time.

> To adopt the objective attitude to another human being is to see him, perhaps, as an object of social policy; as a subject for what, in a wide range of sense, might be called treatment. . . . But it cannot include the range of reactive feelings and attitudes which belong to involvement or participation with others in inter-personal human relationships". (FR, 66)

The moral sceptic holds that because our moral sentiments are never justified, they must be abandoned or suspended altogether. This involves taking up the "objective attitude" toward everybody all of the time. It is Strawson's contention that this is, practically and psychologically speaking, an impossibility for us. We cannot simply suspend our commitment to moral sentiments in this way.

In my view, Strawson's general reply to the position of the moral sceptic and pessimist overstates the case for the naturalistic position.[9] My immediate concern, however, lies with Hume's naturalistic commitments. The question arises as to what extent Hume regards moral sentiment as (somehow) an inescapable feature of human life. If he does, what precisely does he take this to involve? There are certainly a number of passages in Hume's writings which strongly suggest that he does regard moral sentiment (and hence responsibility) as an inescapable feature of human life and society—however varied the forms that it takes may be. Consider, for example, the following passage:

> if ever there was any thing, which cou'd be call'd natural in this sense [*natural*, as opposed to rare and unusual], the sentiments of morality certainly may; since there never was any nation of the world, nor any single person in any nation, who was utterly depriv'd of them, and who never, in any instance, shew'd the least approbation or dislike of manners. These sentiments are so rooted in our constitution and temper, that without entirely confounding the human mind by disease or madness, 'tis impossible to extirpate and destroy them. (T, 474)[10]

Hume believes that the fact of the matter is that human beings naturally become objects of contemplation in the thoughts of their fellows. We find that people universally possess pleasurable and painful qualities of mind and that this inevitably produces moral sentiments in the minds of other people. In this way, and to this extent, therefore, Hume does indeed hold that moral sentiment is a universal and inescapable feature of human life.

However, an important qualification or limitation needs to be noted. According to Hume's account, moral sentiment cannot be abandoned or suspended altogether *so long as we continue to encounter individuals with pleasurable or painful qualities of mind*. It is perfectly consistent with this to grant that *if* we were to find ourselves in circumstances in which individuals lacked these qualities or characteristics—or we believed that they all lacked them—then we would find that our moral sentiments had become completely disengaged. Hume, obviously, believes that it is absurd to suppose that we will ever encounter circumstances of this sort. Nevertheless, this qualification is important, because it indicates that Hume *rejects* the claim— made by Strawson—that we are incapable of altogether ceasing to entertain or feel moral sentiments *even in circumstances in which we understand that they are never in order or called for.*[11] Hume would grant, as Strawson puts it, that the whole framework of moral sentiment "neither calls for, nor permits, an external 'rational' justification" (FR, 78). However, it does not follow from this—and Hume does not suggest that it does—that we will continue to entertain or feel moral sentiment whatever reason suggests our circumstances to be.

Although Hume's naturalism does not commit him to the claim that we will inevitably continue to entertain moral sentiments whatever we may take our circumstances to be, he nevertheless agrees with the general antisceptical, naturalistic thesis that given our actual circumstances, in which we inevitably encounter other people with pleasurable or painful qualities of mind, we will inescapably experience or entertain moral sentiments.[12] This general observation serves to refute or discredit not only the moral sceptic but also the closely related position of the "Spinozist". Unlike the moral sceptic, the Spinozist does not try to show that our moral sentiments are never justified. The Spinozist's goal is to seek to bring about a change in our *perspective* on human conduct so that we are able to remove or eliminate all emotional disturbance and perturbation associated with our involvement with other human beings.[13]

There are two especially important features of this Spinozist shift in perspective on the human situation.[14] First, we are asked to look at individual people, and their thoughts, feelings, and actions, in a strongly "objective" manner. Human beings are to be viewed as natural objects whose thoughts and activities are antecedently conditioned by the natural order. This "objective" perspective, the Spinozist suggests, encourages us to *understand* human beings, not to judge and condemn them.[15] Second, it is argued that this "external" perspective on people—without showing that our moral sentiments are inappropriate or unjustified—nevertheless has a tendency to "dispel" or "drain away" our moral sentiments. We are encouraged, on this account, to abandon our view of the agent as an *individual* whom we are personally involved with and affected by. It is this sort of interpersonal and engaged perspective which gives rise to moral sentiments, and therefore the more we move away from it in favour of the objective perspective, the more our moral sentiments will weaken and fall away.

It seems evident that what the Spinozist shares with the moral sceptic is the supposition that we can, somehow, entirely disengage our moral sentiments. Strawson's response is to grant that it is sometimes possible to disengage our moral sentiments and take up the "objective attitude" toward some individual or group of people even in circumstances in which such sentiments are perfectly appropriate or in order. However, we cannot, he claims, do this systematically in the way that the Spinozist envisions (FR, 66–67). He summarizes his position once again in *Skepticism and Naturalism*:

> I mean that there is open to us the possibility of having deliberate recourse to an objective attitude in perfectly normal cases; that it is a resourse we can sometimes temporarily make use of, for reasons of policy or curiosity or emotional self-defence. I say "temporarily", because I do not think it is a point of view or position which we can hold, or rest in, for very long. The price of doing so would be higher than we are willing, or able, to pay; it would be the loss of all human involvement in personal relationships, of all fully participant social engagement. (SN, 34)

As these remarks suggest, Strawson's response to the Spinozist is two-fold. First, contrary to what the Spinozist supposes, we are not psychologically capable of ceasing entirely to entertain moral sentiments. No perspective which involves "objectivity" of this sort is one that we can sustain all the time toward everybody. Moreover, even if—contrary to fact—we had some "godlike choice" as to whether or not we should entirely suspend our moral sentiments in this way, Strawson argues that we would have good (forward-looking) reason to retain our "commitment" to these sentiments. Without such sentiments, human life would be seriously impoverished. Whatever gains we may realize through the Spinozist ideal, they would not compensate us for the dehumanization which would result.[16]

Hume's general response to Spinozist reasoning is in keeping with Strawson's. First, and most important, he holds that any effort, even by the most disciplined and dedicated mind, to free itself entirely of such emotions is unlikely to succeed. Any project that seeks to eliminate emotional responses of this nature for most or all people for most or all of the time is hopelessly deluded and absurd.[17] Hume, as a student of the science of human nature, does not hesitate to adopt the objective perspective on human nature—that is, he views people as natural objects whose thoughts and actions are antecedently necessitated by the natural order that they belong to. One area of particular importance for Hume's study of man is his investigation of the nature and causes of emotion. These investigations reveal that the mental qualities of human beings inevitably arouse moral sentiments through the mechanism of the indirect passions. In this way, an objective or scientific study of our emotional life indicates that the Spinozist goal of "dispelling" or "draining away" our moral sentiments cannot be achieved. Given the mechanism of the human passions, we can aim only to control and direct our emotions by reason (e.g. through understanding their causes and effects). There is, however, no question of escaping from our emotions simply by adopting a vigorously objective outlook. A Spinozist ideal or goal of this sort is deeply misguided, because it fails to recognize human nature as it actually is.[18]

There is another line of criticism which Hume launches against the Spinozist ideal that appeals to considerations of a rather different nature. In "The Sceptic", in the context of a discussion of the influence of philosophical reflections and systems on actual human feeling and practice, Hume considers the following claim: "*Let not the injuries or violence of men*, say the philosophers [Hume cites Plutarch], *ever discompose you by anger or hatred. Would you be angry at the ape for its malice, or the tyger for its ferocity?*" Hume replies, "This reflection leads us into a bad opinion of human nature, and must extinguish the social affections. It tends also to prevent all remorse for a man's own crimes; when he considers, that vice is as natural to mankind, as the particular instincts to brute-creatures" (ESY, 178). In the passage that follows, Hume repeats a point made in the first *Enquiry* (EU, 102–3): No reflections concerning the (supposed) perfection of the whole universe can in any way undermine the natural basis of the distinction between virtue and vice and the moral sentiments that they produce. In short, it is Hume's view that moral sentiment is an inescapable feature of human life as we find it. Moreover, he argues that any effort to evade or withdraw from such dispositions is corrupting of virtue and therefore wholly undesireable.[19] All this accords with the general position that Strawson has taken against Spinozism.

III

It is quite evident that Hume and Strawson are agreed on the basic issue of compatibilism. The truth of the thesis of determinism, they maintain, would in no way undermine our commitment to the attitudes and practices associated with moral responsibility. Even if human thought and action is part of a wholly determined (natural) order, there is, it is argued, no reason to suspend or abandon entirely these attitudes and practices. Our commitment to them is rooted in human nature. Reason neither can nor should support this natural edifice of responsibility; it can only structure and shape its parts.

Although there is general agreement on the issue of compatibilism, quite different positions are taken on the question of whether or not the truth of the thesis of determinism is required for the functioning of our moral sentiments.[20] Strawson is explicitly agnostic about this issue, and this, in itself, indicates that his specific concerns are more limited in scope than Hume's. Strawson opens his discussion in "Freedom and Resentment" by saying that he is of that "party of [philosophers] . . . who do not know what the thesis of determinism is" (FR, 59). By contrast, Strawson notes, the other parties in this dispute—pessimists, optimists, and sceptics—all seem to know what this thesis involves. In any case, the way in which the truth of this thesis may be relevant to the functioning of moral sentiment is not of any direct concern for Strawson. He points out that his concerns are, first, "the variations to which [our moral sentiments] are subject, the particular conditions in which they do or do not seem natural or reasonable or appropriate", and, second, "what it is like, not to suffer them" (FR, 64). His discussion, he says, is especially concerned with the second issue: circumstances of "objectivity". One question that Strawson says he is not particularly interested to ask is that concerning the "general causes of these reactive attitudes" (FR, 64). This is, clearly, a fundamental difference between his discussion and Hume's. That is, Hume, as we have seen, provides us with a detailed description and analysis of the "general causes" of moral sentiment and how these causes operate and function. His account places heavy emphasis on the role of causal necessity in the operation of this mechanism. Clearly, then, Hume does not avoid the question concerning the truth or falsity of the thesis of determinism. On the contrary, this question is of crucial importance for his discussion.

For Hume, the truth of the thesis of determinism is bound up with the contingent truth that the world exhibits a certain order and regularity—an order and regularity that manifests itself in the uniformity and universality of causation.[21] Hume claims that the operations of our thought and action exhibit the same lawlike order and regularity as the operations of nature.[22] On Hume's principles, if the moral realm did not exhibit this sort of regularity our moral sentiments would never, as a matter of fact, be aroused, or function. They would never be aroused because they require an inference which depends on the experienced uniformity between motive and action or, more generally, between qualities of mind and the "external signs" that they give rise to. Hence, according to Hume, the fact that we are susceptible to moral sentiment is dependent on the prior fact that the moral realm is entirely regular and determined.

There is, however, a certain ambiguity—and vulnerability—in this position as it stands. From the fact that the functioning of our moral sentiments requires regularity in the moral realm, it does not follow that it requires regularity *outside* of this realm. Irregularities in a distant galaxy, for example, need not affect the functioning of our moral sentiments. In this way, even if we were to accept that the functioning of our moral sentiments depends on the fact that the moral realm is determined or exhibits the required regularity, it does not follow that our moral sentiments depend on the truth of the thesis of determinism. The thesis of determinism, after all, is generally understood to involve more than the claim that the *moral realm* is uniform and regular. Hence, even on Hume's principles, it is not evident that the functioning of our moral sentiments depend on the truth of the thesis of determinism.

This objection certainly has some force to it. However, I am not convinced that it gets around the difficulties which most concern us. That is to say, the pessimist is not going to be satisfied by assurances that the thesis of determinism is false if this does not imply that our thoughts and actions are free of the lawlike regularities which Hume ascribes to them. It is the absence of strict regularities in the *moral realm* which the pessimist argues is essential to responsibility, just as it is the opposite thesis which Hume claims is essential to responsibility. Although the thesis that the moral realm is determined might not have the universal scope which the thesis of determinism seems to require, it must be acknowledged that it is the narrower thesis regarding events in the moral realm which concerns the protagonists in this dispute. In light of this, we may call the thesis of narrower scope 'the thesis of *moral* determinism'. Certainly the truth or falsity of this thesis is not, on Hume's principles, irrelevant to the functioning of our moral sentiments. In this way, we preserve the claim that the truth of determinism is essential to the functioning of the moral sentiments by restricting its scope to the relevant realm of events.[23]

On Hume's view, our moral sentiments depend on two sorts of constant conjunction: that between action or behaviour of some sort and a given quality of mind or character trait, and that between these character traits and the sentiments of praise or blame. This second mode of regularity in the moral realm guarantees that, at least to some extent, we *share* with our fellow human beings the same reactions to particular characters or mental qualities. That is, our common humanity ensures that there is not an enormous discrepancy in our emotional needs and responses. Further, this mode of uniformity ensures that our own responses to given characters and mental qualities does not vary too radically from day to day. If our reactive sentiments did not conform to these requirements—that is, that our moral sentiments are on the whole consistent with the moral sentiments of others and that our own reactive sentiments are relatively stable—we could not live in society with these sorts of reactive sentiments. Hence, the relative uniformity and stability which we find in these reactive sentiments is arguably a condition of their existence.[24] Here again, therefore, the truth or falsity of the thesis of determinism—on the (narrow) interpretation that we have given it—does not seem to be obviously irrelevant to the functioning of our moral sentiments.

The above discussion suggests that it may be a mistake to simply *assume* that the truth or falsity of the thesis of determinism is irrelevant to the functioning of our moral sentiments. One does not have to accept all of Hume's more specific claims in order to appreciate this more general point. Before we can properly assess this claim, we must, first, have some idea of what the thesis of determinism is (and what its *status* is), and, second, we must have some understanding of the "general causes" of our moral sentiments. These are, as we have noted, issues which Strawson, unlike Hume, does not pursue.

IV

The overall resemblance between Hume's and Strawson's strategy in dealing with issues of freedom and responsibility is quite striking. The fundamental point that they agree about is that we cannot understand the nature and conditions of moral responsibility without reference to the crucial role that moral sentiment plays in this sphere. This naturalistic approach places Hume and Strawson in similar positions when considered in relation to the views of the pessimist, the optimist, the sceptic, and the Spinozist. The naturalistic approach shows that, in different ways, all these positions fail to properly acknowledge the facts about moral sentiment. Where Hume most noticeably differs from Strawson is on the question of the "general causes" of moral sentiment. Strawson largely bypasses this problem. For Hume, this is a crucial issue that must be settled to understand why necessity is essential to responsibility and why indifference is entirely incompatible with the effective operation of the mechanism that responsibility depends on.

It may be argued that the strategies which Hume and Strawson pursue share something even more fundamental than their naturalism. Both these thinkers, in different ways, shift empahsis and attention from problems of freedom to problems of responsibility. Instead of arguing that we interpret responsibility in terms of the conditions of freedom, it is suggested that we try to understand the conditions of freedom in terms of an empirically better informed theory of responsibility. One consequence of this shift is that what both Hume and Strawson have to say about the nature of moral freedom is rather thin and insubstantial. Moreover, the accounts they offer are quite different. Hume, as we have noted, briefly sketches an account of liberty of spontaneity—a theory of moral freedom which Strawson (along with the pessimist) finds wanting (FR, 60). Strawson, however, does not make much effort to fill this particular gap, because this is not his primary concern. What he does suggest is that a person is morally free insofar as his conduct and behaviour is intelligible to him in terms of his own conscious purposes (FR, 75). In other words, a free agent is one who knows what he is doing and who understands what motivates his conduct. Although this may be an advance on liberty of spontaneity, it leaves a great deal unsaid. It seems evident, then, that there remains a significant gap in the naturalistic approach which still needs to be filled.

These observations concerning the thinness of Hume's and Strawson's accounts of freedom do not discredit the view that the problem of freedom is best understood through a naturalistic approach to the problem of responsibility. On the contrary, what it suggests is that, so described, this project remains incomplete. One point, however, does seem clear. From the perspective of the naturalistic approach, any effort simply to reduce the problem of responsibility to the problem of free will only confuses matters and obscures the relationship that holds between questions of freedom and questions of responsibility. Problems of freedom arise within the framework of our (more general) understanding of responsibility. It is here that investigations into the nature of moral freedom must begin. In my view, this deeper theme constitutes one of the most philosophically interesting and significant aspects of Hume's naturalistic approach.

Notes

1. The fact that several commentators (e.g. Kemp Smith and Flew) dismiss Hume's discussion of the passions as being of little or no interest, and that others (e.g. Mackie and Stroud) ignore or downplay his views on this subject, rather suggests that the philosophical interest of the naturalistic interpretation is not obvious to many philosophers and, hence, must be argued for.

2. An interesting discussion of Strawson's paper, and the responses it has generated, can be found in Fischer and Ravizza, Introduction to *Perspectives on Moral Responsibility*, 14–25.

3. P. F. Strawson cites (FR, 60n) Nowell-Smith's "Freewill and Moral Responsibility". Note, however, that Strawson's principal pessimist target appears to be C. A. Campbell and that Campbell is specifically concerned to reply to Schlick. For another statement of the optimist position roughly contemporary with FR, see, e.g., Smart, "Free Will, Praise and Blame".

4. Strawson's asides concerning "contra-causal freedom" suggest that he has Campbell primarily in mind; cf. FR, 79, with Campbell's remark that "moral responsibility implies a contra-causal type of freedom" ("Is 'Freewill' a Pseudo-Problem?" 126).

5. Hume's scepticism is standardly associated with a range of issues, including induction, the external world, and personal identity, as well as problems of morality. Significantly, however, there is little or nothing about Hume's discussion of freedom and responsibility that suggests a sceptical position—except his scepticism about *libertarian* "free will". In the absence of any "sceptical problem", commentators have neither seen nor looked for an accompanying set of "naturalistic" arguments.

6. There is nothing in either FR or SN to suggest that Strawson challenges or questions the classical interpretation of Hume on free will—and, clearly, Strawson would be aware that this is how Hume is generally read. See, however, Strawson's brief reference to the analogy between Hume's views on *induction* and his own (i.e. Strawson's) naturalism about responsibility (FR, 79n). Strawson suggests that any attempt to justify the general framework of our moral sentiments is misguided in much the same way that any attempt to justify induction is misguided. For Strawson's views on induction, see his *Logical Theory*, chp. 9; see also Beauchamp and Rosenberg, *Hume and the Problem of Causation*, chp. 2, for an interpretation of Hume's views on induction that accords with Strawson's position.

7. Recall Voltaire's observation (*Candide*, chp. 19) that optimism "is a mania for maintaining that all is well when things are going badly".

8. These and related matters will be discussed in further detail in Part II; see esp. chp. 10.

9. See my "Strawson's Way of Naturalizing Responsibility", in which I argue that Strawson fails to properly distinguish two quite different issues. The first issue concerns our natural human liability or proneness to certain *types* of emotion (e.g. moral sentiment) and whether or not dispositions of this kind require some general rational justification. The second issue concerns whether or not we are capable of entirely ceasing to entertain particular *tokens* of some given type of emotion in circumstances in which we recognize that they are never called for or in order. In respect of moral sentiment, the plausible element in Strawson's naturalistic position, I maintain, is the claim that we are naturally liable to emotions of this type and that this disposition requires no "external rational justification". The implausible element, however, is the suggestion that we may continue to entertain and feel tokens of this (type of) emotion even in circumstances in which it is shown that they are never called for or in order. Strawson believes that his observations concerning our natural "commitment" to

moral sentiment serve, on their own, to refute or discredit the view of the pessimist and moral sceptic. This strategy, I point out, commits Strawson to the stronger and less plausible form of naturalism.

10. Cf. T, 619: "It requires but very little knowledge . . ."; EU, 102–3: "What though philosophical meditations establish . . ."; EM, 273: "But the sentiments . . ."; EM, 322: "Every one may employ terms . . ."; ESY, 140 [Stoic]: "When by my will alone . . ."; ESY, 166 [Sceptic]: "The case is the same . . ."; DP, 146–47: "The most probable . . .".

11. Strawson's strategy in FR, as I have noted, commits him to this much stronger (and less plausible) thesis.

12. A major theme that runs throughout Hume's philosophy is, of course, that it is desirable that we live in accordance with our nature and avoid all forms of "excessive scepticism".

13. There is a long succession of thinkers who have endorsed and promoted this kind of project. In the Western context, the Stoics are the most famous proponents of this sort of ideal.

14. In what follows, I draw on Bennett's account of "Spiniozism" in his paper "Accountability", 28. Cf. Spinoza, *Ethics*, V, P1–P20 (esp. P10S and P20S).

15. "I have laboured carefully, not to mock, lament, or execrate but to understand human actions" (Spinoza, *Political Treatise*, I, 4. See also II, 8: "Whenever, then, anything in nature seems to us ridiculous, absurd, or evil . . .".

16. Strawson is perfectly aware that both human nature and human society vary and that this leads to some *variation* in human sentiment—and of moral sentiment in particular. However, as Strawson points out, "an awareness of variety of forms should not prevent us from acknowledging also that in the absence of *any* forms of these [human] attitudes it is doubtful whether we should have anything that *we* could find intelligible as a system of human relationships, as a human society" (FR, 80). This is entirely in accord with Hume's view of the matter.

17. See Hume's remarks as cited in note 10 above.

18. It is, I believe, questionable how far apart Hume and Spinoza actually are on this issue. There are, of course, *some* significant differences between their positions. (See, in particular, Hume's remarks at EU, 102–3, concerning the impossibility of philosophical reflections freeing us from painful reactions to both "physical and moral ill".) Nevertheless, they are agreed about two important matters. First, man is inescapably subject to pleasurable and painful emotions and there are strict limits to the extent to which philosophy can change this state of affairs. Second, philosophy does, however, have two very important roles to play in this context: it can improve our understanding of the nature and causes of emotion, and it can indicate the extent to which reason can control and redirect our emotional lives (see, e.g., Spinoza, *Political Treatise*, I, 5: "For this is certain . . ."). In these important respects, therefore, it would not be inaccurate to describe Hume as a "Spinozist". (I note in passing that until very recently it has been widely held that Hume had little or no direct familiarity with Spinoza's work. It is my view that it is very likely that Hume was familiar with Spinoza's writings and, indeed, that he would have examined them carefully. On this, see my "'Atheism' and the Title-Page of Hume's *Treatise*".)

19. Cf. Hume's remarks at EM, 172: "Extinguish all the warm feelings . . .". Smith, who is generally taken to be much more sympathetic to Stoic moral philosophy than is Hume, nevertheless agrees with Hume that it is psychologically impossible for human beings entirely to overcome their emotional nature and that the success of such a project (i.e. "the entire extirpation and annihilation of all passions") would be "pernicious to society" (TMS, 313; cf. 143, 292–93).

20. Related to this, it is important to draw a distinction between compatibilism and "soft determinism". The compatibilist claims only that freedom and responsibility are not undermined by the truth of determinism. The soft determinist is a compatibilist who also claims

that determinism is true. (As I will explain, although both Hume and Strawson are compatibilists, only Hume is a soft determinist.)

21. Particularly relevant here is Hume's account of the "rules by which to judge of causes and effects" (I, iii, 15), especially principles 4, 5, and 6. According to Hume, the truth of the thesis of determinism—the uniformity and universality of causation—is discovered through experience.

22. An important and influential discussion of "the categorical difference between the mental and the physical" for any attempt to assimilate regularities in the moral realm to regularities in the material realm can be found in Davidson's "Mental Events" and "Psychology as Philosophy".

23. Some philosophers have straightforwardly defined determinism with this narrower scope in mind (no doubt because they rightly perceive that the narrower thesis makes plain the points at issue). Glover, for example, defines determinism as "the thesis that *all human behaviour* is governed by causal laws" (*Responsibility*, 21; my emphasis). One may, I think, have some doubts about the adequacy of this definition as a definition of the thesis of determinism. However, so defined, it certainly is a thesis whose truth or falsity is, on Hume's principles, very relevant to the functioning of our moral sentiments.

24. On this see Gibbard, *Wise Choices, Apt Feelings*, chp. 4, who discusses the evolutionary importance of "social coordination" and "shared evaluation."

II

THE ELEMENTS OF RESPONSIBILITY

And if we can go no farther than this mental geography, or delineation of the distinct parts and powers of the mind, it is at least a satisfaction to go so far; and the more obvious this science may appear (and it is by no means obvious) the more contemptible still must the ignorance of it be esteemed, in all pretenders to learning and philosophy.

Hume, An Enquiry concerning Human Understanding

Philosophers one and all have, with a straitlaced seriousness that provokes laughter, demanded something far more exalted, more pretentious, more solemn of themselves as soon as they have concerned themselves with morality as a science: they wanted to furnish the *rational foundation* of morality. . . . How far from their clumsy pride was that apparently insignificant task left in the dust and mildew—the task of description—although the subtlest fingers and senses can scarcely be subtle enough for it.

Nietzsche, Beyond Good and Evil

6

The Content and Objects
of Moral Sentiment

The final sentence, it is probable, which pronounces characters and actions
amiable or odious, praise-worthy or blameable . . . depends on some internal sense
or feeling, which nature has made universal in the whole species. . . . But in order
to pave the way for such a sentiment, and give it proper discernment of its object,
it is often necessary, we find, that much reasoning should precede . . .

Hume, *An Enquiry concerning the Principles of Morals*

According to Hume, moral sentiment constitutes the key element in any adequate
analysis or description of the nature and circumstances of moral responsibility. There
are, however, a number of problems that arise in connexion with Hume's account of
moral sentiment. In this chapter I am especially concerned with certain difficulties
which Hume encounters concerning his understanding of the nature and content
of moral sentiment, as implied by his general theory of emotion. Related to this, I
examine problems with Hume's account of the objects of moral sentiment. In the
final section of this chapter, I return to the issue of the extent to which, and the way
in which, Hume is committed to the view that moral sentiment is an inescapable feature of human life.

I

Hume's account of the passions suggests that they may be assimilated to sensations.
It is, for Hume, the categories of pleasure and pain which enable us to distinguish
the different emotions. All passions, Hume argues, including the indirect passions,
are "simple and uniform impressions" which are *felt*. Because the passions are simple,
it is "impossible [that] we can ever, by a multitude of words, give a just definition of
them" (T, 277). The most that we can do is describe those circumstances in which
they arise. The various passions are recognized and distinguished primarily by observ-
ing, through introspection, the distinct sensations which "constitute their very being
and essence" (T, 286). On this account, therefore, it is essential that we distinguish
an indirect passion from both the "ideas which give rise to it" (i.e. its "cause") and
from those ideas which it gives rise to (i.e. its "object"). The object of our passion is,

on this account, the *effect* of the passion, and it is, hence, entirely distinct from the cause of the passion.

In light of the above account of Hume's position, it seems evident that he adheres to what is sometimes called the "feeling theory" of emotion. The feeling theory has been subject to a number of penetrating criticisms by various philosophers over the past three decades or so.[1] The fundamental criticism is that it misrepresents emotion as being simple in nature when what is actually required is a complex analysis. For our purposes, there are three general aspects of emotion which are especially important for a proper understanding of the complex nature of moral sentiment: belief, evaluation, and relation to action. Perhaps the most basic element for a proper understanding of emotion is the claim that emotion, generally speaking, involves thought or belief. On this "cognitive" view of emotion, it is argued that our emotions are to be recognized and distinguished, not in terms of sui generis feelings (in the narrow sense of sensations), but rather in terms of the thoughts and beliefs involved in the having of a given emotion. That is to say, in order to ascribe a particular emotion to an individual, we must also ascribe certain relevant or appropriate thoughts to him. In general, our emotions arise out of our beliefs about certain objects. Thus our emotions toward that object are determined by our beliefs about it. This "cognitive" account of emotion, stressing as it does the role of belief in emotion, enables us to explain the ways in which we may intelligibly speak of our emotions as being reasonable or unreasonable, justified or unjustified. It also enables us to account for the "directedness" or "intentionality" of emotion. That is, our emotions are directed toward an object in virtue of the fact that they involve beliefs about that object. In this way, this alternative account of emotion enables us to overcome the well-known difficulties which the feeling theory encounters in explaining both the rationality and intentionality of emotion.

It seems clear, however, that emotion involves much more than the having of certain appropriate or relevant beliefs. Emotions involve favourable or unfavourable ("pro" or "con") attitudes or reactions toward the object as a result of our beliefs.[2] Our beliefs about the object serve as the basis on which we evaluate it. Typically, our evaluative attitude toward the object will be reflected in our beliefs about it. In these circumstances, the beliefs involved in the emotion may be described as evaluative. Such beliefs constitute a conscious appraisal or evaluation of the object in virtue of its perceived characteristics or qualities. This evaluative perspective encourages us to "see" the object in a certain "light" and to *value* it in certain ways. Beyond this, however, it is essential that our evaluation of the object must arouse or cause certain desires, sensations, feelings, dispositions, or physiological changes in us. The ways in which these affective aspects of emotion manifest themselves will, clearly, vary according to the nature and circumstances of the emotion involved (e.g. whether it is "occurrent" or "dispositional", "calm" or "violent"). Usually, however, to have an emotion of a given kind is not only to think about it and value it in certain ways but to be disposed to *act and behave* in certain ways characteristic of the emotion. In being affected by certain objects, we are, generally speaking, through the formation of desires, feelings, and the like, *motivated* to act in given ways toward that object.

What is the significance of these reflections concerning the nature of emotion to Hume's theory of responsibility? Hume's feeling theory of emotion commits him to the view that the moral sentiments *feel* different from all other passions and that this sui generis sensation constitutes the very nature or essence of moral sentiment. Clearly, this account of moral sentiment must be rejected. The key to a proper understanding of this emotion lies, above all, with an adequate description of the cognitive-evaluative factors involved in having a moral sentiment. In developing an account of moral sentiment along these lines, we will be able to sidestep not only difficulties which apply to Hume's feeling theory of emotion in general (e.g. the rationality and intentionality of emotion) but also certain specific difficulties which the feeling theory generates for Hume's naturalistic theory of responsibility.

No adequate theory of responsibility can maintain, as is implied by Hume's theory, that responsibility must be analysed in terms of certain peculiar pleasant or painful feelings. That is to say, according to Hume, whether or not we regard another person as responsible will depend on whether or not a certain sui generis sensation of the appropriate sort arises in us. If we have no such simple and unique impressions, then it would follow, on this account, that no one could be regarded as responsible. Clearly, Hume has gone wrong in this. We may regard other people as responsible without experiencing any particular sensation at all, never mind some unique pleasant or painful sensation. In this way, it seems evident that Hume's feeling theory of emotion encourages him to pursue a somewhat misguided—or misleading—project. The philosopher's concern should not be with the mechanics which generate peculiar, atomistic sensations. It is, rather, the cognitive-evaluative features involved in ascribing responsibility which should be the philosopher's principal concern.[3]

Some qualification of my interpretation of Hume's position on this subject is required. On the whole, it seems clear that Hume's account of the passions commits him to the view which I have been ascribing to him, namely, that moral responsibility necessarily involves certain peculiar pleasant or painful feelings (i.e. sensations). Many passages, such as the following famous passage, can be cited in support of this interpretation: "To have the sense of virtue, is nothing but to *feel* a satisfaction of a particular kind from the contemplation of character. The very *feeling* constitutes our praise or admiration" (T, 471). Clearly, then, on this account when we regard someone as responsible, we are aware or conscious of a peculiar feeling or sensation arising in us when we contemplate that person's character. However, there is an important complexity in Hume's discussion of this issue. The passage cited above appears at III, I, 2. Earlier in the same section of the *Treatise*, Hume makes the following observation: "Morality, therefore, is more properly felt than judg'd of; tho' this feeling or sentiment is *commonly so soft and gentle, that we are apt to confound it with an idea*" (T, 470; my emphasis). The point which Hume is making here is one which we have already noted, namely, that the moral sentiments are *calm* passions (i.e. passions that *tend* to be calm). Hume has the following to say about our experience of passions that are calm:

> every action of the mind, which operates with the same calmness and tranquility, is confounded with reason by all those, who judge of things from the first view and appearance. Now 'tis certain, there are calm desires and tendencies, which, tho' they be real passions, produce little emotion in the mind, *and are more known by their effects than by immediate feeling or sensation*. (T, 417; my emphasis)

In light of these remarks, it would appear that Hume is committed to the view that generally, given the calm nature of moral sentiment, we *do not feel* the moral sentiments but are, rather, aware of them only through "their effects". Insofar as Hume takes this line, he frees himself of the rather implausible claim that moral responsibility necessarily involves certain simple and unique "feelings". It is not obvious, however, that Hume can push this line very far without encountering other difficulties for his position.

Hume seems to be committed to the view that in those circumstances in which we do not directly feel (i.e. experience) the moral sentiments, we *infer* them from the behaviour they have aroused in us (much as we must infer them in the case of other minds). There are, however, one or two immediate difficulties for this view. First, given that we generally do not *experience* calm passions, how, on Humean principles, can they be inferred on the basis of our knowledge of their effects alone. This is not, I believe, an insuperable problem for Hume. That is, it may be argued that the relatively rare occasions when we experience these passions (i.e. when they are violent) suffice to provide us with a basis on which we can make the appropriate inferences in circumstances in which these passions are calm. We are, however, left with a further problem. The same behaviour and conduct, it seems clear, may be aroused by different emotional states. For example, a person's hostile and unkind behaviour toward another individual may be motivated by hatred or jealousy, as well as by moral disapproval. In order to know whether someone has a calm passion of disapproval, rather than some other passion directing his conduct, we need to know more about the beliefs and evaluations that give rise to the hostile behaviour and conduct. Furthermore, it seems clear that the behaviour and attitudes appropriate to moral sentiment must be interpreted as expressions of beliefs and evaluations rather than simply as expressions of sui generis sensations. In this way, in order to infer the presence of (calm) moral sentiments—either in our own case or in the minds of others—we need to be able to identify the beliefs and evaluations which are expressed by the conduct and behaviour of the person who entertains these sentiments.

There are, I believe, two conclusions to be drawn from Hume's retreat from sensations to calm passions in this context. The first is that "feelings" or sensations are not, as such, essential to moral sentiment, and, therefore, they are not required for responsibility. In fact, what is true of moral sentiment in this sphere is true of emotion in general. On the whole, it is neither a necessary nor a sufficient condition of being in a particular emotional state that we experience certain peculiar or unique sensations. Second, insofar as Hume retreats from sensations to the "effects" of calm passions in this context (i.e. to certain modes of behaviour), he takes us in the wrong direction. What is crucial, as I have argued, is an understanding of the cognitive-evaluative aspects of moral sentiment. It is these elements, rather than certain modes of behaviour, which enable us to recognize and distinguish moral sentiment.[4] There may be circumstances in which moral sentiment arouses neither any peculiar sensations nor any relevant actions in us but in which we are, nevertheless, able to identify our emotional state as moral sentiment because of the nature of the beliefs and evaluations involved (along with, perhaps, some physiological changes in our bodies).[5]

II

Hume maintains that the sentiments of love and hatred "are always directed to some sensible being external to us" (T, 329), just as the sentiments of pride and humility are directed at the "self" (T, 277). The moral sentiments, therefore, are directed toward individual people. Moral sentiments are distinguished from other forms of love and hatred by their distinct felt qualities (T, 472, 607, 617; cf. T, 448: "Love may shew itself . . ."). This variation in the kinds of feeling of love and hate that we experience is to be accounted for, Hume says, by the causes of these feelings. In particular, the beliefs which give rise to love and hate vary insofar as they range over different types of "subjects" (e.g. physical qualities, mental qualities, property) belonging to or related to the person who is the object of our love or hatred (see *Treatise*, II, I, esp. pp. 278–79). In the case of our moral sentiments, our beliefs concern the "mental qualities" of the individual in question (as opposed to, e.g., their physical characteristics, property). These qualities constitute, on Hume's account, the individual's virtues and vices. Hume holds, in other words, that the virtues and vices are mental qualities (e.g. "passions, habits, turns of character" [T, 295]) which have a "tendency" to produce pleasure or pain either in the person himself (i.e. the possessor) or in others.

The first thing to note about this account is that the understanding of the nature of virtue and vice appears to be too wide.[6] More specifically, Hume's account of the nature of virtue and vice makes it impossible to identify and discriminate appropriate and inappropriate objects of moral sentiment. That is to say, we are, on this view of things, encouraged to hold a whole range of individuals responsible who are (self-evidently) inappropriate objects of moral sentiment.

Hume claims that any individual whose "mental qualities" tend to produce pleasure or pain in himself or others will inevitably arouse moral sentiments in a disinterested observer (i.e. insofar as that person becomes an object of contemplation). It would seem to follow that children, the insane, and those with mental disabilities are (psychologically speaking) considered responsible. Nor is it clear, on this view of things, why animals do not arouse our moral sentiments given that they, too, possess pleasurable and painful "mental qualities".[7] According to Hume, it is simply an ultimate, inexplicable fact about moral sentiments (qua feelings) that they are directed toward people. Clearly, however, quite apart from anything else, this approach leaves us entirely unable to say why some people are *not* appropriate objects of moral sentiment. Hume provides us with no adequate account of the nature of moral capacities required for a person (or creature) to be deemed an appropriate object of moral sentiment. Indeed, this issue is not directly tackled by Hume at all. This is a very deep flaw in his general theory of responsibility, and it is closely connected with his similarly inadequate description of virtue and vice understood in terms of pleasurable and painful qualities of mind. The capacities which render an agent an appropriate object of moral sentiment are the same as those which render an agent capable of moral virtue and vice. We require, therefore, some more adequate account of the nature of these capacities.[8]

It is not possible, in the present context, to provide a full description of the nature of the moral capacities required to render an agent *capable* of virtue and vice, and thus an appropriate object of moral sentiment. A few general points may, neverthe-less, be noted. A person who is a moral agent must be capable of being *self-conscious* about her actions, motives, and feelings, and their associated character traits. This requires that the agent be able to *articulate* her motives and actions under some rele-vant description and that she be able to deliberate and choose or reject action or courses of conduct on this basis. An intentional agent is always able to say what she is doing insofar as she is acting intentionally.[9] This mode of self-knowledge or self-understanding requires *language*. On the basis of the capacity to articulate the nature of actions, desires, and feelings, it is possible for a moral agent to engage in self-criticism and self-evaluation. In other words, through her capacity for self-knowledge, the agent becomes an object for her own reflective self-criticism and moral evaluation. Among other things, this capacity enables the agent to recognize herself as one among others with similar capacities.

A moral agent not only must have the capacity or ability to "step back" and con-sider her character and qualities of mind in a critical light but must be able to take measures to put this self-criticism into effect. This requires, in the first place, that a moral agent be able to formulate desires and preferences about the kind of character that she has or is acquiring.[10] The moral agent, unlike the nonmoral agent, has the ca-pacity to care about which desires move her to action and which feelings animate and affect her. Such an agent may be said to *identify* herself with her actions and feelings insofar as they are what she wants them to be. To be a moral agent, therefore, a person must be able to reflectively endorse or repudiate her own established moral traits and characteristics. When these traits and characteristics are not as the person wants them to be, then reflective ("second-order") desires may effect a change or alteration in the structure of the person's will and disposition. So described, a moral agent must be able to formulate a set of standards she expects to live by and be judged by (or at least judge herself by). These standards constitute the parameters outside of which certain breaches of conduct or behaviour would be viewed as a blow to her self-respect or dignity.

This general framework constitutes, I suggest, the essentials of some adequate account of the capacities required of moral agents—individuals who are appropriate objects of moral sentiments. On the basis of these sorts of considerations, we are able to draw the relevant distinctions between normal, adult human beings (i.e. moral agents) and those with whom we wish to contrast them: children, animals, the men-tally ill, those with mental disabilities, and so on. This general description of our moral capacities does not, however, make any appeal to "free will" (i.e. categorical or contra-causal freedom) as the distinguishing characteristic of moral agents. Through our shared, reciprocal capacity for language and reasoning, we form a "moral commu-nity". Insofar as an individual is recognized as a member of this community, she is viewed as someone who is not an appropriate object for manipulation and "treatment". Rather, we recognize the individual as a person who must be reasoned with and, thus, treated with the dignity due to such an agent. Membership in the moral community, so described, admits of *degrees*. That is, there are degrees to which an agent may be deemed an appropriate or inappropriate object of moral sentiment, because there are degrees to which such agents possess the requisite capacities. This view contrasts sharply with the view that responsibility is an all-or-nothing affair in virtue of the agent's either possessing or not possessing "free will".[11]

Hume, quite simply, has much too little to say on these difficult and complicated matters. Some commentators have suggested that Hume was aware of the importance of language to moral capacity and moral community.[12] On the whole, however, what Hume has to say in this regard is rather thin and sketchy. Similarly, although Hume does not ignore the fact that we have a capacity to reflect critically on our moral character and can in some measure alter or amend our character on this basis, he nevertheless downplays the significance of such capacities and suggests that they do not have a central role to play in moral life.[13] What he does say on this issue—that the objects of moral sentiment should be understood, simply, as creatures who possess pleasurable or painful mental qualities—is plainly inadequate and unacceptable. Accordingly, it seems clear that if we are to further advance the naturalistic theory, we must rectify this shortcoming in Hume's account.[14]

Notes

1. Two relatively recent studies that are particularly relevant to the discussion in this chapter are Lyons, *Emotion*, and Taylor, *Pride, Shame and Guilt*. Helpful discussions of Hume's views can be found in Penelhum, *Hume*, chp. 5, and Neu, *Emotion, Thought and Therapy*, Pt. 1. Hume is widely regarded as "the most notable exponent" of the feeling theory (Lyons, *Emotion*, 8; Alston, "Emotion and Feeling", 480). However, it is important not to lose sight of the extent to which Hume argues that our emotional states are directly determined by our thoughts and beliefs. It is misleading, therefore, to present Hume as holding the view that our emotions are unregulated by reason—his view is quite the contrary. On this, see Baier, *A Progress of Sentiments*, esp. 158–60, 180–81. (Baier, I think, rather downplays Hume's difficulties in this area, but she correctly argues that for Hume "passions incorporate the influence of reason, since they presuppose beliefs" [p. 159].) Note also that it would be incorrect to suppose that criticism of Hume's feeling theory of emotion is entirely recent. See, e.g., Reid's criticism of Hume's "use of the word *sentiment*, to express feeling without judgment" (*Active Powers*, 468–69).

2. Indeed, it may be argued, as Lyons argues, that it is the "evaluative category" involved in emotion which enables us to identify it as an emotion of a given type. Cf. Lyons, *Emotion*, esp. chps. 3 and 4.

3. A very illuminating effort to account for the cognitive-evaluative elements in "emotions of self-assessment" is presented in Taylor, *Pride, Shame and Guilt*. Taylor draws a useful distinction between what she terms "identificatory" and "explanatory" beliefs, which are, she claims, constitutive of the emotional experience in question (see esp. *Pride, Shame and Guilt*, chp. 2). I think that it is possible to provide an analysis of the cognitive-evaluative elements of moral sentiment along the lines Taylor suggests. Very briefly, the identificatory belief may be characterized as the belief that some person is morally praiseworthy or blameworthy, admirable or contemptible. The explanatory beliefs will provide the grounds on which we hold this identificatory belief. Thus the explanatory beliefs will point to the moral characteristics or qualities in virtue of which we value the person as we do. In reconstructing our understanding of the nature of moral sentiment along these lines, we come closer, I suggest, to a proper analysis of the cognitive-evaluative aspects involved in moral sentiment. As Taylor points out, this is not an exhaustive analysis of what is involved in emotions of this kind, but it serves to identify those beliefs which make the emotional experience what it is. (Note that Taylor's identificatory/explanatory belief distinction draws attention to a point that is fundamental to Hume's position, namely, that moral evaluation is directed toward the [whole] *person* but is grounded on our beliefs about the person's specific character traits.)

4. Consider, for example, our emotional reactions when we contemplate evil characters in fiction or in historical eras far removed from us (see, e.g., T 470, 584). In these circumstances there may be no felt disturbance or affect at all, nor any change in our practical attitude and disposition. We nevertheless recognize when we contemplate these characters that they produce an emotional response in us.

5. Hume does, of course, have something substantial to say about what the cognitive-evaluative aspects involved in moral sentiment are—they are beliefs which concern the moral virtues and vices of the individual who is the object of our moral sentiment. His mistake, I have argued, is to suggest that these beliefs are not an essential element of moral sentiment. I argue below that Hume's account of the content of these beliefs (i.e. that they concern pleasurable or painful qualities of mind) is also faulty.

6. It includes, for example, "natural abilities", on the grounds that they, too, are mental qualities which give rise to pleasure and pain and, thus, generate moral sentiments (*Treatise*, III, iii, 4). I return to this issue in chapter 9.

7. As already indicated (chp. 4, n.5), Hume holds that "animals have little or no sense of virtue or vice" and that they cannot feel any pride or humility in their qualities of mind or in their possessions (T, 326). This suggests that animals do not themselves experience moral sentiments, but it does not show that human beings cannot entertain moral sentiments toward animals for the same reason that they entertain them toward other people (i.e. on the basis of their perceived pleasurable or painful qualities of mind). Hume could, like Descartes, deny that animals have any mind and that they are mere "machines"—but this is clearly not his view, since he thinks that they are like people in that they have thoughts and feelings. On this general issue, see Pitson, "Humean Animals", 308–12. (Pitson makes some effort to help Hume out of his difficulties, but I am not convinced that this can be done.)

8. The seriousness of this flaw in Hume's position can be properly gauged when we consider that, standardly, libertarians will argue that the relevant moral capacity is some form of categorical or "contra-causal" freedom. As it stands, Hume's response to this alternative view remains feeble insofar as he has failed to provide any plausible alternative account of the capacities in question. (Similar weaknesses can be seen in Strawson's naturalistic theory; on this, see my "Strawson's Way of Naturalizing Responsibility".)

9. A classic discussion of these matters is presented in Hampshire, *Thought and Action*, esp. chps. 2 and 3. Hampshire states, "A man becomes more and more a free and responsible agent the more he at all times knows what he is doing . . . and the more he acts with a definite and clearly formed intention" (p. 177).

10. This is a large literature that has appeared in the last two decades on these matters. See especially the papers by Frankfurt, Watson, and Taylor in Watson, ed., *Free Will* and also Dennett, *Elbow Room*, esp. chps. 2–5.

11. The claim that it is a matter of degree whether one is or is not an appropriate object of moral sentiment accords, I believe, with our everyday intuitions on this subject. In particular, it accords with the ambiguous moral status which we attribute to children and the mentally ill and disabled.

12. See, e.g., Baier, *A Progress of Sentiments*, 190. Baier cites an interesting and relevant passage at EM, 274.

13. This is discussed in more detail in chp. 9 of this volume.

14. Smith makes an important advance on Hume's theory insofar as he emphasizes the point that it is essential that the objects of our moral sentiments—in particular, our feelings of merit and demerit—be able to *understand why we feel about them as we do* (TMS, 69; cf. 95–96, 111n). In other words, on Smith's account legitimate objects of moral sentiment must be capable of *interpreting* the way that others in their moral community react to them.

7

Action, Character, and Excuses

> It seems ridiculous to infer an excellency in ourselves from an object which is of so much shorter duration, and attends us during so small a part of our existence.
>
> Hume, *A Treatise of Human Nature*

> We are never to consider any single action in our enquiries concerning the origin of morals; but only the quality or character from which the action proceeded. These alone are durable enough to affect our sentiments concerning the person.
>
> Hume, *A Treatise of Human Nature*

Hume's understanding of how moral sentiment is aroused commits him to some puzzling and controversial views about responsibility and excusing considerations. More specifically, Hume maintains that people are responsible for actions only insofar as they reveal enduring qualities of mind or character.[1] He also holds that agents cannot be held responsible for actions that were produced by qualities of mind that they no longer possess (T, 412; EU, 99). In this chapter I examine the basis of these claims and consider how they relate to Hume's naturalistic principles.

I

Hume's remarks about the nature of character are both brief and fragmentary, and thus it is not easy to say exactly how he understands the concept of character.[2] He speaks of 'character' in two quite different senses. The narrower sense refers to a specific character *trait* (e.g. honesty, courage). The wider sense, by contrast, means a person's *complete* set of moral traits and qualities—that is, his whole set of character traits. It is clear enough that when Hume is speaking of virtues and vices, he is referring to specific traits of character which are, for him, "durable principles of the mind" (T, 575). A person's character traits, Hume observes, are neither fixed nor unalterable. It is to be expected that a person's character will change through time (EU, 86, 99; T, 261, 349, 412).

Character, we have noted, is known primarily through the actions that it produces or gives rise to. That is to say, our knowledge of character depends very largely on causal inferences from actions. So understood, character is distinct from, and thus not reducible to, action. This leaves us with a problem: What does character *consist* in? The most plausible answer to this question is that traits of character are constituted by passions. In certain contexts, Hume quite explicitly identifies virtues and vices with specific passions (e.g. EU, 83, where ambition, avarice, self-love, etc., are described as "passions"; see also EM, 271; T, 602–3, 604). On this interpretation, then, it is perceptions that constitute the ontological basis of qualities of character—because passions are one kind of perception. A passion, Hume suggests, may become "a settled principle of action" and, as such, may be "the predominant inclination of the soul" (T, 419). In this way, a passion can serve as an enduring or persisting cause of actions. This observation explains the very important connexion between character and action.

On the account offered, character traits are interpreted as enduring or persisting passions.[3] So considered, they are, typically, tied to a disposition to act in certain relevant ways. It follows from this that a person's character in the wide sense is constituted by a certain structure or pattern of the various passions that animate that person and direct her conduct and behaviour. An understanding of a person's character in these terms generally involves identifying the ways in which the various passions are related to each other and shape the person's will. Hume points out, for example, that some passions prevail or dominate in the mind of an agent and thereby direct the person's conduct one way rather than another.[4] It is, then, according to Hume's account, this pattern and structure of the passions, and the way that it relates to conduct, that is of the very essence of moral character.

The above account of Hume's conception of character, although it clearly captures much of what Hume has to say about character, requires some significant qualification. First, it is important that we do not construe Hume's understanding of character entirely in terms of its relation to *action*. An individual can entertain passions that never give rise to intentional action. It is, moreover, obvious that passions may be manifested by a person without being expressed in action. Indeed, a person's gestures, mannerisms, and countenance can betray a passion even when the person prefers to conceal the passion or feign a different one. It is a mistake, therefore, to assume that character traits must always be manifested through intentional action.

There is another important aspect of Hume's account of character to consider. In a variety of contexts, Hume suggests that our natural abilities and talents constitute important aspects of character and that they are, as such, liable to moral evaluation (T, 606–14; EM, 312–17; LET, I/33–34). For example, according to Hume, intelligence and imagination are no less aspects of a person's character (i.e. considered as enduring principles of mind) than are, say, honesty and compassion. Clearly, however, intelligence and imagination cannot be construed as passions of any sort. It is a mistake, therefore, to interpret Hume's account of character *exclusively* in terms of the passions (and the way that they relate to intentional action). On the contrary, Hume's views about the relevance of natural abilities to the interpretation of character commit him to a more complex account than this.[5] This specific feature of Hume's conception of character, however, is essential to his moral philosophy, in general, and his theory of responsibility in particular.

II

Hume maintains that people are responsible for actions only insofar as they reveal enduring qualities of mind or character. He makes this claim in several different contexts. It first appears in the important passage in the *Treatise* near the end of his discussion of liberty and necessity.

> Actions are by their very nature temporary and perishing; and where they proceed not from some *cause in the character and disposition of the person*, who perform'd them, they infix not themselves upon him, and can neither redound to his honour, if good, nor infamy, if evil. The action itself may be blameable. . . . *But the person is not responsible for it; and as it proceeded from nothing in him, that is durable or constant,* and leaves nothing of that nature behind it, 'tis impossible he can, upon its account, become the object of punishment or vengeance. (T, 411; my emphasis; cf. EU, 98)[6]

The same general points are discussed in some further detail in his discussion of the natural virtues and vices in Book III.

> If any action be either virtuous or vicious, 'tis only as a sign of some quality or character. *It must depend upon durable principles of the mind, which extend over the whole conduct, and enter into the personal character.* Actions themselves, not proceeding from any constant principle, *have no influence on love or hatred, pride or humility*; and consequently are never consider'd in morality. (T, 575; my emphasis)

Hume continues,

> This reflexion is self-evident, and deserves to be attended to, *as being of the utmost importance in the present subject.* We are never to consider any single action in our enquiries concerning the origin of morals; but *only the quality or character from which the action proceeded. These alone are durable enough to affect our sentiments concerning the person.* Actions are, indeed, better indications of a character than words, or even wishes and sentiments; but 'tis only so far as they are such indications, that they are attended with love or hatred, praise or blame. (T, 575; my emphasis)

In another passage, placed between the two passages that I have cited, Hume gives these observations a slightly different twist.

> 'Tis evident, that when we praise any actions, *we regard only the motives that produced them, and consider the actions as signs or indications of certain principles in the mind and temper. The external performance has no merit.* We must look within to find the moral quality. This we cannot do directly; and therefore fix our attention on actions, as on external signs. But these actions are still considered as signs; and *the ultimate object of our praise and approbation is the motive, that produc'd them.* (T, 477; my emphasis; cf. T, 479; EU, 99)

In all these passages, Hume is making two distinct, although related, points. First, he is concerned to argue that the "action", considered as an "external performance" without reference to the motive or intention that produced and guided it, is not, as such, of moral concern. It is, rather, the "internal" cause of the action which arouses our moral sentiment. It is these aspects of action which inform us about the mind and moral character of the agent.[7] Second, the moral qualities of an agent which arouse our moral sentiments must be "durable or constant"—they cannot be "temporary and perishing" in nature in the way that actions are. Hume, evidently, regards these points as linked, but he does not distinguish them as sharply as he should do.[8]

Hume says that it is a matter of "the utmost importance" for moral philosophy that action be indicative of durable qualities of mind if a person is to be held accountable for it (T, 575).[9] On the basis of such remarks, some may argue that when explaining Hume's commitments it is inappropriate to speak of "responsibility for action"—because it is character, not action, that we are *ultimately* accountable for. However, I think that this puts the point too strongly. On Hume's theory, as I have explained, action *in itself* (i.e. "the external performance") does not give rise to moral sentiment. In this sense, strictly speaking, agents are not responsible for actions per se. Nevertheless, clearly Hume holds that action does arouse moral sentiment *under the relevant circumstances*, and he recognizes that people are, plainly, praised and blamed for their conduct (crimes, etc.). More specifically, what Hume maintains is that a person is accountable for action *only so far as* such action is (taken as) a *sign* of some *lasting* principle of *mind*. The important point here is that it is the (double) proviso that requires careful explanation in terms of the principles of Hume's system. Clearly, then, it is not illegitimate to speak of "responsibility for action" *so long as* one keeps in mind the relevant (double) proviso. Indeed, speaking this way is entirely consistent with Hume's own way of expressing himself.

The claim that moral evaluation of action requires that we consider the motive or intention which produced the action is easy to explain in terms of the general principles of Hume's system. Moral sentiments, he holds, are aroused only by mental qualities, and thus if action is not indicative of the mind of the agent no moral sentiment will be generated. However, the further claim that action must be indicative of some *persisting* or *enduring* character trait is both puzzling and controversial. Moreover, it seems clear that the first condition does not, in itself, imply the second. That is, we can grant that the moral evaluation of an action requires that we consider the motive or intention which produced the action and yet reject the *further* claim that the action must be indicative of some persisting or enduring character trait if the agent is to be held responsible for it. Many commentators who accept the first claim have argued that the further, stronger claim is wholly implausible and must be rejected.

What, then, is the *basis* of this puzzling and controversial claim concerning the need for *enduring* principles of mind if moral sentiment is to be aroused? One commentator, in a recent article, has suggested that Hume fails to provide this claim with any support. Hume's position on this issue, it is said, is "merely asserted" and lacks any "clear theoretical backing in [his] work".[10] However, according to the classical interpretation of Hume on responsibility, there is a plausible explanation for this claim.

The classical view is clearly stated by Philippa Foot in an influential paper written some thirty years ago.[11] Foot discusses Hume's claim concerning the relationship between responsibility and character in the context of her criticism of the general thesis that freedom and responsibility require the truth of determinism. She takes Hume to be supporting this thesis by way of arguing that "an undetermined action would be one for which it would be impossible to praise or blame, punish or reward a man, because it would be connected with nothing permanent in his nature" (p. 105).

She then quotes from the passage at T, 411, that is cited above, and comments on it as follows.

> Hume is surely wrong in saying that we could not praise or blame, punish or reward, a person in whose character there was nothing 'permanent or durable'. . . . We honor people as well as nations for what they have done in the past and do not consider what has been done *merely as an indication of what may be expected in the future*. Moreover, it is perfectly rational to punish people for what they have done, even if there is no reason to think that they would be likely to do it again. (Foot, "Free Will", 105; my emphasis)[12]

Foot presents Hume, in line with other thinkers in the classical compatibilist tradition, such as Schlick, as taking an essentially forward-looking and utilitarian view about responsibility. That is, Foot's remarks imply that Hume is concerned primarily with the efficaciousness of praise or blame, and rewards or punishments, in order to secure desirable conduct and behaviour. Hume's claim about the relevance of character for the purpose of moral evaluation does indeed seem to make sense in this context. If an action is not in character, or reveals no durable principle of mind, then we have no reason to expect that the agent will repeat such actions in the future.[13] To blame or punish the agent in these circumstances, therefore, is unnecessary and pointless insofar as we are concerned to prevent or deter the agent from acting in these ways in the future.[14]

The difficulty with Foot's account is that it depends on a mistaken interpretation of Hume's wider position on responsibility. As I have argued, it is a mistake to read Hume as taking a Schlickean (forward-looking, utilitarian) position on responsibility. According to Hume, our sentiments of praise and blame, on the basis of which we hold people responsible (and thus liable to reward and punishment), are naturally aroused by the pleasant or painful qualities of mind of the person who is the object of these sentiments. Moral sentiments, on Hume's account, arise in us spontaneously, without a view to the sort of forward-looking, utilitarian considerations that concern Schlick. On the contrary, it is entirely consistent with Hume's naturalistic principles for moral sentiments to be aroused in us by individuals who are characters in (remote) history or fiction and from whom we have no expectation of actions of a given kind being repeated in the future. Indeed, this is Hume's explicitly expressed position on this matter.[15] In general, we may morally evaluate a person without any practical interest in how we may influence future action by means of praise or blame, rewards or punishments. This is not the "general point of view" from which moral evaluation takes place (T, 580–87). It follows, then, that Hume's view that we praise or blame a person for action only if it reveals a durable principle of mind cannot be explained in these terms.

These observations present us with a quite specific problem of interpretation and exegesis in respect of Hume's position. Foot's Schlickean interpretation provides us with a prima facie plausible explanation for Hume's claim regarding the relationship between responsibility and character. In the absence of some relevant (forward-looking, utilitarian) Schlickean framework, Hume's claim seems to lack any intelligible foundation in his system. The interesting question, therefore, is can the *naturalistic* interpretation make any better sense of this important aspect of Hume's theory of responsibility?

III

In order to understand Hume's position, we need to examine, once again, the details of his account of the indirect passions. Hume claims that for an indirect passion to be aroused in us, the "cause" of the passion (i.e. some item or feature which we find independently pleasurable or painful) must stand in some relevant and appropriate relations to the "object" of the passion (i.e. oneself or someone else). The "most obvious causes of these passions", it is said, are virtue and vice, or our various qualities of mind (T, 279, 295; DP, 146–47). In general, this relationship between the cause and the object of the passion, Hume argues, must be *close* (T, 291). The quality or feature must be "part of ourselves, or something nearly related to us" if it is to produce these passions (T, 285; cf. T, 296, 298, 331). Failing this, the quality or feature will not be closely enough related to the "object" of the indirect passion (i.e. oneself or someone else) to move the mind (naturally) from the idea of the one to the idea of the other. Related to this point, Hume also notes that the relationship between the quality or feature which gives rise to the passion and the person who is the object of the passion must not be "casual and inconstant" (T, 293). If the relationship between them is of "short duration", then the transition or association of ideas required to generate the sentiment will be weakened or may even entirely fail its effect (T, 349; cf. DP, 146).

In the following passage, Hume points out what happens when the relationship between the cause and object of the passion is brief and temporary (in this context he is concerned specifically with pride):

> What is casual and inconstant gives but little joy, and less pride. We are not much satisfy'd with the thing itself; and are still less apt to feel any new degrees of self-satisfaction upon its account. We foresee and anticipate its change by the imagination; which makes us little satisfy'd with the thing: We compare it to ourselves, whose existence is more durable; by which means its inconstancy appears still greater. *It seems ridiculous to infer an excellency in ourselves from an object, which is of so much shorter duration, and attends us during so small a part of our existence.* (T, 293; cf. DP, 146, 153–54)

The language here is closely in accord with the language Hume employs when he is arguing that a person is responsible for an action only when it reveals durable principles of mind (e.g. T, 349, 411, 575). The reason for this is that the latter claim is simply a particular application of the general claim that Hume makes in respect of the indirect passions: Any object or quality which bears only a casual or inconstant relation to us will be unable to generate an indirect passion. Actions are by their very nature "temporary and perishing". In order to generate a moral sentiment, they must proceed from something that stands in the required close and *lasting* relation to the agent. Only constant and enduring principles of mind satisfy this demand, and, hence, only they will serve to arouse moral sentiment. It is now clear, at least, why Hume claims that we are responsible for actions only insofar as they reveal *durable* principles of mind.

Hume's claim concerning character and responsibility is much more intelligible when considered within this naturalistic framework. Note, for example, the parallels with other kinds of causes of the indirect passions, such as bodily beauty. Hume maintains, by analogy, that someone who is physically beautiful momentarily, or at infrequent intervals of time, will not thereby become the object of our love. The reason for this is that the beauty that arouses our love for the person must be a persisting or enduring quality that they possess. "Flashes" of beauty might impress us briefly, but they will not, of themselves, sustain our sentiments toward that person.[16] Clearly, then, to the extent that we view Hume's claim concerning the relationship between responsibility and character in terms of the general principles of his system, his claim is not entirely implausible.

IV

I have argued that Hume's claim concerning responsibility and character has its foundation in the details of his account of the mechanism that produces the moral sentiments. In this respect, his claim is entirely intelligible within the framework of his own naturalistic principles. I have also suggested that Hume's claim has a certain plausibility when we consider the parallels that hold between moral evaluation and certain other forms of personal evaluation. In order to feel love for a beautiful person, the quality of beauty must be lasting. To feel esteem for the rich and powerful, a person must possess these goods and qualities in a manner that endures beyond "a small part of [their own] existence". Similarly, for us to feel moral approval or disapproval toward a person, that person must possess lasting and constant pleasurable or painful qualities of mind.

Although this position seems clear enough, there are significant ambiguities in what Hume is saying. On one interpretation, Hume may be taken to claim that our moral sentiments toward a person will vary in *duration* depending on how durable and constant the quality possessed is found to be. On this account, our moral sentiments toward a person are only as lasting as the quality that gives rise to them. This, however, is not entirely consistent with Hume's remarks on the subject. He does not claim that moral sentiments are "temporary and perishing" unless they are aroused by durable qualities of mind. He claims that if qualities of mind are not enduring in nature, then moral sentiments simply will not be produced (see, e.g., T, 411; EU, 98).

Another interpretation, given the principles suggested, is that our sentiments toward a person will vary in *quality* (i.e. degree of pleasure or pain) depending on how durable and constant the quality possessed is found to be. On this account, we naturally approve or disapprove of a person more *intensely* depending on how lasting the quality of mind in question may be. This interpretation is also at odds with Hume's remarks. Hume does not claim that "temporary and perishing" episodes *weaken the intensity* of our moral sentiments. He holds that they do not arouse our moral sentiments. Hume is not claiming that the felt pleasure or pain of our moral sentiments varies with the *duration* of the character trait that produces them. On the contrary, his claim is that only durable character traits engage our moral sentiments (and hence action gives rise to moral sentiment only insofar as it reveals qualities of mind of this sort).

Hume's position on this matter is stark. His analysis presupposes that actions either reveal durable qualities of mind or they do not. This implies that actions can be neatly placed into one of two categories: "in" or "out" of character.[17] If an action belongs to the first category, then it reveals durable qualities of mind which we can evaluate the person for; otherwise there is no durable quality of mind that will arouse our moral sentiment. Clearly, this is to oversimplify matters. In at least one passage (T, 349), Hume suggests that *all* intentional action reveals durable qualities of mind. If this is his considered view, then he is simply mistaken. The extent to which an action reveals durable and persisting qualities of mind varies greatly. It is, moreover, quite evident that some character traits are more deeply entrenched in the mind of a person than are others. The general difficulty with Hume's position is, then, that the requirement that we consider action in relation to character (i.e. enduring qualities of mind) raises issues that are considerably more complex and subtle than Hume's remarks suggest.[18] Given the importance that Hume attaches to this claim, it must be judged one of the weaker aspects of his general theory of responsibility.[19]

V

Hume's view about the relationship between responsibility and character provides the background for his most detailed discussion of excusing considerations. These passages appear at T, 412 and EU, 98–99. They follow immediately after Hume's claim that actions are "temporary and perishing" and give rise to our sense of merit or demerit only insofar as such action proceeds from "some cause in the character and disposition of the person" (T, 411; EU, 98). Consistent with this, Hume holds that excusing considerations must be explained or accounted for with reference to character. The significance of excusing considerations is that they alter or change our beliefs about an agent's *character* in some relevant way. By this means they alter our moral sentiments toward the person.

In the passages referred to above (T, 412; EU, 98–99) Hume cites three fundamental categories of excusing consideration: (1) "Men are not blam'd for such evil actions as they perform ignorantly and casually, whatever may be their consequences." (2) "Men are less blam'd for such evil actions, as they perform hastily and unpremeditatedly, than for such as proceed from thought and deliberation." (3) "Repentance wipes off every crime, [especially] if attended with [an evident] reformation of life and manners." Each of these claims is followed by a brief explanation of the principles involved. In each case Hume connects the excusing consideration to some relevant consideration about the agent's character or durable principles of mind.

There is a significant difference between the first two and the third kind of excuse. In the case of the latter—repentance accompanied with a change of character—what affects and alters our sentiments toward the agent is a consideration respecting the agent's character that arises *subsequent* to the actions in question. In the case of the first two excuses, however, we are to look carefully at the character of the agent *at the time of action*. In other words, excusing considerations of the first two kinds do not draw attention to subsequent changes or developments in the agent's character but rather suggest that when the action is properly interpreted in terms of its relevant causes, it is evident that the character of the agent is significantly different from what initial appearances may suggest.[20]

In the next chapter, I discuss Hume's account of the first two excusing considerations. Here I confine my attention to the third excusing consideration: repentance and changes of character. What Hume says on this subject is in certain respects closely related to his claim that we are responsible for action only insofar as it reveals enduring and constant qualities of mind. It is this relationship that I am particularly concerned to examine.

Insofar as repentance and a change of character is put forward as an excusing consideration, no effort is made to show that the "crime" was not indicative of vicious principles of mind. Rather, a change of sentiment is produced by showing that the agent repents of his action and has subsequently altered his character in this respect. In other words, it is not denied that a crime has taken place, nor that the agent was animated by "criminal [passions or] principles in the mind" (T, 412; EU, 99]. What is asserted is that the agent has *ceased* to be criminal in character and thus is no longer blameworthy.

Hume's comments link repentance and changes of character in a way that raises several difficulties of interpretation and criticism. There is, in the first place, a difference between the *Treatise* and *Enquiry* accounts of this matter. In the *Treatise*, Hume says that "repentance wipes off every crime, *especially if* attended with an evident reformation of life and manners" (my emphasis). In the *Enquiry*, he says that "repentance wipes off every crime, *if* attended with a reformation of life and manners" (my emphasis).[21] The *Enquiry* version suggests that repentance excuses *only if* it is accompanied by a relevant change of character; whereas the *Treatise* version suggests that a change of character *further supports*, but is not required, for repentance to excuse. The significance of the linkage between repentance and alteration of character is clearly problematic. One way of reading Hume's remarks in the *Enquiry* is that repentance excuses to the extent that it involves some relevant character change—and that it is the latter feature which is of significance for the modification of our moral evaluation of the agent. Clearly, however, the *Treatise* version separates these issues and suggests that repentance *independently* excuses, even though a change of character reinforces excusing considerations of this nature.

It seems clear that the *Treatise* version is preferable because it keeps considerations of repentance and change of character distinct. Obviously a person may repent of his crimes without any appropriate change in disposition. Similarly, a subsequent change in character or disposition might, in certain circumstances, not be accompanied by an appropriate attitude of repentance. The relationship, however, appears to be this. Generally speaking, repentance will *motivate* a change in character. In other words, repentance serves as a very important avenue through which a person may come to alter his character and disposition after due reflection on his crimes. So there is something of a natural link between repentance and changes of character. Typically, we expect the one to be accompanied by the other.

Is it correct to present repentance as independently excusing? Certainly sincere repentance is evidence that a person does not reflectively identify with his actions. In these circumstances, we understand the agent to take the view that the action does not reflect his deepest values and that he would *prefer* that the structure of his will was otherwise than it is (or was). The person repudiates such action as morally unacceptable and indicative of qualities he does not approve of. Certainly these are important observations, and they show that considerations of this kind affect our moral sentiments toward the agent. It seems too strong, however, to present repentance, so interpreted, as *excusing* a person from all responsibility for a crime. Rather, the appropriate point to make—even from within the framework of Hume's principles—is that such considerations serve to *mitigate* and reduce the degree of blameworthiness for the crime. In other words, repentance serves to put some "distance" between the agent and his crime—but it does not, in itself, sever the tie.[22] As I have indicated, a person may sincerely repent and yet still retain "criminal passions or principles of mind".

A further difficult question raised by Hume's discussion is whether or not changes of character serve by themselves to excuse agents of responsibility for actions that were *at the time that they were performed* indicative of the agent's durable qualities of mind. Let us suppose that a person commits a vicious crime at a certain time and subsequently there is a relevant change in character. The person, then, no longer possesses the vicious quality of mind that gave rise to the crime. Hume is committed to the view that after the change in character takes place it would be inappropriate to blame the person for the crime, because the person no longer possesses the relevant blameworthy character. His discussion suggests, moreover, that this conclusion is a straightforward corollary of the more general principle that we are accountable for actions only insofar as they reveal durable and constant qualities of mind.

It is evident that on Hume's account the conditions of responsibility extend beyond the initial (double) proviso that he lays down—that is, that an agent is responsible for an action only if it reveals durable and constant principles of mind. Hume's comments suggest that the principles or qualities involved must also *continue* or *persist* in the mind of the agent (otherwise no appropriate moral sentiment will be aroused). It is important to note, however, that the first requirement does not imply the second. That is, we may accept that there must be some enduring quality of mind that belongs to an agent for the person to be morally evaluated, and still, consistently, reject the further, stronger demand that any such enduring quality of mind must *continue* to belong to the mind of the person being evaluated (i.e. praised or blamed). Nothing about Hume's system concerning the mechanism of the indirect passions gives us reason to accept this stronger demand. An established, enduring quality of mind may have persisted through time in such a way that we naturally and reasonably associate it with the person long after the character trait has altered or changed. Hume is mistaken if he supposes that a change in character shows that there ceases to be any durable connexion or relation between the agent and the character trait that the person once possessed. I conclude, therefore, that according to Hume's own principles a change of character will not, in itself, release an agent of responsibility for past crimes, so long as those crimes were indeed produced by durable principles of mind possessed by the agent at the time.[23]

It seems reasonable to suppose that an alteration in character must lead to an appropriate *modification* or *moderation* of our moral sentiments toward the agent. In this sense, there is a parallel between cases of this sort and cases of repentance (and, indeed, cases of out-of-character action). On this view of things, the moral evaluation of the agent requires that we take note of the fact that this is a person who no longer possesses such a vicious quality of mind, and we are thus required to *tem-*

per our sentiments accordingly. We can, therefore, agree with Hume that changes of character are directly relevant to the way in which we hold agents responsible for crimes that have occurred in the past. However, as I have argued, this is not to say, with Hume, that an alteration in character (along with repentance) requires us to withdraw all sense of blame toward the criminal.[24] Observation of ordinary life makes plain that the truth is not so simple as this.[25]

VI

In this chapter, I have been primarily concerned with a problem of interpretation. Specifically, I have been concerned to identify the basis of two controversial claims that feature prominently in Hume's rationale of excuses: the claim that we are responsible for action only insofar as it reveals durable qualities of character; and the claim that an agent ceases to be responsible for a crime when there is an alteration in the qualities of character that gave rise to it. These claims are closely related insofar as Hume appears to regard the latter claim as a simple corollary of the first. I have argued that the first claim is not to be explained in terms of forward-looking, utilitarian considerations. On the contrary, the basis of this claim lies with Hume's naturalistic commitments and is to be accounted for in terms of his description of the mechanism that produces moral sentiment. Hume's second claim cannot be accounted for in these terms. Contrary to what Hume supposes, it has no basis in the principles of his system.[26]

Insofar as Hume provides support for his claims concerning the relevance of character to issues of responsibility, it is offered in terms of his naturalistic principles. I have argued, however, that Hume's account of the relation between action and character depends on an in/out-of-character distinction that oversimplifies these matters and obscures significant difficulties that arise in this area. Beyond this, the specific theses which Hume advances are implausibly strong and at odds with the sort of ordinary moral experience that he claims to be drawing from. On these matters, I side with Hume's critics. Nevertheless, Hume may well be correct in maintaining that when considering the actions of an agent our moral sentiments should be modified or moderated with a view to that person's wider character. This (weaker) aspect of Hume's position is not implausible. Moreover, as Hume indicates, it touches on important issues in moral philosophy. It is a mistake, therefore, to dismiss this aspect of Hume's theory of responsibility casually. A proper understanding of his position shows that what he has to say—however flawed—is intricately linked with other features of his system and touches on problems that are both difficult and important.

Notes

1. It is surprising to find that this claim has been dismissed rather casually by a number of commentators—particularly since Hume says that it is a matter of "the utmost importance" for moral philosophy (T, 575). Flew's comments are quite typical of the sort of treatment that Hume's claim has received. Flew says, "Every action has of course to be the action of some person. If anyone is to be fairly credited with an action he has to be the person who did it. But it is not essential for the action to be in character" (*Hume's Philosophy of Belief*, 160). Flew

then dismisses this aspect of Hume's discussion as a "feeble foray" and drops the matter completely. Stroud, in his influential commentary, altogether ignores Hume's claim concerning the importance of character to ascriptions of responsibility (*Hume*, chp. 7).

2. In what follows I draw on the helpful discussions of this matter in McIntyre, "Character: A Humean Account" and Baier, *A Progress of Sentiments*, 188–99.

3. Precisely *how* passions are understood to "endure" is a matter requiring some further interpretation and discussion. We need, for example, to distinguish "types" and "tokens" of a given passion. McIntyre clearly reads Hume as holding that specific *tokens* of the passions are "more durable than other perceptions" ("Character: A Humean Account", 200). On a different reading, however, Hume may be understood to be claiming that a person has a given character insofar as a particular *type* of passion regularly appears in her mind and influences her behaviour and conduct. This account allows Hume to acknowledge that specific *tokens* of the passion may not be enduring and constant.

4. "Almost every one has a predominant inclination, to which his other desires and affections submit, and which governs him, though, perhaps, with some intervals, through the whole course of his life" (ESY, 160 [Sceptic]). See also Hume's remarks concerning the prevalence of the calm passions over the violent (T, 418).

5. McIntyre notes that Hume views natural abilities as "powers" and that both "powers and character traits are commonly described as existing unexercised" ("Character: A Humean Account", 198–99). This raises further difficulties regarding the interpretation of Hume's conception of character which I will not pursue.

6. It should be clear that Hume does not express himself carefully enough when he says that the "action itself may be blameable". Clearly, for Hume, blame is not aroused by "actions" as such but only by actions *insofar as they reveal character*. What he should say in this context, therefore, is that the action itself may be pleasurable or painful in nature but that this *alone* will not arouse a sentiment of praise or blame toward the agent. The discussion below will further clarify this point.

7. Note also, however, that Hume says, "Actions are at first only consider'd as signs of motives: But 'tis usual, in this case, as in all others, to fix our attention on the signs, and neglect, in some measure, the thing signify'd" (T, 479). Clearly, then, Hume holds that we need to check our (natural) tendency to "fix attention" on the action and "neglect" the motive that caused it. See chp. 8 in this volume for a further discussion of the interpretation of action in terms of its causes and the relevance of this to issues of responsibility.

8. The linkage for Hume is to be explained in part by the fact that he holds that intentional action *always* reveals or manifests some *durable* principle of mind—i.e. a character trait of some kind (T, 349). It is important to note, however, that this claim is distinct from the claim that only durable principles of mind give rise to moral sentiments. Hume, as I will show, does provide some rationale for the latter claim, although there is no support offered for the thesis that intentional action is always indicative of durable principles of mind. The significant point here is that we must distinguish the thesis that only durable principles of mind give rise to moral sentiment from the thesis that intentional action always reveals durable principles of mind if we are to properly assess the rationale, or lack of rationale, which Hume (independently) provides for each of these theses.

9. Hume touches on this point in a letter written to Hutcheson in September 1739. The letter is a reply to Hutcheson's comments on the (as yet unpublished) manuscript of Book III of the *Treatise*. The relevant passage occurs at the beginning of a long postscript to the letter. It reads, "Actions are not virtuous nor vicious; but *only so far as* they are proofs of certain Qualitys or durable Principles in the Mind. This is a Point I shou'd have established more expressly than I have done" (LET, I/34; my emphasis). The passage at T, 575, as subsequently published (November 1740), duly emphasizes this point.

10. Davie, "Hume on Morality, Action and Character", 339 and 345.

11. Foot, "Free Will as Involving Determinism". Foot's interpretation of this issue is neither recent nor detailed. I discuss her remarks only because they are both influential and representative of the classical view on this matter. In general, in this context I am not concerned to discuss or closely examine the secondary literature on this subject. I note, however, that there is a more detailed criticism of Foot's discussion of Hume in Helm, "Hume on Exculpation". Helm agrees with Foot that Hume is mistaken in holding that we should excuse agents for "out-of-character" action, but he argues that Foot misrepresents Hume's position on this issue insofar as she presents it as grounded in forward-looking, utilitarian considerations. Unlike Foot, however, Helm offers no explanation for why Hume makes this claim.

In the more recent literature, Bricke has made some effort to explain the basis of Hume's position on this subject ("Hume on Freedom to Act and Personal Evaluation", 148–50). Bricke's particular concern, however, is to explain why Hume holds that "an action provides a basis for personal evaluation of a certain sort only insofar as it is intentional". He does, nevertheless, touch on several of the points which I pursue concerning the basis of Hume's understanding of the relationship between responsibility and character.

12. Foot misrepresents the passage that she cites from the *Treatise*. The first sentence she quotes from the passage at T, 411 should appear at the *end*, not the beginning, of this quotation (see Foot, "Free Will as Involving Determinism", 105).

13. The reverse, however, does not hold. That is, it does not follow from the fact that an action is indicative of an agent's persisting character that it is, therefore, one that we have reason to expect to be repeated. On the contrary, external circumstances might have altered, or might be expected to alter, in such a way that we think that the action will not be performed again in the future by the agent. Continuity or persistence of character, therefore, does not imply that we always expect similar actions in the future.

14. It is worth noting, however, that such punishment might still serve to deter *others* from acting in these ways.

15. In a variety of contexts, Hume makes reference to characters in history and literature whom we morally evaluate without any practical interest in changing or influencing their conduct or behaviour (T, 470, 584). He does, of course, discuss at some length how distance in time and space can affect our moral sentiments through a variation of sympathy (e.g. T, 580–87; EM, 222–23, 225–31, 275).

16. Cf. EM, 269: "That sudden flash struck . . .".

17. Helm presents telling criticism of Hume along these lines. He argues that it is "not possible precisely to identify an action as 'in character' or not". There are, in other words, no necessary and sufficient conditions on the basis of which we can judge whether an agent should be excused for an evil action on the ground that it was not "in character". Helm doubts, therefore, that there is any serviceable distinction to be drawn of the kind that is presupposed by Hume's position. Whenever we excuse or mitigate an action, Helm argues, it is on the basis of some quite distinct and independent consideration from that of being "out of character" (e.g. compulsion, accident; "Hume on Exculpation", 268–69). I think that Helm's scepticism about the possibility of distinguishing in- and out-of-character action is excessive, as are his doubts about the direct relevance of this issue to questions of responsibility. As I suggest, however, Helm's criticism does show that Hume's position on this matter is unacceptably crude.

18. For a more general discussion of this problem, see Flanagan, *Varieties of Moral Personality*, pt. 4. Flanagan points out that contemporary virtue theory is unclear regarding the nature and ontology of character or "traits" (see esp. pp. 22, 281, 292, 331–32). The point that I am concerned to make is that this shortcoming is manifest in Hume's philosophy, and it leads to a series of related problems in his account of responsibility.

19. Davie, as I have noted, suggests that Hume provides no "adequate theoretical foundation" for his position concerning the relationship between responsibility and character. I have argued that Davie is wrong about *this*. Davie, however, believes that there is truth in Hume's position, and he makes an effort to provide some independent support for it. He contrasts the moral evaluation of persons with the moral evaluation of actions, and he argues that the former "are more essential to moral life than assessments of actions are". When we praise or blame actions, "it is usually the case that our interest lies not merely with the action itself, but in the character of the person who acts". Moreover, "even in cases where our interest lies in the action alone, we do assume that it is the action of a person [a coherent and enduring self]" (Davie, "Hume on Morality, Action and Character", 347). These observations may well indicate that Hume's claim touches on interesting and important matters concerning moral evaluation. They also make plain, however, that these problems are considerably more complex than Hume's discussion suggests.

20. Such excuses, we may say, are intrinsic to the interpretation of the agent's character at the time the action was performed, rather than extrinsic considerations that make reference to the agent's character and attitude after the performance.

21. Cf. T, 349. In this context, Hume speaks of "repentance *and* a change of life" producing an alteration in our sentiments toward a person. Clearly this accords more with the formulation at EU, 99, rather than that of T, 412.

22. There has not been a great deal of work done on repentance viewed as an excusing consideration. Generally, repentance is discussed in relation to "forgiveness". The difficulty here is whether genuine repentance *demands* forgiveness. On this, see Hampton and Murphy, *Forgiveness and Mercy*, 29–30, 41–42, and 154.

23. The parallels between moral evaluation and other forms of personal evaluation support this point. An individual who was at one time a great athlete may no longer be capable of such athletic activity or achievements, but we nevertheless have reason to continue to regard the person with admiration and esteem for her past achievements and qualities. Similarly, someone who loses her beautiful appearance might continue to arouse admiration, because people remember the beauty which the person once possessed. These sorts of considerations suggest, contrary to Hume's remarks, that we might continue to approve or disapprove of an individual for character traits that were once, but are no longer, possessed—and that this is, indeed, as I have indicated, quite consistent with the view that we can evaluate people only for qualities of mind that are durable and constant.

24. The claim that continuity of responsibility presupposes or requires continuity and persistence of character is, I have argued, not demanded by Hume's general principles, nor is it entirely plausible considered on its own merits. It is worth noting, however, that the claim is more intelligible if we (mistakenly) *confuse* continuity of character with continuity of self or personal identity. Clearly, if the person who is or was accountable for some action or character trait is someone *other than myself*, then *I* cannot be accountable for the action or trait in question. In this way, if a change in character involved or constituted a change in personal identity, then we could make some sense of Hume's further claim regarding the supposed significance of changes of character for ascriptions of responsibility. Certainly some contemporary philosophers have sought to develop arguments along these general lines (e.g. Parfit, *Reasons and Persons*, pt. 3, and his "Later Selves and Moral Principles"). As things stand, however, this particular strategy is not available to Hume. He makes it very clear that the *same person* can alter or change character (T, 261, 349, 412). If there is some foundation for this claim, then it must lie elsewhere. (It is worth noting that Parfit's views about personal identity are greatly influenced by Hume's discussion of this issue in Book I of the *Treatise*. Nevertheless, the significant point is that Parfit draws conclusions that Hume explicitly resists.)

25. Contrast, for example, Smith's very different account of how particular actions give rise to our sense of merit and demerit (TMS, II, i, 5). From Smith's perspective, Hume's claim that it is only actions that are indicative of (persisting) durable qualities of mind that arouse moral sentiment is simply at odds with the relevant psychological facts about human feeling in these circumstances. Insofar as we are concerned with descriptive psychology—as Hume and Smith are—Smith seems very largely right about this matter.

26. Clearly, the second claim cannot be accounted for in terms of the sort of forward-looking, utilitarian position which Foot attributes to Hume. As I have indicated, this is to misrepresent Hume's wider position on moral responsibility.

8

Will, Intention, Feeling:
The Indications of Character

By the intention we judge of the actions, and according as that is good or bad, they become causes of love or hatred.

Hume, *A Treatise of Human Nature*

But you'll please to observe that 'tis with Nations as with particular Man, where one Trifle frequently serves more to discover the Character, than a whole Train of considerable Actions.

Hume, letter to Michael Ramsay

The way that we *interpret* action shapes our judgments about a person's character and thereby affects our moral sentiments. On Hume's account, an accurate interpretation of action requires that we carefully identify the motives and intentions that caused it. In this chapter, I examine these aspects of Hume's account of action and the way that they relate to his theory of responsibility. More specifically, I explain the role of will and intention in this sphere and show that according to Hume a person can be held responsible for aspects of character that are manifested involuntarily. These are, clearly, matters of considerable importance for an understanding of the relationship between responsibility and freedom.

I

"Actions are, indeed", Hume says, "*better* indications of a character than words, or even wishes and sentiments" (T, 575; my emphasis). Action, then, although not the only evidence that we have concerning the nature of a person's character, is nevertheless the principal sign of character that we have available to us. Indeed, on Hume's account, to have knowledge of a person's character presupposes that we know how he will *act* in some relevant circumstances (T, 401–5; EU, 83–86).[1] Moral evaluation of character, therefore, is based primarily on action. What is it about action that is relevant to generating moral sentiment?

Several of the elements of Hume's answer are now clear. In the first place, we are concerned with action or conduct as it tends to produce pleasure or pain. This, however, is too wide as it stands. Not all pleasurable or painful conduct or behaviour— fortunate or unfortunate as it may be—reveals, or is indicative of, the mind of the agent. When a person's behaviour is due to physical violence or force, for example, we may regret the consequences, but we do not regard the person as accountable. Action of this nature is, obviously, wholly involuntary. More importantly, in these circumstances we cannot infer anything about the mind of the person insofar as the source of such behaviour lies elsewhere. Behaviour of this kind, therefore, cannot be indicative of a vicious motive or character. Similarly, action done in ignorance or accidently, although it, too, may have terrible consequences, does not reveal the sort of vicious nature or character which it would had the action been preformed *intentionally* (T, 412; EU, 98–99). In general, then, our moral evaluation of people depends on how we interpret their action or behaviour. It depends, in particular, on our understanding of the *causes* of their conduct.

If an action of any sort can be attributed to an agent then, according to Hume, it must be produced voluntarily by the agent. Voluntary action is produced through the "will" or "volition" of the agent. That is to say, on this account, voluntariness depends on the activity or causal influence of the agent's will.[2] Hume's specific remarks on this matter are limited, very largely, to the opening paragraph of the *Treatise* discussion of "liberty and necessity" (T, 399; cf. T, 413–18, 437–39). "By the will", he says, "I mean nothing but the internal impression we feel and are conscious of, when we knowingly give rise to any new motion of our body, or new perception of our mind". Although the will is not to be "comprehended among the passions", it is nevertheless like the passions insofar as it is an internal impression that has no representative qualities. It is, accordingly, "impossible to define, and needless to describe any further".

What is significant about the will, as Hume understands it, is that it is the causal intermediary between our desires and motives, on the one hand, and our actions, on the other. Not all desires or motives affect the will and lead to action. The will, therefore, is of vital importance in distinguishing those desires that are *effective in action* and those that are not. Also of importance is Hume's suggestion that our thoughts and feelings (i.e. our perceptions) are *in some measure* under the influence of the will. Our "actions" are not limited to the external public world, because we may control our own states of mind in some degree as well (EU, 67–69). In this way, the will, on this account, is the causal object through which our desires and motives take effect in bodily or mental action. As our will varies so, too, must our actions. Two individuals with similar desires and motives may nevertheless have wills that are structured very differently, and this, clearly, reflects fundamental differences in their moral character.[3] The pleasurable and painful influence which they have on themselves and others will vary accordingly.

Conduct or behaviour that is not produced by means of, or through, the will of the agent is not voluntary and is not, strictly speaking, *action* at all. Some involuntary behaviour may be indicative of certain qualities of mind in a person, but it cannot inform us about the nature of her will. By contrast, the voluntary conduct of an agent does indicate something about the structure of the agent's will (and the nature of her motives and intentions). Nevertheless, not all voluntary conduct that produces harmful consequences will be blameworthy. The reason for this is that the consequences may have been unintended even though the action was voluntary (i.e. produced by the will of the agent). Intention, therefore, is crucial to the interpretation of action considered as a basis for moral evaluation.

Hume explains in some detail how intention relates to ascriptions of responsibility through the mechanism of the indirect passions. The double association between impressions and ideas involved in generating moral sentiments forms the framework for his analysis. We judge actions, Hume says, by the intention "and according as that is good or bad, they become *causes of love or hatred*" (T, 348; my emphasis). Intention, he says, involves "a particular fore-thought and design" (T, 349; cf. T, 475: "For however it may . . ."). In other words, we must have some conception of what we are doing, and we perform the action *because* it secures ends or results of some (favoured) kind. Intention is crucial to the moral evaluation of action, because, as Hume notes, the mind of the agent varies with the motive or intention which produces the action (T, 348–50, 477).[4]

How do (beliefs about) intentions generate love or hatred? Two things are required: a relation between the person and some enduring quality of mind or character; and a resemblance between the independently painful or pleasant effects of the quality of mind and the painful or pleasant nature of the moral sentiment itself. The first is required to produce the relation of *ideas* involved in the mechanism of the indirect passions, and the second is required to produce the accompanying association of *impressions* involved in the mechanism of the indirect passions. Hume argues that intention has a role to play in both spheres.

In respect of the relation of ideas, Hume makes two related points that we have already discussed. First, it is "not enough, that the action arise from the person", because, in itself, such "action" may not reach "the sensible and thinking part" of the person (T, 349).[5] In other words, an action, considered merely as an "external performance", may lack some relevant mental cause. That is why a motive or intention is required.[6] Second, the relation between the cause and the object of the passion must be durable and constant. An action "is produc'd and annihilated in a moment", but "an intention shews certain qualities, which remaining after the action is perform'd, connect it with the person, and facilitate the transition of ideas from one to the other" (T, 349). In short, an intention serves to "connect" our idea of some pleasant or painful quality of mind with our idea of the agent or the person who is the object of the moral sentiment. If this connexion were to be severed in our thought, the person would cease to be an object of our moral sentiment.

Similar considerations explain the role of intention in producing the required association of impressions. An intention, Hume says, "besides its strengthening the relation of ideas, is often necessary to produce a relation of impressions, and give rise to pleasure and uneasiness" (T, 349). Hume explains this by noting that "the principal part of an injury is the contempt and hatred, which it shews in the person, that injures us; and without that, *the mere harm gives us a less sensible uneasiness*" (T, 349; my emphasis). In other words, it is not the injury or benefit as such which we find particularly painful or pleasant, but rather the good or ill will which is manifest through the agent's actions. If this good or ill will is lacking, then our very *feeling* of harm or benefit is reduced or weakened, and this in turn weakens the required association of impressions. Clearly, then, intention has a two-fold role in the production of moral sentiment. By its removal, we "cause a remarkable diminution in the passions of love and hatred" (T, 350).

Having made these observations—observations which suggest that it is motives and intentions, rather than consequences of our conduct, which determine the quality of our moral sentiments—Hume proceeds to qualify his position. The "removal of design", he points out, does not entirely "remove the passion of love or hatred" (T, 350; cf. 479: "Actions are at first . . ."). Even involuntary and accidental injuries may arouse hatred and anger. Although in these circumstances the relation of ideas is altogether feeble (i.e. the relation between the agent and his qualities of mind and character), there can nevertheless be a stronger natural connexion between the painful injury or hurt and the sentiments of hatred and anger. The influence of such sentiments is, however, somewhat limited. That is, according to Hume, a little reflection quickly reveals that "the character of the person is no wise interested", and the effect of such reflections is to weaken the sentiments that have been generated. We find, therefore, that any hatred or anger aroused by injuries that are "casual and involuntary" do not lead to "lasting enmity" and that the emotions involved "cannot be of long continuance" (T, 350).[7]

It is evident, I think, that this passage (i.e. T, 348–50) raises issues of fundamental importance for Hume's theory of responsibility. Most important, Hume is concerned to argue that our moral sentiments, steadied by reflection and careful attention to all the relevant features of action, are not (in any lasting manner) swayed by the good or bad consequences of action considered independently of the motive and intentions which produced them. All sorts of good or bad consequences may follow in the train of involuntary or accidental conduct. What affects our moral sentiment, Hume maintains, is the quality of mind lying behind the action—all else, he argues, is irrelevant.[8]

According to Hume, it is through action that we principally or primarily express or manifest qualities of mind and character. Action is produced by the causal influence of our desires and will. The interpretation and evaluation of action, therefore, must take note of the intention or design with which the action was undertaken. Failing this, we are liable to misrepresent the agent's character and, hence, entertain inappropriate and unjust sentiments toward that person. The specific consequences or effects of an agent's conduct are relevant to the moral evaluation of action only insofar as they indicate the motive and intention that the agent was acting on.[9]

II

Hume's views concerning the role of will and intention in relation to the interpretation human conduct and behaviour are directly relevant to his account of excusing considerations. When evaluating an agent on the basis of her conduct and action, it is essential that we properly identify the nature and structure of her will and intentions. As indicated, if a person's behaviour is produced entirely by external causes (or is wholly uncaused), then it does not reflect on the mind of that person, and it will not arouse (any lasting) moral sentiment. A person can, therefore, be excused for conduct on this basis. What is relevant in such cases, according to Hume, is not simply that such behaviour is involuntary, but rather that it does not reflect on the person's qualities of character. (I explain below that on Hume's account involuntariness as such does not excuse.)

Consider, again, the two excusing considerations that were left unexamined in the previous chapter: that people are not blamed for "such evil actions as they perform ignorantly and casually, whatever may be their consequences"; and that people are blamed less for "evil actions" that are done in haste and without premeditation (T, 412; EU, 98–99). In the first case, it is argued that the action is produced by principles of mind that are not blameworthy at all. In the second case, the principles of mind that produce the action are less blameworthy when compared to some other relevant set of character traits. In both cases, it is suggested that a person's character is significantly different from what her conduct seems to indicate on the basis of initial appearances.

Take the first excusing consideration. Hume argues that the reason people are not blamed for "evil actions" (i.e. actions with bad consequences) that are performed in ignorance or casually is that "the causes [principles] of these actions are only *momentary*, and terminate in them alone" (T, 412; EU, 98; my emphasis). Hume evidently understands a "casual" action to be an *accidental* action (cf. T, 350). In both the case of accidents and action done in ignorance, what is relevant is that the action lacks any vicious intention and hence reveals no blameworthy principles of mind. If the agent intends to cause injury or harm, then, clearly, very different principles of mind are at work.

In this context, Hume emphasizes the claim that the causes of actions of these kinds are "only momentary" and terminate with the action (cf. T, 349–50, 412; EU, 98–99). This is, however, mistaken and misleading. What is relevant is that when the action is properly interpreted—in terms of the motives and intentions that produced it—we have no basis for inferring some *vicious* principles of mind of the sort that could be inferred if the action had been intended to cause harm or injury. The general point is, then, that conduct of this nature cannot be understood as a "sign" of a *vicious* character unless it is misrepresented. To blame an agent in these circumstances would be to entertain negative sentiments toward a person who does not have the required unpleasant qualities of mind.[10]

In the case of action done in ignorance, it is generally assumed that the agent acted voluntarily (i.e. according to her own will) but lacked any vicious intention. In the case of accidental injury, the harm caused is not intended and is often not even the result of voluntary conduct (i.e. the agent's will may not have produced the behaviour that caused the injury or harm). The analysis of Hume's second category of excusing consideration is more complicated than this. Hume claims that people are *less* blamed for evil actions that they perform in haste and without premeditation "because a hasty temper, tho' a constant cause [or principle] in the mind, operates only by intervals, and infects not the whole character" (T, 412; EU, 98–99). Hume's account of the rationale of this kind of excusing consideration is, again, less than convincing.

Hume's explanation is given in terms of the claim that the underlying principle of mind (i.e. a "hasty temper") operates "only by intervals" and does not "infect the whole character". There are several points to make in criticism of this. First, any trait of character may operate "only at intervals"—in fact this is typically the case. Whether or not there is an *occasion* for character to produce action depends very largely on external circumstances. This is not unique to a "hasty temper" (see, e.g., T, 584; EM, 228n). Second, there is no basis for claiming that a "hasty temper" does not "infect the whole character" if indeed, as Hume claims, such a character trait is "a constant cause or principle in the mind". Third, and most important, it is misleading to account for excuses in these circumstances in terms of the character trait of a "hasty temper". An agent may perform a particular action in a hasty and unpremeditated manner and yet not have a "hasty temper". These are separate issues which Hume confuses.[11]

The principal significance of the premeditated/unpremeditated distinction for moral evaluation of an agent does not lie with the question of whether or not the agent possesses a "hasty temper" (Although it is true that hasty action may be a sign of a hasty temper, and this is something that is blameworthy in itself.) Rather, the principal significance of premeditation is that it indicates the way in which the "criminal passion" that produced the crime structures the agent's will and animates her conduct. The circumstances in which an agent will act on a "criminal passion" will vary depending on what role premeditation plays in the agent's conduct. In the case of premeditation, the crime cannot be dismissed as a product of immediate provocation or temptation. On the contrary, prior thought and deliberation is a sign that the criminal passion engages the will of the agent on an ongoing basis. A person who acts in haste and without premeditation, therefore, does not have the same kind of disposition as a person who performs similar crimes in a premeditated manner. In general, individuals who differ in these respects differ in the way that their (vicious) passions produce criminal conduct. Lack of premeditation, therefore, is a *mitigating* consideration, because it indicates that there is a relevant difference in the agent's moral character.[12]

III

According to Hume's philosophy, virtuous dispositions manifest themselves not only through our (voluntary, intentional) actions but also through our feelings and desires (i.e. our emotional reactions and attitudes). That is to say, a virtuous and vicious character can be distinguished by reference to its "wishes and sentiments", as well as by the nature of the person's will (T, 575). Feelings, desires, and sentiments manifest themselves in a whole range of ways—not just through willing and acting. Bodily signs of mental features or episodes of this nature appear in the manner and style of our "countenance and conversation" (T, 317), our deportment, our "carriage" (EU, 88) and "gesture" (EU, 85), and, in general terms, simply by our mere look and expression. To a limited extent, of course, we are able to control the expression or public manifestation of such sentiments and desires, and, similarly, we are able to feign or pretend that we have sentiments and desires that we do not have.[13] In large measure, however, we find that sentiments and desires arise in us spontaneously, without our exercising any immediate control or direction over them. We generally exhibit or manifest these psychological states and attitudes involuntarily. Nevertheless, considered as aspects or qualities of mind, our emotional states and attitudes, no less than our actions, may serve as a basis for moral evaluation—both for ourselves and for others.

There is a strong and deep tradition in moral philosophy which maintains that a person cannot be held accountable for what is not under voluntary control or the influence of the will.[14] It follows, on this view, that we cannot be held accountable for emotions, feelings, and desires insofar as they come on us or arise involuntarily.[15]

Clearly, this thesis is rejected by Hume's naturalistic theory. People of a certain constitution and temper are just as prone or disposed to certain kinds of feeling and emotion, Hume maintains, as they are to certain kinds of action. These dispositions of feeling and emotion, moreover, may or may not be agreeable or useful to the person himself and to those who live with him and share his company. In other words, experience teaches us that the emotional life of an individual is itself pleasant or painful, agreeable or disagreeable, and that we react to people accordingly. For Hume, this is a plain matter of fact and experience. The scope of our moral sentiments, therefore, extends well beyond the sphere of voluntary action.[16]

This particular aspect of Hume's naturalistic theory of responsibility is perhaps most apparent in his discussion "Qualities Immediately Agreeable to Ourselves", in Section 7 of the second *Enquiry*. In this context, Hume contrasts the virtue "cheerfulness"—a "playful", "jovial", and "affable" disposition—with the vice of being gloomy and morose (EM, 250–51; cf. EM, 279, where Hume speaks of play, frolic, and gaiety at "proper intervals"). However correct the conduct of a person may be we find that we cannot enjoy his company if he presents us with "a melancholy, dejected, sullen, anxious temper" (EM, 251). In a similar vein, Hume points out that the same person may possess mixed qualities in respect of his conduct and his emotional disposition.

> A gloomy and melancholy disposition is certainly, *to our sentiments*, a vice or imperfection; but as it may be accompanied with great sense of honour and great integrity, it may be found in very worthy characters; though it is sufficient alone to imbitter life, and render the person affected with it completely miserable. On the other hand, a selfish villain may possess, a spring and alacrity of temper, a certain *gaiety of heart*, which is indeed a good quality, but which is rewarded much beyond its merit, and when attended with good fortune, will compensate for the uneasiness and remorse arising from all the other vices. (ESY, 179 [Sceptic])

Hume directs these observations particularly against the "monkish" morality of Christian divines. These gloomy, morose individuals—with their concern to preach a morality of "celibacy, fasting, mortification, self-denial, humility, silence, solitude"— are hardly fit or acceptable social company (EM, 270, 279). The "dismal dress" which these individuals wear, we observe, serves to "stupify the understanding and harden the heart, obscure the fancy and sour the temper" (EM, 270). These characteristics can be contrasted with the affable and easy manner of a cheerful person.

The good humour of the cheerful person, Hume observes, "is lov'd and esteem'd, because it is *immediately agreeable* to the person himself" (T, 611). That is to say, the contrast between these personality types (i.e. the cheerful and the morose) manifests itself, first and foremost, in their different states of felicity or happiness. The cheerful person, we see, unlike the gloomy individual, is happy in himself and with himself.[17] The happiness which a person enjoys by means of his cheerful disposition very quickly affects all those around him. A "cheerful good-humour'd companion", says Hume, "diffuses a joy over the whole company, from a sympathy with his gaiety". "These qualities", he continues, "being agreeable, they naturally beget love and esteem, and *answer to all the characters of virtue*" (T, 611; my emphasis). In other words, according to Hume, a person is accountable for his emotional disposition because, through our common human capacity for sympathy, we affect others and thereby engage their moral sentiments. Hume repeatedly emphasizes the point that our private or personal emotional states influence and affect all those who must deal with us or think about us. He uses the analogy of a "flame" or the "sun" in describing a "merry" or "jolly" individual—such a person warms and brightens all who come into contact with him (EM, 250; cf. EM, 178; ESY, 151 [Stoic]). In summary, a person's emotional dispositions are, in the first instance, a source of happiness or unhappiness to himself. No person is completely insensitive to the happiness of others, because sympathy has some influence on us all. These qualities of mind, accordingly, affect us all. It is on this natural basis, concerning the workings of the human mind, that we find ourselves accountable to other people for emotional states and attitudes over which we may have little or no control.[18]

Hume's claims on the subject of responsibility for our emotional states and dispositions raise a number of difficulties. For the present purposes, however, I would like to note briefly certain difficulties that arise in respect of Hume's account of *how* we (morally) evaluate people's feelings and desires. Hume takes the passions to be pleasant or painful. A person of a gloomy disposition shuns those activities and objects that might provide pleasure and, instead, is preoccupied with thoughts and reflections that generate painful and unpleasant emotions. Thus, for example, the "monkish divine" concerns himself with the evil and suffering which he observes in the world and with his own inevitable decline and death. Such an outlook, evidently, secures little happiness for the individual concerned.[19] Clearly, then, a turn of mind that *seeks out and indulges* miserable and unpleasant thoughts and reflections is objectionable. Nevertheless, as Hume's analysis makes plain, there are many circumstances in which sad, painful, unhappy emotions are both the *natural and the appropriate response* to certain situations and experiences.[20] There is, in other words, a fundamental and important difference between an individual who is in a gloomy and dejected state of mind because of, say, some tragic death or illness that has overtaken a relative or friend, and a person who is prone to thinking pointlessly and gratuitously about the evil and suffering in the world.

Given Hume's basic principles, it is not obvious that we can draw necessary distinctions in this area. Hume's analysis suggests that we approve or disapprove of certain passions or states of mind primarily with a view to their (pleasant or unpleasant) *effects*. We may find, however, that the person who has good reason for being dejected is no less unhappy than the person who is inappropriately gloomy and morose. Moreover, an unhappy individual—whether there is good reason for his emotional condition or not—is in a state of mind that is unpleasant not only for himself but also (through the influence of sympathy) for all those who deal with him or think about him.[21] Hume's account, therefore, implies that an unhappy individual, whether there is due cause for his condition of mind or not, will naturally arouse sentiments of blame. It follows from Hume's principles, in other words, that we would be prone to blame people for unhappy states of mind that are perfectly understandable and appropriate in the circumstances and, likewise, to praise people for being cheerful and content, even when these emotions and attitudes are clearly inappropriate and out of place. In general, it is a mistake to suggest that we should (morally) assess or judge a person's emotions and feelings primarily with a view to their effects on the happiness of the person and those who deal with him. Whether a passion is "appropriate" or not depends on whether or not it is well-grounded and suitable to its object. Putting this point in terms of Hume's mechanical analysis, we may say that it is the *cause* and not the effects of the passion that determines whether or not it is reasonable and appropriate.[22]

Hume's analysis seems to confuse or obscure the following two issues: the circumstances under which certain feelings and emotions are appropriate or in order; and the circumstances under which we have reason to inhibit these emotions or curb or limit our *expression* of them? It is the beliefs and evaluations that give rise to, or are constitutive of, our feelings and emotions that determine to what extent these aspects of our mental life are appropriate and (morally) acceptable. By contrast, forward-looking, utilitarian considerations are of some direct and immediate relevance in assessing the (further and distinct) aspects of our emotional lives concerning the entertainment and expression of these emotions. These two distinct spheres of our emotional and affective life can move in quite different directions. That is to say, we can have utilitarian reasons for not entertaining, or for disguising, perfectly reasonable and appropriate feelings and emotions. Similarly, we can have utilitarian reasons for feigning or affecting emotions and sentiments that are nevertheless wholly inappropriate and unreasonable. The general conclusion, therefore, is that Hume tends to misrepresent and oversimplify the basis on which we judge and hold people accountable for their emotional life. In particular, it is incorrect to suggest that our emotional dispositions are to be praised or blamed, approved or disapproved of, simply on the basis of whether or not they are conducive to the happiness of ourselves and those who share our company. The problem is more complicated than this.[23]

One way of approaching Hume's claim that we are responsible for feelings and desires, as well as intentional actions, is to ask what it is that they *share* in virtue of which we hold a person responsible. That is, what is it about our feelings and desires that makes them of *moral* concern? Hume's answer is that both manifest pleasurable or painful qualities of mind. I think that there is an alternative answer to this question which is considerably more plausible. Our feelings and desires, no less than our intentional action, reveal or indicate how, and to what extent, we *value ourselves and others*.[24] An involuntary expression of emotion, no less than an intentional action, can manifest contempt, malice, or an uncaring attitude. Moral sentiment is best understood, in general terms, as *reactive* value—valuing people for the way in which they do or do not manifest value for other people or themselves. Clearly this leaves a great deal unsaid. It does, however, suggest in general terms *why* we react to someone's involuntary feelings and desires no less than to their intentional actions—both can equally manifest the value which the person or agent places on the interests and concerns of other people as well as himself. This general analysis takes us in a very different direction from concern with pleasurable or painful qualities of mind.[25] It nevertheless accords with Hume's views insofar as it does not limit moral concern to what we do or do not do voluntarily.

IV

The above account of Hume's system shows that intention and voluntariness are important aspects of mind which affect the way in which our moral sentiments are produced and the form that they take. These aspects of mind are not, however, essential to producing moral sentiment. On the contrary, as I have argued, Hume holds that feelings and desires, even though they might never engage the will or direct our intentions, are distinct and vital indications or signs of a person's character and qualities of mind, and, as such, they are quite capable of arousing moral sentiments toward the person. What, then, is the relationship between Hume's conception of moral freedom (i.e. liberty of spontaneity) and his account of the "signs" of moral character?

I have already explained why liberty of spontaneity is essential to the moral evaluation of *action*. Any action that is either caused by factors external to the agent (i.e. physical force or violence) or is entirely uncaused (i.e. due to "indifference") reveals nothing about the mind of the agent and therefore will not arouse our moral sentiments. More specifically, the action must reveal the will and (some relevant) intention of the agent. In the absence of these causes, there is no "action" for us to attribute to the person. Accordingly, without liberty of spontaneity—the ability to act according to the determination of our own will, unimpeded by external obstacles—it is not possible to make any inference about the willings and intentions of the agent. Clearly, then, liberty of spontaneity is essential for the moral evaluation of action considered as a sign of character.

Desires and feelings are not always expressed or manifested through the will and intentions of the agent. For this reason liberty of spontaneity is not necessarily required for the moral evaluation of a person in *this respect*. It is, accordingly, Hume's considered opinion that moral evaluation is not concerned *exclusively* with the structure of an agent's will and the intentions that guide her actions. The sphere of responsibility, therefore, extends *beyond* the sphere of action and liberty of spontaneity.[26] That is to say, on Hume's account, there are other channels, independent of will and intention, through which an agent can reveal her moral character and qualities of mind.[27]

The basic points that I am concerned to establish in respect of Hume's conception of moral freedom and his account of the signs of moral character can be summarized as follows:

1. For any item of behaviour or conduct to be relevant to the moral evaluation of a person, it must reflect some (pleasant or painful) quality of mind or character.

2. The most notable "signs" of mind and character are actions, which are produced by the will of the agent and are directed by some relevant intention (i.e. forethought and design).

3. In the absence of liberty of spontaneity, no "action" or piece of conduct can be read or interpreted as indicative of the agent's will and intentions.

4. Some items of behaviour or bodily movements, that are neither produced by a person's will nor guided by any intention, can nevertheless express or reveal a person's desires and feelings. As such, they constitute reliable and pertinent information concerning the person's moral character.

5. Liberty of spontaneity, therefore, although essential to the interpretation and evaluation of action, is not, on Hume's account, essential to all forms of moral evaluation. Some "signs" of moral character bypass liberty of spontaneity and do not require it.

6. Clearly, Hume rejects the view that involuntariness as such constitutes an excuse, since some involuntary behaviour is indeed an indication of a person's char-

acter. Accordingly, insofar as an agent may be excused for involuntary conduct, it is only on the ground that it is not indicative of the mind of the agent (i.e. it has external causes).[28]

The discussion above leaves open a fundamental question: To what extent do people have voluntary control over their moral character? Closely related to this issue is the problem of our (supposed) accountability for our natural abilities (T, 606–14; EM, 312–23). In the following chapter I take up these issues.

Notes

1. Cf. esp. T, 403: "The knowledge of these characters is founded on the observation of an uniformity in the actions, that flow from them . . .".

2. Hume's remarks about the nature and influence of the will are far from satisfactory. See Penelhum, *Hume*, 111–17 (esp. p. 113: "What follows . . ." and p. 116: "From these scattered comments . . ."); Stalley, "The Will in Hume's *Treatise*". Stalley notes that, on Hume's account, there is a sharp distinction to be drawn between our desires and the will and that Hume has, thus, a "two-stage theory of action" (p. 44 and p. 47). He says, "Implicit in Hume's treatment of the will and the passions is a two-stage account of the causes of action. We first experience various passions which provide the impulse or motivation to act. There follows a volition which is in turn followed by a bodily movement. . . . The will is thus necessarily differentiated from the passions because it occupies a different place in the causal process. Passions cause and are motives to the will; the will in turn causes movements of the body but is not a motive to anything" (p. 44).

3. In speaking of the "structure" of an agent's will, I am not referring to any sort of "faculty". Rather, I am speaking only of the *causal* structure or pattern of an agent's (particular) willings considered in relation to her motives and actions.

4. Hume's views about the nature of intention—and how it relates to volition and action—are not developed in any detail. For our purposes, I take Humean intentions to involve a belief-desire complex that engages the agent's will (i.e. I take a broadly Davidsonian view of Hume's position; see note 6). Note in particular that Hume is committed to the view that intentions involve "a particular fore-thought and design", and thus they must have some propositional content. On this account, then, Hume's understanding of intention is more complex than his account of the passions and the will (which are, he says, simple impressions and incapable of further analysis [T, 399]).

5. In the context of Book II, Hume presents human persons as "essentially incarnate" or embodied beings (cf., e.g., T, 298, 303). On this, see Baier, *A Progress of Sentiments*, 131–43.

6. In Davidson's terms, we can interpret Hume as saying that from the moral point of view we are not concerned with an action considered under any *description*. We are, rather, concerned with the action primarily in terms of the desires and beliefs which *caused* it (i.e. the motive which produced it). It is these desires and beliefs which "rationalize" the action and render it intentional under some description. Depending on the relevant description, our moral evaluation can (and must) vary. To consider an action merely as an "external performance", as Hume describes it, is to ignore the relevant intentional description and, indeed, to fail to ask even if there is one. See esp. Davidson, "Actions, Reasons, and Causes".

7. Hume's account of the way in which our feelings of hate and anger may be aroused by injury alone, without due consideration of the agent's intention, is not altogether convincing within the framework of the mechanism that he provides us with. In particular, Hume suggests that "the relation of impressions will operate upon a *very small* relation of ideas" (my emphasis) but that "the defect" of the relation of ideas ensures that this emotion "cannot

be of long continuance" (T, 350). The question is, however, how can such an emotion arise *at all* when the relevant and required relation is *entirely lacking*?

8. It is interesting to contrast Hume's position on this issue with Smith's very different account. Smith agrees with Hume that most people, on reflection, would accept the "equitable maxim" of justice that "all praise or blame, all approbation or disapprobation, of any kind, which can justly be bestowed upon any action, must ultimately belong" to the beneficence or hurtfulness of the design or intention (TMS, 93). Nevertheless, the fact is, Smith claims, that our moral sentiments do not operate according to such a principle. Actual consequences immediately affect our sense of merit and demerit, and thus influence to what extent we deem a person liable to reward or punishment. Smith acknowledges that this leaves all moral agents subject to the mercy of fate and fortune. He maintains, however, that there is a hidden or indirect value in this "irregularity" of human sentiment insofar as it restricts the disposition of resentment and retribution to actions (i.e. we are not vulnerable to resentment and retribution for mere thoughts and feelings), and it also forces us to take consequences seriously. (I discuss Smith's views on these matters in more detail in "Smith on Moral Sentiment and Moral Luck".)

9. As I have already indicated, much of what Hume is driving at in this context can be presented in the contemporary idiom of Davidson's theory of action. In more general terms, Hume claims that moral evaluation is concerned with the mind of the agent. It is crucial, therefore, that our moral sentiments are conditioned by some relevant and accurate beliefs about the mental state or motive which produced the action. In order to properly assess the mind of the agent, and the way that it is disposed to act, we must be careful to identify the agent's actual reasons for acting in the circumstances. In Davidson's terms, therefore, it is crucial that the action be intentional under some relevant description and that it be correctly "rationalized".

10. Hume's position needs some further qualification. An individual might be careless or negligent in disposition. Actions done accidently or out of ignorance might reveal a painful quality of mind of *this sort*—and this is, independently, a blameworthy character trait for a person to possess.

11. The more general point is made by Bayles: "there is no necessary connection between a person performing a particular action of a certain type and his having a certain mental quality or character trait" ("Hume on Blame and Excuse", 28).

12. Hume's specific remarks about the nature of intention and the nature of premeditation make it difficult to draw necessary distinctions in this sphere with any precision. When an agent acts viciously but without premeditation, it is not the case that the action was either involuntary or lacked any relevant criminal intention (i.e. such agents know what they are doing and why). According to Hume, however, all intentional action is "deriv'd from a particular fore-thought and design" (T, 349)—this being what it is for an act to be intentional. Evidently, then, there is a difference between an action that is simply guided by forethought and design and one that is produced after thought and deliberation. Failing this, we could not distinguish between premeditated and unpremeditated intentional action. Hume's remarks on this subject are too slight to make the distinction as clear as it needs to be.

13. "It is harder to disguise feelings we have than to put on those we have not" (La Rochfoucauld, *Maxims*, no. 559).

14. This view, of course, constitutes a key foundation stone for Kantian moral philosophy. See also Nagel, "Moral Luck", 174: "Prior to reflection it is intuitively plausible that people cannot be morally assessed for what is not their fault, or for what is due to factors beyond their control".

15. Interesting recent discussions of this matter can be found in, e.g., Lyons, *Emotion*, chp. 13; Adams, "Involuntary Sin"; and Schlossberger, "Why We Are Responsible for Our

Emotions". Schlossberger presents a fairly lengthy discussion of Hume's views on this matter and incorrectly, in my view, interprets Hume as denying that we are responsible for our emotions and desires.

16. See the following passage at EM, 321–22: "In general, we may observe, that the distinction of voluntary or involuntary was little regarded by the ancients in their moral reasonings".

17. An important sub-theme of this discussion is, of course, Hume's defence of "well-regulated" pride against the "monkish" *vice* of humility (T, 594–602; EM, 253, 264–66). Whereas the proud person, on Hume's account, finds pleasure when he thinks of himself (which we all naturally do), the humble individual is literally a source of pain to himself. (I discuss these issues at further length in chp. 11 in this volume.)

18. Hume, of course, need not deny the (obvious) fact that we have some indirect control over our emotional lives. In the first place, we can, as I have noted, hide or feign emotion in order to make ourselves more acceptable and pleasant company for others. Beyond this, however, we can also, to some extent, control emotional states as they arise within us. Hume allows, for example, that the will has some "command" of the mind as well as of the body (EU, 68). By controlling and directing our thoughts, we may exercise some (indirect) influence over our feelings and desires. There are, nevertheless, strict limits to such policies or goals. In this spirit, Hume says, rather too strongly, that it is "certain we can naturally no more change our own sentiments, than the motions of the heavens" (T, 517). See also ESY, 140 [Epicurean]: "When by my will alone . . .".

19. See Hume's description of Pascal's Christian character in "A Dialogue" (EM, 342–43) and the way that he contrasts it with the philosopher Diogenes. Hume's distaste for the character of Pascal could hardly be stronger. He observes Pascal's "contempt and hatred of himself", his "indifference towards his nearest relations", and his "extreme contempt of this life, in comparison of the future"—this being "the chief foundation of his conduct". The fact that Pascal's character is a model of virtue to some is to be explained by the perversion of human sentiment created by "the most ridiculous superstition that directed Pascal's faith and practice". Related to this matter, see also Hume's comments in "The Sceptic", in which he takes up the issue of excessive concern with evil and suffering in the world (ESY, 174).

20. Cf. EM, 251n: "There is no man, who, on particular occasions, is not affected with all the disagreeable passions, fear, anger, dejection, grief, melancholy, anxiety, &c. But these, so far as they are natural, and universal, make no difference between one man and another, and can never be the object of blame. It is only when the disposition gives a *propensity* to any of these disagreeable passions, that they disfigure the character, and by giving uneasiness, convey the sentiment of disapprobation to the spectator". As already noted (chp. 5), Hume emphasizes the point that it is impossible for philosophy to make us indifferent to the pains and sufferings of human life. More specifically, he rejects Stoic-Spinozist principles as both unlivable in practice and as destructive of virtue. (See also, e.g., T, 605: "We are not . . ."; ESY, 150–53 [Stoic]; ESY, 172 and 179n [Sceptic]; ESY, 539 [Moral Prejudices]; EU, 102: "What though . . ."; EM, 272: "While the human heart . . ."; EM, 281: "Now if life . . ."; EM, 301: "In the same manner . . .".)

21. Hume does allow, of course, that we may receive some indirect pleasure from the pain and unhappiness of others by way of *comparison* with our own situation. He notes, in particular, that the pain of another "consider'd in itself, is painful to us, but augments the idea of our own happiness, and gives us pleasure" (T, 376). In this way, comparison can produce a kind of reversal of sympathy.

22. This general line of criticism is pursued in some detail by Adam Smith. See, e.g., TMS, 18: "Philosophers of late years . . ." and TMS, 20: "The utility of those qualities . . .". Smith takes the view that the tendency of Hume's system is to assess motives and sentiments

by their (forward-looking) utility rather than in terms of their "suitableness or unsuitableness . . . to the cause or object which excites [them]". It is this sort of concern which leads Smith to draw a fundamental distinction between two kinds of moral sentiment. (1) Propriety and impropriety are concerned with the "suitableness" of motives and sentiments considered in relation to their causes or the objects that excite them. (2) Merit and demerit, by contrast, take into consideration "the beneficial or hurtful nature of the effects which the affection aims at, or tends to produce" (TMS, 18; cf. 67).

23. In a letter to Smith (July 1759), Hume wryly observes that if Smith were correct in claiming "that all kinds of Sympathy are necessarily Agreeable", then it would follow that "an Hospital would be a more entertaining place than a Ball" (LET, I/313). This criticism has force. Nevertheless, it might be said, in reply to Hume, that on his account we are naturally disposed to *disapprove* of the miserable and unfortunate individuals who populate hospitals— because their painful and unhappy condition affects all those who have contact with them.

24. Clearly, as with intentional action, not all feelings and desires are concerned with the ways that we value ourselves and others. We are, in other words, concerned with only a limited range of feelings and desires. Obviously, there are many feelings and desires that we may find unreasonable and inappropriate but not in themselves morally blameworthy.

25. As I argue in chp. 9, this analysis also suggests, contrary to Hume's position, that natural abilities, however painful or pleasurable they may be, are not a suitable basis for the *moral* evaluation of a person.

26. In the following chapter, I take up the general issue of what Hume has to say about the possibility of our desires and willings operating on themselves (i.e. "second-order" desires and willings)—especially as it relates to the question of shaping our own character. Suffice it to say, however, that Hume's remarks on the subject of freedom seem to suggest that he takes the classical line of Hobbes that it is only our (bodily) actions that can strictly be called "free" or "unfree" and that it is improper to speak of the will itself as being free or unfree. This position is not so easy or straightforward for Hume, because he very specifically allows that there are actions of mind as well as body.

27. The involuntary and spontaneous physical and bodily expression of a person's desires and feelings must still, on Hume's account, be regularly or constantly conjoined in such a way that the observer can *infer* what these feelings and desires are. Clearly, liberty of *indifference* would make all such inferences impossible. In other words, *necessity* is still required in this sphere, even though liberty of spontaneity is not.

28. This point is noted by Bayles, in "Hume on Blame and Excuse", 23. In general, involuntary behaviour cannot be indicative of the agent's will and intentions; thus, strictly speaking, it cannot be an *action* of the agent. However, as I have explained, it does not follow from this that such behaviour is never indicative of the agent's mind.

9

The Involuntary Nature
of Moral Character

> The fabric and constitution of our mind no more depends on our choice, than
> that of our body.
>
> Hume, "The Sceptic"

Hume claims that we are responsible for those qualities of mind or character that
affect ourselves and others in pleasurable or painful ways. Insofar as our action and
deportment *express* our character, so to that extent we are accountable for it. The
question arises, therefore, to what extent are our traits of character—our virtues and
vices—shaped and conditioned by our own choices and willings? In other words, is
our moral character *voluntarily acquired*? In this chapter, I explore and critically
evaluate Hume's view on this matter.

I

Hume, as I have pointed out, believes that we are responsible *for character* in the
sense that it is (beliefs about) character that generate moral sentiment. He does not
take the view, however, that responsibility, so interpreted, presupposes that we made
or shaped our own character. Our character is not, Hume maintains, acquired through
our own choices and decisions. The most substantial discussion of this matter appears
at *Treatise* III, iii, 4, in the context of his account of natural abilities and the way that
they generate moral sentiments (cf. EM, 312–23). Also relevant to this issue are those
passages in which Hume emphasizes the influence of various external conditions—
beyond the reach of the will—which condition and determine moral character.

In the passages entitled "Of liberty and necessity", Hume argues that not only do
we observe how certain characters will act in specific circumstances but we also
observe how circumstances condition character. Among the factors that Hume claims
determine character are bodily condition, age, sex, occupation and social station,
climate, religion, government, and education (T, 401–3; EU, 83–88; see esp. EU,
85–86: "Are the manners . . ."). Hume observes that although "mankind are so much
the same, in all times and places, that history informs us of nothing new or strange in
this particular" (EU, 83), we must, nevertheless, be alive to the varied and complex
influences at work in this sphere. These various causal influences, it is claimed,

account "for the diversity of characters, prejudices, and opinions" (EU, 85). The same sorts of *apparent* "irregularities" which we discover in the physical world are present in the moral world. In both cases, however, the unexpected or uncertain course of events is to be accounted for by the influence or operation of "contrary and concealed causes" (T, 403–4; EU, 86–88; cf. T, 132). The "internal principles and motives", Hume argues, "may operate in a uniform manner, notwithstanding these seeming irregularities; in the same manner as the winds, rain, clouds, and other variations of the weather are supposed to be governed by steady principles; though not easily discoverable by human sagacity and enquiry" (EU, 88; cf. T, 313: "Nothing is more fluctuating . . ."). In summary, according to Hume, there are "characters peculiar to different nations and particular persons, as well as common to mankind" (T, 403). Any accurate moral philosophy, it is argued, must acknowledge and take note of the forces that "mould the human mind from its infancy" and which account for "the gradual change in our sentiments and inclinations" through time (EU, 86).[1]

In the *Treatise*, as I have indicated, Hume takes up the issue of the involuntariness of moral character primarily in the context of discussing accountability for natural virtues. Hume rejects the suggestion that the distinction between natural abilities, such as intelligence and imagination, and moral virtues, such as courage and honesty, is to be accounted for in terms of the voluntary/involuntary distinction. The moral virtues and the natural abilities are both acquired involuntarily for the most part. It is, Hume says, "almost impossible for the mind to change its character in any considerable article, or cure itself of a passionate or splenetic temper, when they are natural to it" (T, 608). Our will has little influence over such matters. In this sense, natural abilities and moral virtues are on "the same footing with bodily endowments" (T, 606). The fundamental distinctions in this sphere, as with beauty and deformity, depend on "the natural distinctions of pain and pleasure" (T, 608). Just as bodily qualities produce a different *sort* of love or hate (i.e. in respect of *feeling*), so too, Hume allows, natural abilities can generate their own peculiar form of moral sentiment. However, each of the virtues, he claims, "even benevolence, justice, gratitude, integrity, excites a different sentiment or feeling in the spectator" (T, 607; cf. T, 617: "On the other hand . . .").

What is significant for Hume is the extent to which moral virtues (narrowly conceived) and natural abilities are "on the same footing". He makes two points in this regard: moral virtues and natural abilities are "equally mental qualities"; and both of them "equally produce pleasure" and thus have "an equal tendency to produce the love and esteem of mankind" (T, 606–7).[2] Natural abilities are valued primarily because of "the *importance* and *weight*, which they bestow on the person possess'd of them" (T, 613). Such an individual acquires great influence, and his conduct and character affect the lives of many. All of this, naturally, engages our sympathy and hence arouses our moral sentiment. In short, in common life, people "naturally praise or blame whatever pleases or displeases them" and thus regard prudence and penetration as no less virtues than benevolence and justice (T, 609).[3]

Hume claims that the voluntary/involuntary distinction does explain "why moralists have invented" the distinction between natural abilities and moral virtues. Natural abilities, unlike moral qualities, "are almost invariable by any art or industry" (T, 609). By contrast, moral qualities, "or at least, the actions, that proceed from them, may be chang'd by the motives of rewards and punishments, praise and blame" (T, 609).[4] We cannot, in other words, make people intelligent, imaginative, and so on, by the application of rewards and punishments, but we can (in some measure) regulate their voluntary actions and thus direct their conduct with respect to moral virtues, such as justice.[5] In this way, according to Hume, the significance of the voluntary/involuntary distinction is largely limited to our concern with the *regulation of conduct* in society. To confine morality to these frontiers is, Hume maintains, to distort its very nature and foundation. It is, therefore, a mistake to view the voluntary/involuntary distinction as constituting the boundary of moral concern (cf. T, 609 and EM, 322).

There are two issues that need to be carefully separated in Hume's discussion:

1. the claim that we are (morally) accountable for our natural abilities;
2. the claim that our accountability for our moral qualities does not depend on their being voluntarily acquired.[6]

The first claim can be rejected without rejecting the second. That is to say, we can agree with Hume that we are accountable for our qualities of character whether they are acquired voluntarily or not but reject the further suggestion that we are accountable for our natural abilities. Clearly, however, if we take this view, our reason for *denying* that we are accountable for our natural abilities cannot be that they are *involuntarily* acquired. There must be, therefore, some further and distinct reason for holding, contrary to Hume, that we are not (morally) accountable for our natural abilities.

I have already indicated, in general terms, why I think that the former claim should be rejected. Moral sentiment should be understood in terms of reactive value—we value people according to how they express or manifest value for themselves and others. In this sense, bodily beauty, although it certainly gives pleasure to others, as well as the person possessed of it, nevertheless does not manifest or express any particular mode or way of valuing the interests and concerns of others.[7] So from the point of view of *morals*, there is nothing to *react* to. Unlike our actions and feelings, bodily characteristics will not, on this account, give rise to *moral* sentiments, however pleasurable or painful such characteristics may be. When we consider things in this light, it is clear, I think, that natural abilities are more on "the same footing" with bodily endowments than they are with moral qualities. That is to say, when a person acts or conducts himself in a way that shows that he is stupid, dull, or unimaginative, we might well find it unpleasant to contemplate, but we do not take the person, thereby, to manifest or express some lack of due care or concern for himself and others. (Indeed, things might be quite otherwise in respect of this person's attitude to his fellows. The stupid and dull person might be acutely aware of these shortcomings, and his affect on others, and might well be mortified by them.) In these circumstances, we might regret the lack of some desirable natural ability—in the way that we regret physical ugliness—but we do not *blame* the person for these failings. Hume's conception of moral sentiment, and its essentially utilitarian foundation in human nature, again misleads him.

Clearly, then, something has gone *wrong* with Hume's discussion in respect of accountability for natural abilities. There is, nevertheless, a great deal of insight in his discussion. More specifically, Hume is right in pointing out that *we value people for more than their moral qualities*. Although we do not *blame* the ugly or unintelligent person, we clearly value people favourably or unfavourably in these respects. Where people are found to be ugly or stupid, we, typically, shun their company—or seek and enjoy their company for *other* reasons. Whether we should, as Hume does, describe behaviour and attitudes of this nature in terms of the language of "love" and "hate" does not matter much. The deep point which Hume is driving at—a very important point—is that moral sentiments are just *one mode* of valuing people. Moreover, so considered, this way of evaluating people is naturally related to other ways of valuing and caring about human beings on the basis of their qualities and characteristics. These other modes of valuing people for the qualities that they possess do not depend on their being acquired voluntarily. We might conceal these facts about human life in our (moral) theory, but it is very obvious in our experience and practice. What Hume has got right on this issue is every bit as important as what he has got wrong.

I have argued that it is misleading and incorrect for Hume to claim that we are morally accountable for our natural abilities. This, however, does not show that it is misleading or incorrect to claim that we are accountable for a moral character that is involuntarily acquired. In order to establish this point, some separate line of criticism must be established. Libertarian and incompatibilist critics would, I believe, argue in the following general terms. Hume maintains that we are responsible for actions, feelings, and desires insofar as they *express* our moral character. He also holds that individuals have little or no influence over those factors and forces that shape our character. This, however, is more than paradoxical—it is inconsistent. How can an agent be held responsible for the character his actions and feelings express or manifest if the person has no control or influence over the *nature* of that character? In these circumstances, the virtuous person can no more claim merit than the vicious need accept any demerit. You cannot, it is argued, claim or accept merit and demerit over matters that do not relate to your own will and choices in life. Virtue and vice really would be, in these circumstances, matters of mere fortune that are as entirely removed from the scope of moral concern as bodily beauty or ugliness. If people are responsible for the characters their actions and feelings express, then they must have acquired that character voluntarily. The two issues stand or fall together.[8]

Hume's own line of response to this sort of criticism is, I think, clear enough. The criticism presupposes that the distinction between virtue and vice depends on, or arises out of, the *way* in which our character is formed. That is, on this view the *source* of our moral character is relevant to an evaluation of its nature and quality. The libertarian or incompatibilist holds, in other words, that unless the source of our character is our *self*, then it has no *moral* quality whatsoever. From a Humean perspective, such an account wholly misrepresents the issue. We can perfectly well distinguish virtue and vice without making any reference to the *way that character is acquired*. Indeed, we may well disagree about *this matter* and still agree about which actions and feelings represent or manifest a virtuous or vicious character. Thus, for example, we must all acknowledge and recognize the virtuous nature of Cato's character *whatever we believe* about its origins or source. Clearly, then, our moral sentiments are in order, and reflect relevant distinctions regarding moral character, irrespective of the way that these traits and qualities are themselves conditioned. A character that tends to produce pleasure will also produce love and, similarly, a character that tends to produce pain will arouse hate. These are natural principles of the human mind.

We can reject Hume's utilitarian framework of analysis in this matter and still accept the general point that is being made: Our moral sentiments are reactions or responses to the moral qualities and character traits that people manifest and thus need not be withdrawn simply because people do not choose or voluntarily acquire these moral characteristics. In other words, from a Humean perspective, responsibility for those actions and feelings that express character does not depend on or require that the person involved *made* his own character what it is. It is because incompatibilists *confuse* these matters, we may take Hume to argue, that they find themselves constrained to accept claims that are at odds with ordinary moral feeling and experience.[9]

II

Hume's remarks in the *Treatise*, and elsewhere, suggest very strongly that human beings are essentially *passive* with respect to their own moral character. Clearly many would argue that it is a mistake to present moral character as fixed and unalterable in this way. More specifically, Hume's theory, it may be said, is wholly insensitive to the ways in which character is, or can be, shaped and conditioned *by the person who possesses it*. Hume, however, does not entirely overlook this problem. It is taken up, quite directly, in his essay "The Sceptic". In this context, he argues that "the happiest disposition of the mind is the virtuous" (ESY, 168).[10] Why, then, Hume asks, do we not all simply alter "the fabric and constitution of our mind" so that we may be virtuous, and hence happy? Hume observes, in reply, that anyone who considers "the course of human actions, will find, that mankind are almost entirely guided by constitution and temper" (ESY, 169). No amount of philosophical reflection and training—including Hume's own theorizing on this subject—can change this basic fact about human beings. The influence of philosophy in promoting virtue, Hume claims, is very limited—"even upon the wise and thoughtful, nature has a prodigious influence" (ESY, 169). In any case, the influence and authority of "the empire of philosophy" is not only weak and limited in itself, it extends to only a few individuals. The "ignorant and thoughtless" constitute the majority of mankind, and they are "actuated by their natural propensities" without any benefit from philosophy. In this way, although philosophy might enlighten a few minds about the value of virtue, its role in the broad stream of human life is of little consequence. Most people know nothing of philosophy, and those who do are largely unaffected by it.[11]

These claims provide further evidence that Hume takes the view that we can do little or nothing to alter or change our basic moral character. Hume does, however, qualify these remarks in some important ways. Philosophy—more generally, self-criticism and reflection—does have some *indirect* influence on our lives (ESY, 170). "Serious attention to the sciences and liberal arts", says Hume, "softens and humanizes the temper, and cherishes those fine emotions, in which true virtue and honour consists", and it leads us to "feel more fully a moral distinction in characters and manners" (ESY, 170). By means of education, moral exemplars, and careful and conscious self-criticism, a person will find that, in time, there will be "an alteration for the better" in respect of his temper and character. Finally, Hume notes that habit "is another powerful means of reforming the mind, and implanting in.it good dispositions and inclinations" (ESY, 170–71). All these reflections substantially qualify the claim which Hume makes elsewhere to the effect that it is "almost impossible for the mind to change its character in any *considerable* article" (T, 608; my emphasis) and that "the fabric and constitution of our mind no more depends on our choice, than that of our body" (ESY, 168).[12] Hume does not deny, therefore, that we can to some limited extent alter or cultivate our moral character through self-criticism, self-discipline, and self-understanding. This, however, is entirely consistent with the basic point that he is concerned to establish: It is wholly misleading to suggest that our moral character is a product of our own choices and voluntary conduct and that we are accountable for our character only to the extent that we exercise control over it.

It is interesting to contrast Hume's views on this subject with two rather different approaches—one ancient, and one rather more modern. Aristotle, famously, maintains that our character is produced or determined by our own voluntary actions (*Nicomachean Ethics* [hereafter NE], 1114a3–1114b25). More specifically, the nature of our moral character depends, crucially, on those actions which *shape* our moral character in our formative years. These actions, it is claimed, are (categorically) open to us (NE, 1114a20), and, hence, no (responsible) person's moral character is determined or necessitated by any factors other than his own choices and decisions in life. In other words, the nature of our moral character, Aristotle claims, is "originally open" to us even though, with time and habit, it becomes increasingly fixed (i.e. unchangeable through our own efforts).[13] An agent, then, may find that he is *no longer* able to alter his character at will but is responsible for actions that *express* this character only insofar as there was a time when the actions which *formed* the character were "open" to him.[14]

It is clear that Hume rejects this position. Two points are especially important. First, as I have indicated, Hume can concede that there are some actions and choices that we make in life that contribute—in some *limited* measure—to making our character what it is.[15] Nevertheless, this granted, Hume would argue that the fact of the matter is that our moral character is determined and conditioned by a whole range and variety of factors, most of which have little to do with a person's choices and actions early on in life. Insofar as there is any truth in Aristotle's claim, therefore, it is exaggerated in a very misleading way. Second, and more important, even if we grant (contrary to what Hume thinks is true) that our moral character is determined and "fixed" very largely by choices and actions undertaken in our formative years, the fact of the matter is that these (formative) choices and actions have themselves antecedent, necessitating causes that lie outside or beyond the agent. It follows from this that it is a mistake to suggest that our character was "originally open" in the (categorical) sense implied on Aristotle's account.[16] In short, it is Hume's view that a person has little direct and immediate influence over the nature and quality of his moral character. What influence a person does have can itself be accounted for by causal factors that lie outside of him. Inevitably, however, whatever the (complex) causes at work in this sphere, a person's moral qualities will continue to arouse moral sentiments in other human beings.

Over the past two decades or so a number of writers have developed an alternative account of how it is that a moral agent can be said to have some control or influence over her moral character. In general terms, the thesis is that human beings have a capacity to reflect on their desires and willings (i.e. those desires that are effective in action), and they can form second-order desires about what (first-order) desires and willings they entertain or act on.[17] On the basis of critical reflection of this nature, it is possible for human beings to *restructure* their own will. That is to say, our second-order desires may lead to or produce a change in what we want to do. In this way, it is argued that to the extent that a person has the capacity to alter and amend the structure of her will by means of second-order desires, so that person is not passive in relation to her established moral character. To enjoy freedom of action is to be able to do what one wants to do. To enjoy freedom of will, however, is to have the will which one (reflectively) wants to have. Clearly, then, on this account, much more is required of moral agents than that they simply enjoy liberty of spontaneity—they must also have the capacity to form desires and preferences about their moral character, and they must be able to restructure their character on this basis. None of this, however, presupposes the libertarian metaphysics of unnecessitated events or "breaks" in the chain of causation.[18]

"Two-level" theories of this sort are, obviously, more in line with Hume's general position on this subject insofar as they do not suggest that indeterminism is required for moral responsibility. However, I think that Hume's position is plainly at odds with two-level theories in some important respects. Hume can (and does) readily accept that human beings are capable, on occasion, of "reforming" themselves and that they may self-consciously and successfully cultivate good dispositions and inclinations. Second-order desires, in other words, certainly have some influence on (some people's) moral development and character traits. Nevertheless, Hume suggests that the influence of critical reflection of this nature is rather limited—even for those (few) individuals who are disposed through philosophy to give proper care and attention to these matters. Moreover, the fact that a person is disposed to reflect on these matters, and does make an effort to alter or improve himself in this respect, can itself be accounted for by factors that have nothing to do with the mind of the agent.[19] Hence, from a Humean perspective, a strategy of this sort tends to *exaggerate* the role of second-order reflection in moral life and, indeed, misleadingly implies that the possession of this capacity somehow turns human beings into "self-made selves".[20] For Hume, the basic fact of the matter is that moral character is very largely determined and conditioned by factors that are quite independent of the agent, and any effort to change or alter our moral character in fundamental respects is difficult and rarely achieved. The crucial point remains, however, that when such a change is brought about by the person herself, it can still be attributed to factors that, eventually, lie beyond her.[21] There is, as it were, no escaping the grip of "fate" in this respect.[22]

III

Hume's view that moral character is (very largely) involuntarily acquired raises the more general problem of moral luck. This problem can be interpreted in terms of what Thomas Nagel has called "the condition of control".[23] People cannot be held responsible, according to this view, for factors that are beyond their control. When we discover that some feature of an action, or attribute of an agent, whether good or bad, is not under the person's control, then, it is claimed, we naturally feel that the appropriateness of moral assessment is to that degree undermined. Insofar as we view people as accountable for "external" factors that lie beyond their control, we render them "morally at the mercy of fate".[24] Nagel sums up the problem as follows:

> If the condition of control is consistently applied, it threatens to erode most of the moral assessments we find it natural to make. The things for which people are morally judged are determined in more ways than we at first realize by what is beyond their control. And when the seemingly natural requirement of fault or responsibility is applied in light of these facts, it leaves few pre-reflective moral judgements intact. *Ultimately, nothing or almost nothing about what a person does seems to be under his control.* ("Moral Luck", 176; my emphasis)

The particular form of moral luck which seems directly relevant to Hume's views concerning the involuntariness of character may be described as "constitutive luck". Constitutive luck concerns the sort of person that we are. It includes our desires and feelings, abilities and dispositions, as well as our deliberate actions. There are, however, two further forms of moral luck which are relevant to Hume's general theory of responsibility. First, "consequential luck" concerns how our actions actually turn out. The specific outcome of an action, it is said, is very often not under our own control, but these outcomes determine what we have *done* and therefore how we will be morally judged.[25] Secondly, there is "circumstantial luck", which concerns the sorts of (moral) problems and situations a person may face. Some people may be more severely "tested"—faced with greater moral hardship—than others. What we succeed in doing depends very largely on the circumstances and opportunities presented to us, but these conditions are very largely beyond our control.[26] Moral assessment of a person, therefore, may vary because of factors that have nothing to do with the person as such.

As regards "constitutive luck", it is plainly Hume's view that we are all subject to "moral luck" in *this* respect. That is to say, by and large, we have little or no control over the kind of person that we turn out to be. Nevertheless, Hume rejects the suggestion that this erodes our responsibility for what we are. "Moral beauty" no less than natural beauty may be largely beyond our own control, but we naturally arouse the sentiments of our fellow human beings on this basis (cf. EM, 291–93). Hume therefore rejects "the condition of control". Not only does this principle have no intuitive appeal, on Hume's account, it is, indeed, directly at odds with everyday human experience.[27]

Although Hume rejects the condition of control, in several very important ways, he holds that we are *not* held (morally) at "the mercy of contributions of fate". The two further forms of moral luck bring this point clearly to light. According to Hume's principles, neither "consequential" nor "circumstantial" luck should have any influence on our moral sentiments. As I explained in the previous chapter, Hume argues that moral sentiments are aroused by qualities of mind or character and are not affected (in any lasting way) by consequences of action as such. Similarly, Hume also maintains that variations in the circumstances that a person finds himself placed in do not alter our sentiments toward the person, because we are interested in the *tendencies* of qualities of character, whether or not the particular circumstances that a person is placed in result in specific actions of some kind. A virtuous character will not always produce good; nor will a vicious character always produce evil. Thus Hume observes, "Virtue in rags is still virtue; and the love, which it procures, attends a man into a dungeon or desart, where the virtue can no longer be exerted in action, and is lost to all the world" (T, 584). He continues, "Where a character is, in every respect, fitted to be beneficial to society, the imagination passes easily from the cause to the effect, without considering that there are still circumstances waiting to render the cause a complete one" (T, 585).[28]

Hume points out, however, that it takes some effort to ensure that our moral sentiments are not influenced by good or bad fortune. He says,

> 'Tis true, when the cause is compleat, and a good disposition is attended with good fortune, which renders it really beneficial to society, it gives a *stronger pleasure* to the spectator, and is attended with a more lively sympathy. We are more affected by it; and yet we do not say that it is more virtuous, or that we esteem it more. We know that an alteration of fortune may render the benevolent disposition entirely impotent; and therefore we separate as much as possible, the fortune from the disposition. (T, 585; my emphasis)[29]

In this way, Hume maintains that the *strength* of our sentiments is naturally affected by whether or not a character's pleasurable or painful tendencies are actually realized in practice, but our considered moral judgment "corrects" this natural bias due to sympathy.[30] It takes only, he claims, "an easy and necessary effort of thought" to separate "character from fortune" (EM, 228n). Moral evaluation of persons, therefore, does not leave them at the mercy of circumstantial luck.[31]

Hume's position on the problem of moral luck is, evidently, complex. It is a basic principle of Hume's system that it is qualities of mind and character that give rise to moral sentiment. These character traits are evaluated on the basis of their pleasurable or painful tendencies. Clearly, however, the particular circumstances that a person is placed in may or may not allow these traits of character to achieve or realize good or bad results through action. Similarly, specific actions that we undertake may or may not secure their ends and objectives. Nevertheless, in both these cases, Hume argues, it is perfectly possible for a moral spectator to make the relevant and required distinctions and to form, on this basis, moral sentiments with a view only to the tendency of the character in question. In other words, how a person has behaved and acted in particular circumstances, or what specific results her actions have had, is not in itself the appropriate basis for moral evaluation. The relevant issue is, rather, what the general influence of such a character is likely to be, considered more abstractly. For Hume, this is a *requirement* of the (impartial and disinterested) moral perspective, and it is not difficult to satisfy.

Hume does not make these demands on moral thinking and feeling because he accepts the condition of control. On the contrary, he makes them because he thinks that they are required for an accurate assessment of a person's moral qualities. We must, therefore, overlook extraneous factors that do not reflect on the mind of the agent. To be subject to moral luck in this regard, as Hume would interpret it (i.e. qua "fortune"), is to be (illegitimately) praised or blamed for things that do not reflect our character and qualities of mind. There is, however, no demand that whatever reflects our mind or character be under our control, much less that our mind and character must themselves be products of our own will. Because Hume rejects the condition of control, he can accept that we are all, more or less, subject to "constitutive luck" while insisting that "circumstantial" and "consequential" luck have no place in moral life.[32]

Notes

1. In the essay "National Characters", Hume distinguishes between the "physical" and the "moral" causes that condition character (ESY, 198). He states, "By *moral* causes, I mean all circumstances, which are fitted to work on the mind as motives or reasons, and which render a particular set of manners habitual to us. Of this kind are, the nature of government, the revolutions of public affairs, the plenty or penury in which people live, the situation of the nation with regard to its neighbours, and such like circumstances. By *physical* causes I mean those qualities of the air and climate, which are supposed to work insensibly on the temper, by altering the tone and habit of the body, and giving a particular complexion, which, though reflection and reason may sometimes overcome it, will yet prevail among the generality of mankind, and have an influence on their manners." The general drift of Hume's discussion is to emphasize the importance of moral, as opposed to physical, causes in shaping the character of nations.

2. Related to this point, Hume also suggests, plausibly, that many people would be every bit as mortified if they were thought to be stupid as they would be if they were thought to be dishonest (cf. T, 587–88, 607; EM, 240, 315–16). It is not clear, however, what this establishes except that we *care* about natural abilities as well as—or perhaps more than—moral virtues. Many people would prefer to be thought dishonest than physically ugly, but this hardly shows that moral and physical beauty stand on "the same footing".

3. Smith objects to these claims in the following terms: "it seems impossible that the approbation of virtue should be a sentiment of the same kind with that by which we approve of a convenient and well-contrived building; or that we should have no other reason for praising a man than that for which we commend a chest of drawers" (TMS, 188; cf. TMS, 327: "There is another system . . .").

4. Hume's qualification in this context (i.e. "at least the actions that proceed from them") seems to mean that rewards and punishments typically serve the function of influencing which desires and dispositions we act on, rather than changing our underlying desires and dispositions as such.

5. It is not obvious that the contrast between moral virtues and natural abilities can be explained with reference to the efficaciousness of rewards and punishments in the straightforward way implied by Hume's remarks. First, as Hume recognizes in other contexts, the efficaciousness of rewards and punishments on a given individual will depend very largely on that person's established character. A wholly vicious character may be impossible to influence or deter even by means of the most severe punishments. Second, rewards and punishments may, clearly, have some influence in *cultivating* and *developing* a person's natural abilities. The "regulation of conduct" by means of rewards and punishments, therefore, is not without application and relevance to the natural abilities. (I note in passing that it is a mistake to interpret Hume as claiming that it is *in principle* wrong to *punish* people for "that which they cannot control" [Bayles, "Hume on Blame and Excuse", 30, 32]. The principle that Hume

embraces is, rather, that we should not punish people when it is of no social utility *and* punishment for involuntary conduct or behaviour is not efficacious. The issue is whether Hume is correct about the latter supposition. See the discussion in the following chapter.)

6. We also need to distinguish the second claim from the claim that we may be held accountable for involuntary manifestations or features of moral character. It may be argued, for example, that we are accountable for involuntary feelings and desires if such feelings and desires arise from character traits that we have voluntarily acquired (this is the general position of Aristotle, which is discussed later in this chapter).

7. Even here, however, careful qualification is required. Consider, for example, how grooming, cleanliness, and so on, reflect consideration for the feelings and sensibilities of others.

8. Reid makes this general point with reference to the example of the character of Cato. "What was, by an ancient author, said of Cato, might indeed be said of him. *He was good because he could not be otherwise.* But this saying, if understood literally and strictly, is not the praise of Cato, but of his constitution, which was no more the work of Cato, than his existence" (*Active Powers*, 261). The same view has been stated more recently by Berlin: "Nevertheless, if I literally cannot make my character or behaviour other than it is by an act of choice (or a whole pattern of such acts) which is itself not fully determined by causal antecedents, then I do not see in what normal sense a rational person could hold me morally responsible either for my character or for my conduct" (*Four Essays*, xvii).

9. It is, in particular, at odds with ordinary moral feeling and practice to claim that responsibility *demands* that we can act *contrary* to our established character. Consider, for example, Campbell's well-known statement of Kantian-libertarianism. Campbell offers an account of the nature and conditions of responsibility that is *diametrically* opposed to Hume's position. Freedom and responsibility, he holds, depend on our capacity to act *contrary* to our established (or "given") character. The "self", as Campbell puts it, must be able to "transcend" its character in order to act "creatively" (Campbell, "Is 'Freewill' a Pseudo-Problem?" 132). Responsibility on this view presupposes that we can act according to the dictates of "duty" *in opposition* to desire as conditioned by our established character. Clearly, then, on this view, an agent who is capable of acting only in ways that express his character can *never* be morally responsible for his actions.

10. Hume describes the virtuous mind as follows: "[It is] that which leads to action and employment, renders us sensible to the social passions, steels the heart against the assaults of fortune, reduces the affections to a just moderation, makes our own thoughts an entertainment to us, and inclines us rather to the pleasures of society and conversation, than to those of the senses" (ESY, 168).

11. "Men may well be sensible of the value of virtue, and may desire to attain it; but it is not always certain, that they will be successful in their wishes." (ESY, 169).

12. Cf. Spinoza's strikingly similar remark: "That it is not within the competence of any man's nature that he should be of strong character, and that it is no more within our power to have a healthy body than to have a healthy mind, nobody can deny without flying in the face of both experience and reason" (letter to Henry Oldenburg, February 7, 1676; trans. S. Shirley).

13. Terence Irwin translates the relevant passage from Aristotle as follows: "Similarly, then, it was originally open to the person who is [now] unjust or intemperate not to acquire this character; hence he has it willingly, though once he has acquired it he can no longer get rid of it" (NE, 1114a20–22).

14. Hardie describes Aristotle's position as follows: "Aristotle suggests that a stand can be made on the distinction between actions which express a well or badly formed character and the actions which formed it well or badly" (*Aristotle's Ethical Theory*, 175).

15. Hume can, of course, allow that our character is in some measure acquired voluntarily if all that is implied by this is that *one* of the causal influences on our mature, established

moral character is the set of choices and actions that we have made earlier in life. The crucial point for Hume, however, is that *these* choices and actions also have antecedent, necessitating causes.

16. Hardie neatly summarizes these difficulties in Aristotle's position in the following way: "The idea that a man is a responsible agent cannot be defended by pushing back his responsibility to a time when his character was unformed. For the objector will reply that, if the earlier actions cannot be traced to character, they can be traced to the joint efficacy of natural innate tendencies and environmental influences. Again there is no clear or sharp division of actions into those which form and those which express character" (*Aristotle's Ethical Theory*, 175). For an attempt to defend Aristotle along rather different lines—i.e. as concerned with interruptions in *necessitation*, rather than causation—see Sorabji, *Necessity, Cause and Blame*, 229–33.

17. See, e.g., Frankfurt, "Freedom of the Will" and Dennett, *Elbow Room*, esp. chps. 2–5. (See the related discussion at chp. 6, sec. 2 in this volume.)

18. This alternative account of "free will" is thought by many of its proponents to avoid the (crude) oversimplifications of classical compatibilist accounts of freedom (i.e. liberty of spontaneity) without falling into the obscure metaphysics of libertarianism. "Two-level" theories of this nature are, in this way, generally presented as more sophisticated forms of compatibilism.

19. See, e.g., ESY, 171, where Hume grants that we can reform ourselves but that this cannot take place "unless a man be, before-hand, tolerably virtuous".

20. The expression "self-made selves" is taken from Dennett (*Elbow Room*, chp. 4). Hume does acknowledge, however, the very important role which human beings have in the education and upbringing of children (i.e. as parents, members of society, officeholders, etc.; see, e.g., T, 500–501). To this extent, therefore, it can be argued that *other* people have had more influence in making us what we are than we have had on ourselves. The irony is, then, that we may have greater opportunity to "make" *others* as we want them to be than we have to make *ourselves* what we want to be. Accordingly, insofar as moral character is shaped by human beings and human arrangements, I think that Hume would argue that it would be more accurate to describe us as either "selves made by others" or "makers of other selves".

21. The gist of Hume's outlook is well captured in the following passage from Nietzsche: "The individual is, in his future and his past, a piece of fate. . . . To say to him 'change yourself' means to demand that everything should change, even in the past" (*Twilight of the Idols*, "Morality as Anti-Nature", sec. 6).

22. I believe that these general observations show that "two-level" theories are not entirely successful in avoiding some of the well-known difficulties of traditional compatibilism. However, as I have indicated in chp. 6, theories of this nature do bring to light the significant weaknesses in Hume's own account of moral freedom and, more generally, his failure to provide any convincing and plausible account of the capacities required of moral agents. Two-level theories of freedom are at least a good place to *begin* when it comes to improving on Hume's position in this respect.

23. Nagel, "Moral Luck", 176.

24. Nagel's expression ("Moral Luck", 182).

25. Nagel provides a number of examples, including the difference between "successful murder" and attempted murder, and reckless or drunken driving that kills someone and similar driving that does not ("Moral Luck", 175, 177–78).

26. Nagel notes, for example, that "someone who was an officer in a concentration camp might have led a quiet life and harmless life if the Nazis had never come to power", or if the person had emigrated to Argentina before the Nazis did come to power ("Moral Luck", 175, 182).

27. Nagel concedes this point ("Moral Luck", 181–82: "Nevertheless, Kant's conclusion . . .") but maintains that our natural disposition to regard each other as responsible in these circumstances will, reflectively, strike us as irrational.

28. In the passage immediately preceding, Hume argues that there are "general rules" on the basis of which we can arrive at a common or shared perspective on a person's character (T, 581f). Such a perspective allows for some stability and agreement in our moral sentiments. In circumstances in which an object is "fitted to an agreeable end" but is placed in external conditions which make it impossible to realize these ends, "general rules" influence the imagination and enable us to infer the effect (i.e. some measure of utility) from the cause (i.e. the object suited to these ends).

29. Hume continues, "The case is the same, as when we correct the different sentiments of virtue, which proceed from its different distances from ourselves. The passions do not always follow our corrections; but these corrections serve sufficiently to regulate our abstract notions, and are alone regarded, when we pronounce in general concerning the degrees of vice and virtue." See also the lengthy footnote at EM, 228n, in which Hume makes similar points.

30. Hume's position on this issue is similar to what he has to say about unintended injuries arousing moral sentiments (T, 350). Here, too, we find that our moral sentiments are (naturally) influenced by factors that are not strictly relevant to the moral assessment of a person; but this, Hume claims, can be "corrected" with a little thought and reflection.

31. It is obvious that Smith takes a very different view about the influence of both consequential and circumstantial luck on our moral sentiments. According to Smith, our sense of merit and demerit is directly aroused by the *actual* consequences of *particular* actions. (See esp. TMS, 97–99.) In the absence of real achievement, "merit seems imperfect"; in the face of an unsuccessful attempt to do evil, "demerit is incomplete".

32. Hume's views on these matters place him in a position which is quite different from that of either Kant (the champion of the condition of control) or Smith (who maintains that we are inescapably subject to *all* three forms of moral luck discussed above). The fundamental tension in Hume's position—one that he never quite resolves—is reconciling how he thinks our moral sentiments *should* behave in this respect, with how he thinks they do as a matter of fact behave. It is one of Smith's more interesting insights to see these tensions in Hume's discussion and to argue, on this basis, that in moral life psychological nature may prove too strong for reflective (rational) principle. (On this see my "Smith on Moral Sentiment and Moral Luck".)

10

Retributive Feeling and the
Utility of Punishment

As to the good or ill desert of virtue or vice, 'tis an evident consequence of the
sentiments of pleasure or uneasiness. These sentiments produce love or hatred;
and love or hatred, by the original constitution of human passion, is attended
with benevolence or anger; that is, with a desire of making happy the person we
love, and miserable the person we hate.

Hume, *A Treatise of Human Nature*

Punishment, without any proper end or purpose, is inconsistent with *our* ideas
of goodness and justice.

Hume, "Of the Immortality of the Soul"

I have argued that we fundamentally misrepresent Hume's account of responsibility
if we interpret it as essentially "forward-looking" and utilitarian. However, some of
Hume's remarks appear to lend support to the view that his position on *punishment*
is essentially "forward-looking" and utilitarian—and thus suggest that, to this extent,
his views on responsibility are close to those of Hobbes and Schlick. In this chapter,
I articulate Hume's theory of punishment. I argue that Hume seeks to develop an
account of punishment on the foundations of the naturalistic theory of responsibility. Although this naturalistic aspect of Hume's theory of punishment has been largely
overlooked by commentators, I maintain that it is, nevertheless, precisely this aspect
of Hume's position that is especially interesting from a contemporary perspective.

I

It would seem reasonable to assume that *if* Hume does have a clear position on the
subject of punishment, then it is most likely to be found in his major works, the *Treatise* and the *Enquiries*. When we turn to these works, however, we find that what
Hume has to say on this subject is both fragmented and cursory.[1] His brief remarks
on this issue largely emphasize the social utility of punishment. Punishment, he claims,
is justified primarily on the ground that it motivates people to obey those rules of
justice which are essential to "the peace and security of human society" (T, 526).[2]
Clearly, then, punishment must be justified, at least in part, in terms of a "forward-
looking" rationale. Given this, it would seem safe to conclude that Hume unambigu-

137

ously rejects *pure* retributivism. That is, punishment cannot, on this account, be justified simply on the basis of guilt or wrongdoing, without any reference to consequentialist considerations.

This general interpretation of Hume's position on punishment certainly accords with the views of Hobbes and Schlick—two thinkers with whom Hume is closely associated in this context. More specifically, like Hume, Hobbes and Schlick are primarily concerned to emphasize the social utility of punishment. Both argue that punishment without any view to reform or deterrence is simply an act of "hostility" or "vengeance".[3] It is important to note, however, that Hobbes's theory of punishment is not *purely* utilitarian. According to Hobbes, punishment is, by definition, for a "transgression of the law" and thus (necessarily) has a retributive element. Although Schlick's remarks are less clear on this point, it would seem that he is willing to dispense with all retributive elements from punishment. To the extent that Hume's views are identified with those of Schlick, therefore, he would appear to be committed to a (purely) utilitarian theory of punishment.[4]

Although there is, evidently, a strong utilitarian element in Hume's account of punishment, it seems equally clear that his remarks on this subject are not unequivocally utilitarian. Moreover, it may be argued that there are several passages in the *Treatise* which lend support to an account of punishment that is essentially retributivist, rather than utilitarian. Hume suggests, for example, that in regard to *divine* laws, God may act not only in his "magisterial capacity", with a view to producing obedience, but also "as the avenger of crimes *merely on account of their odiousness and deformity*" (T, 410–11; my emphasis). In several other passages, Hume further suggests that we are naturally or psychologically disposed to retributive attitudes and practices. More specifically, he argues that our moral sentiments naturally give rise to "benevolence or anger; that is, with a desire of making happy the person we love, and miserable the person we hate" (T, 591).[5] In this way, we find that Hume's remarks in the *Treatise* and the *Enquiries* lend some support to *both* (backward-looking) retributivist and (forward-looking) utilitarian interpretations. Nor is it clear how these divergent elements of his account of punishment are supposed to merge together into one unified theory. These tensions in Hume's position have led some commentators to conclude that "it is not easy to say where Hume stood" on this issue.[6] A more severe critic might argue that Hume simply oscillates between utilitarian and retributivist views on punishment, and he has, therefore, *no* clear position for us to articulate. In order to resolve this problem, we must, I suggest, look elsewhere in the corpus of Hume's writings.

It is, perhaps, surprising to find that Hume's most coherent remarks on the subject of punishment appear in his posthumously published essay "Of the Immortality of the Soul". In the second section of this essay, Hume turns his attention to the "moral arguments" which are supposed to prove the immortality of the soul. These arguments, he notes, are "chiefly those derived from the justice of God, which is supposed to be further interested in the further punishment of the vicious and reward of the virtuous" (ESY, 592). In this context, Hume is especially concerned to argue that responsibility and punishment can be understood only within the fabric of human nature and human society. To this end, Hume launches a number of arguments against the orthodox theological position. For our purposes, the following three points are the most important.

First, Hume maintains that the distribution of rewards and punishments is determined on the basis of our (human) moral sentiments. He says,

> By what rule are punishments and rewards distributed? What is the divine standard of merit and demerit? Shall we suppose, that human sentiments have place in the deity? However bold that hypothesis, we have no conception of any other sentiments. . . . To suppose measures of approbation and blame, different from the human, confounds every thing. Whence do we learn, that there is such a thing as moral distinctions, but from our own sentiments? (ESY, 594–95)

In a letter to Francis Hutcheson (March 1740), Hume touches on the same point. He states, "since Morality, according to your Opinion as well as mine, is determin'd merely by Sentiment, it regards only human Nature & human Life. This has been often urg'd against you, & the Consequences are very momentous. . . . If Morality were determined by Reason, that is the same to all rational Beings: But nothing but Experience can assure us, that Sentiments are the same. What Experience have we with regard to superior Beings? How can we ascribe to them any Sentiments at all?" (LET, 1/40).[7]

In this way, Hume is arguing that the moral sentiments serve as the foundation on which we distribute rewards and punishments. Given that we have no knowledge of God's sentiments—or even if he has any sentiments—it is quite impossible for us to make any sense of the basis on which God is supposed to distribute rewards and punishments in a future state.

Second, Hume argues that the point or purpose of punishment is that it secures or produces benefits for human society. He says,

> Punishment, without any proper end or purpose, is inconsistent with *our* ideas of goodness and justice; and no end can be served by it after the whole scene [this world] is closed. . . . What man, who has not met with personal provocation (or what good-natur'd man who has) could inflict on crimes, from the sense of blame alone, even the common, legal, frivolous punishments? And does anything steel the breast of judges and juries against the sentiments of humanity but reflections on necessity and public interest? (ESY, 594–95)

In other words, Hume maintains that a future state in which the wicked are punished would serve no end or purpose and thus would lack any proper or appropriate justification.[8] The only proper end or purpose of punishment, he holds, is that it serves the interests of human society.

Third, Hume points out that punishment must not be disproportionate to the offence.

> Punishment, according to *our* conception, should bear some proportion to the offence. Why then eternal punishment for the temporary offences of so frail a creature as man? . . . The chief source of moral ideas is the reflection on the interests of human society. Ought these interests, so short, so frivolous, to be guarded by punishments, eternal and infinite? The damnation of one man is an infinitely greater evil in the universe, than the subversion of a thousand million of kingdoms. (ESY, 594–95)

Clearly, then, Hume is concerned to show that divine punishment, being "infinite and eternal", is bound to be grossly disproportionate even when inflicted on the worst of criminals.

It seems clear that Hume launches what is essentially a two-pronged attack on the theological position. First, given that we have no evidence of the nature or existence of God's sentiments, there is no accounting for the basis on which we can be responsible to him, and, therefore, there is no accounting for the basis on which he distributes rewards and punishments. Second, insofar as we suppose God to distribute eternal punishments to those he disapproves of, such divine punishment: (a) lacks any point or purpose, because it produces no benefits for human society; and, (b) given that it is infinite in duration, it will inevitably be excessive in the extreme. It would seem to follow, therefore, that according to Hume the theological doctrine of eternal rewards and punishments in a future life is from one point of view unintelligible, from another, morally repugnant.

Given this more elaborate statement of Hume's views on punishment, how should we characterize the general nature of his position? There are, I believe, two features of Hume's discussion which merit particular attention: his "mixed" or teleological retributivist account of punishment; and the "naturalistic" theory of responsibility which serves as the foundation of his teleological retributivism. I will begin by describing in more detail the nature of Hume's teleological retributivism.

Our analysis of Hume's remarks on punishment suggest that we must approach this issue by way of distinguishing several different questions, each of which requires, on Hume's account, a different answer.[9] More specifically, there are at least two significantly different questions which Hume appears to be addressing in this context. The first asks: What is the end or purpose of punishment? In other words, what is the general justifying aim of punishment considered as an institution or practice? The second asks: On what basis are punishments to be *distributed*? That is, who may be punished (i.e. who is *liable* to punishment), and how severely may we punish them (i.e. what *amount* of punishment are they liable to)? Hume, as has been noted, provides us with different answers to these different questions. According to his account, therefore, it is a mistake to assume that the justification of punishment involves an appeal to a single value or aim (e.g. deterrence, retribution, reform). In addressing ourselves to the issue of the general justifying aim, for example, we must appeal to considerations of social utility (i.e. deterrence and reform). Such (forward-looking) considerations, however, are not relevant or appropriate when we turn to the question of the distribution of punishment (i.e. liability and amount). Here we must take note of (backward-looking) retributivist considerations. Considerations of this nature, Hume suggests, must be interpreted in terms of our moral sentiments.

The moral sentiments, it is claimed, provide us with a framework within which it may be determined who *deserves* to be punished and who does not. That is, according to this account, there is an intimate connexion between the question of whether or not we deem someone liable to punishment and the question of whether or not that person arouses the appropriate negative moral sentiments in us. Someone who does not arouse such sentiments in us when we contemplate his actions or character cannot justly be punished *even if* the infliction of punishment would, all things considered, produce beneficial consequences. In other words, it is a necessary condition of being justly punished that you are also justly disapproved of or blamed. Further, the *degree* to which a person whom we disapprove of is liable to punishment will clearly be limited by the degree to which we disapprove of or blame him (i.e. the amount of punishment must not be out of proportion to the strength of our disapproval).[10] In this way, we find that it is our moral sentiments which account for the principles which govern and limit the distribution of punishment.

Hume maintains that punishment is justified only if it serves the public interest. It would seem to follow, therefore, that where punishment does not serve the public interest it cannot be justified *even if it is deserved*. That is to say, from the fact that someone arouses negative moral sentiments in us, it does not straightforwardly follow that we are justified in punishing him. It follows only that he is *liable* to the *appropriate degree* of punishment. On this account, then, the question of whether or not the person *deserves* to be punished should be kept distinct from the question of whether or not the infliction of punishment would produce some beneficial consequences.[11] It is, accordingly, especially important to note that on this view the general justifying aim of punishment cannot be accounted for simply in terms of our negative moral sentiments toward the individual concerned. Although our moral sentiments can serve as an adequate basis on which to account for the distribution of punishment, they do not, of themselves, provide us with any adequate account of the *purpose* or *point* of punishment. It would be a mistake, in other words, to attempt to justify the practice of punishment by referring solely to our (negative) moral sentiments without making any reference to the utility of such a practice. To this extent, Hume's theory is not committed to, and does not license, any crude form of retributivism. Should we find, for example, that the institution or practice of punishment lacks any satisfactory teleological rationale (i.e. it is of no social utility), then Hume can consistently maintain that such an institution or practice should be suspended or abandoned altogether.

Hume's position on this issue may be further clarified by way of distinguishing between two very different modes of retributivism. That is to say, it is crucial that we distinguish between "negative retributivism", the doctrine that we must not punish the innocent (nor excessively punish the guilty), and "positive retributivism", the doctrine that we have an obligation to punish the guilty. Our moral sentiments toward an individual do not, of themselves, generate an obligation to punish that individual. That is to say, as I have noted, it does not follow from the fact that an individual *deserves* to be punished that we are, necessarily, justified in punishing him (because such punishment may be of no social utility). Hume's theory, therefore, does not lend any support to "positive retributivism". It does, however, account for the "negative" retributive principle which is essential to the teleological retributivist position. That is, our moral sentiments, by way of determining the distribution of punishment, ensure that the innocent must not be punished, nor the guilty excessively punished. On the other side of the same coin, our moral sentiments also enable us to determine who we are *permitted* to punish (i.e. who is liable to punishment). In this way, the moral sentiments provide what may be described as the "negative" rationale of punishment. They indicate the *limits* within which the attitudes and practices associated with punishment must take place. Theories and systems of punishment which try to ignore the limits imposed by moral sentiments are, on this account, fundamentally flawed.

The framework which the moral sentiments impose on any system of punishment cannot be ignored, because this framework constitutes the very foundation on which any adequate or plausible theory of punishment must be erected.

It is widely held that Hume's theory of justice is a form of rule utilitarianism. It should be clear, however, that, as regards punishment, Hume's position is more complex than this. In particular, as I have emphasized, the principles governing the distribution of punishment reflect considerations of desert, interpreted in terms of moral sentiment, rather than those of utility. In this regard, the obvious point of comparison is John Rawls's well-known rule-utilitarian approach to punishment.[12] According to this account, no rule or practice permitting punishment of the innocent (i.e. "telishment") is likely to have any utilitarian justification. In this way, for the rule utilitarian, it is considerations of social utility which are the ground of our prohibition against punishing the innocent. We misrepresent Hume's analysis of the retributive element of punishment if we interpret him along these lines.

It is evident that Hume's naturalistic account of responsibility serves as the foundation of his theory of punishment. Hume suggests, in particular, that we must interpret the retributive features of punishment in terms of our moral sentiments. This important feature of Hume's discussion of punishment (i.e. his concern with the moral sentiments) is entirely absent from Hobbes's and Schlick's discussions. To this extent, therefore, it seems evident that Hume develops his theory of punishment along fundamentally different lines from those pursued by Hobbes and Schlick.[13] Moreover, whatever objections Hume's theory is vulnerable to, it is *not* vulnerable to the standard objection levelled against purely utilitarian theories, namely, that they license the punishment of the innocent or the excessive punishment of the guilty.[14]

II

Hume has not been alone in his efforts to construct a theory of punishment on the basis of naturalistic foundations. On the contrary, Adam Smith, his friend and fellow Scot, developed a theory of punishment along very similar lines. Indeed, on the face of it, Smith's position is very close to that of Hume's insofar as he, too, is concerned to *describe* the moral psychology on which our practices of reward and punishment rest.[15] In light of this, it may be suggested that Hume's theory of punishment is best understood as being simply an (underdeveloped) variant of the sort of (naturalistic) theory that Smith describes. Such an interpretation, however, would be mistaken. The differences between Hume's and Smith's theories are at least as instructive as their similarities.

According to Smith, we regard punishment as just and deserved in those circumstances in which an impartial spectator would sympathize with (i.e. share) the resentment felt by the injured party.[16] More precisely, an action deserves punishment when it "appears to be the proper and approved object of resentment" (TMS, 68). It is the sentiment of resentment "which most *immediately and directly* prompts us to punish". To punish, Smith maintains, is simply "to return evil for evil that has been done" (TMS, 68). In this way, we find that an offender is deemed "the proper object of punishment, when we thus entirely sympathize with, and thereby approve of, that sentiment which prompts us to punish" (TMS, 74). In other words, Smith claims that in "going along" with the sentiment of resentment from which the action of punishment "proceeds", we must necessarily *approve of the punishment* and regard the person against whom it is directed as its proper and suitable object.

Smith's retributivism is in no way half-hearted. An action surely deserves punishment, he says, "which every body who hears of it is angry with, and upon that account *rejoices* to see punished" (TMS, 70; my emphasis). Smith continues in this vein:

> When we see one man oppressed or injured by another, the sympathy which we feel with the distress of the sufferer seems to serve only to animate our fellow-feeling with his resentment against the offender. We are rejoiced to see him attack his adversary in his turn, and eager and ready to assist him whenever he exerts himself for defence, or even for vengeance within a certain degree. (TMS, 70–71)

These retributivist sentiments are given full vent by Smith when he turns to consider our reaction to murder and our sympathy with the victim.

> We feel that resentment which we imagine he ought to feel. . . . His blood, we think, *calls aloud for vengeance*. The very ashes of the dead seem to be disturbed at the thought that his injuries are to pass unrevenged. . . . And with regard, at least, to this most dreadful of all crimes, *Nature, antecedent to all reflections upon the utility of punishment, has in this manner stamped upon the human heart, in the strongest and most indelible characters,, an immediate and instinctive approbation of the sacred and necessary law of retaliation.* (TMS, 71; my emphasis)

In light of passages like this, it would be hard to overstate the strength of Smith's (positive) retributivism. The contrast with Hume, in this respect, is perfectly clear.

Although Smith, unlike Hume, rejects any role for forward-looking consequentialist considerations in *justifying* punishment, he, nevertheless, does not entirely overlook such considerations.[17] A number of philosophers, he notes, have suggested that it is consideration of the public good which is "the real source of the punishment of crimes".[18] Smith, as we have seen, rejects this suggestion. However, he does acknowledge that there is an *indirect* connexion between our retributive practices and the welfare of society. Indeed, Smith points out that there can be no doubt "that we frequently have occasion to confirm *our natural sense of the propriety and fitness of punishment*, by reflecting how necessary it is for preserving the order of society" (TMS, 88; cf. TMS, 77: "The very existence of society . . ."). Be this as it may, "the Author of nature", Smith suggests, "has not entrusted it" to man's reason to find out that a certain application of punishments is the proper means of attaining the welfare and preservation of society. In order to secure the preservation of society—an end which we all naturally desire—nature has not only "endowed mankind with an appetite for the end which she proposes, but *likewise with an appetite for the means by which alone this end can be brought about, for their own sakes, and independent of their tendency to produce it*" (TMS, 77; my emphasis). In other words, according to Smith, we naturally and instinctively approve of those punishments which secure an end which we also, independently, desire, namely, the welfare of society. On this basis, Smith argues that "revenge of the injured" will "regulate" our practice of punishment in such a way that it (indirectly) secures precisely those ends (i.e. deterrence, reform, etc.) which such philosophers as Hume have *mistakenly* suggested are the source of our "original interest" in the punishment of crimes (LJ, 105; TMS, 89).[19]

It seems clear that despite their obvious similarities there are, nevertheless, significant differences between Hume and Smith on the subject of punishment. There are three particularly important general points to be noted. First, both thinkers are concerned to develop a theory of punishment on the basis of a naturalistic account of the moral sentiments. More specifically, for both Hume and Smith, it is crucial that we interpret the retributive features of punishment in terms of our moral sentiments. In this respect, their approach to the problem of punishment is fundamentally different from that of Hobbes and Schlick. Second, Hume, following Hobbes, and unlike Smith, develops a "mixed" or teleological retributivist theory of punishment. Both Hobbes and Hume are agreed that any adequate theory of punishment must appeal to utilitarian considerations as the general justifying aim of punishment. Neither, accordingly, would accept Smith's form of positive retributivism. Third, Hume, along with both Hobbes and Smith, rejects any *purely* utilitarian approach to punishment. For all three thinkers, there is an ineliminable retributive element involved in punishment.

It seems clear, in light of these observations, that Hume's account of punishment differs in significant respects from both that of Hobbes and that of Smith. We may conclude that Hume has a theory of punishment which is not only distinctive but also far richer and more complex than has hitherto been recognized.[20]

III

In my opening remarks to this chapter, I suggested that the most interesting aspect of Hume's discussion, from a contemporary perspective, lies in his effort to develop a theory of punishment on naturalistic foundations (i.e. his effort to account for the role that moral sentiment plays in this sphere). The contemporary significance of this aspect of Hume's discussion can be better appreciated if we compare Hume's and Smith's views with reference to certain difficulties that Strawson encounters in this sphere. Behind the specific issues separating Hume and Smith lies the deeper and wider problem of how we are to understand the relationship between responsibility and punishment. Both Hume and Smith, as I have indicated, agree that punishment must be understood as resting on, or developing out of, the fabric of our moral sentiments. Beyond this, however, there is deep disagreement about how we should interpret the implications of a naturalistic theory of responsibility for the problem of punishment.

This is a problem which Strawson does not adequately address. Strawson's remarks regarding the implications of his views for the problem of punishment are both brief and obscure.[21] It is, more specifically, unclear whether his remarks should be interpreted as lending support to a form of positive retributivism, along the lines of Smith, or to a form of teleological retributivism, along the lines of Hume. If it is the former theory which Strawson is embracing, then it may be argued, for reasons which I will explore, that such an account is not satisfactory. More generally, it may be argued that until it is shown that a naturalistic account of responsibility can be rendered consistent with a plausible theory of punishment, then such an account remains suspect.[22] In this way, it seems clear that the issues which separate Hume and Smith reappear at the very heart of Strawson's discussion. Granted the contemporary importance of Strawson's views on this subject, we cannot, I suggest, afford to overlook Hume's and Smith's rival positions on this matter.[23]

My analysis of the contrast between Hume's and Smith's views will focus on two closely related issues: (1) the relationship between moral sentiments and the justification of punishment; and (2) the relationship between retributive practices and the will.

Hume, along with Smith, takes the view that it is impossible to develop a convincing or plausible "forward-looking" or consequentialist rationale for our moral sentiments. That is, they agree that our moral sentiments are essentially retrospective. Moreover, they agree that such sentiments arise naturally and spontaneously in reaction to the perceived moral qualities of another person.[24] However, Hume also maintains, contrary to Smith's view, that a wholly "backward-looking" or retributive account of *punishment* would be equally inadequate and implausible. The rationale of punishment, it is argued, raises separate issues from those which arise solely within the framework of our moral sentiments. That is to say, there exists what may be described as a "justificatory gap" between our moral sentiments and our practice of punishment. The only way to bridge this gap is by taking note of the relevance of forward-looking, consequentialist considerations.

Where, according to Hume, does this "justificatory gap" arise? Fundamental to Smith's position, as we have noted, is the claim that, in blaming an individual (i.e. regarding him as an appropriate object of resentment), we inevitably or necessarily approve of inflicting punishment on that individual. In other words, according to Smith, if our sentiments of blame or resentment are appropriate and suitable to their object, then so, too, are those actions of punishment which are motivated by these sentiments. Punishment, it appears, requires no further or independent justification than that which is already presupposed in viewing someone as a reasonable or appropriate object of blame or resentment. It is, therefore, a mistake to seek to provide some further or independent justification for inflicting punishment, beyond reference to the appropriate or suitable nature of those sentiments which motivate such actions. Resentment and retribution, on this account, come in one indivisible package. To regard resentment as justified and appropriate is, ipso facto, to regard punishment as justified and appropriate.

It is precisely at this stage that Hume rejects Smith's model. It simply does not follow from the fact that our sentiments of blame or resentment are justified that we are therefore justified in intentionally inflicting suffering or pain on the individual concerned.[25] The backward-looking, retributive considerations which serve to justify our moral sentiments cannot, of themselves, bridge this gap. At the very least, we require some further argument here to show how, or why, such considerations can be "extended" to cover the further issue of punishment. Simply to make reference to the "necessary law of retaliation" (TMS, 71, 82), or to the principle of "returning evil for evil done" (TMS, 68), is either to provide no further justification at all or, worse still, to misrepresent such practices as, psychologically or practically speaking, inescapable features of human life.[26]

This "gap" in Smith's account of punishment is most apparent when we focus attention on the institution or practice of punishment taken as a whole. That is to say, the obvious question to raise at this juncture is why should society spend its energies and resources on constructing and maintaining institutions and practices of this nature? Smith's response here, such as it is, seems sorely inadequate. In respect of this issue, it is wholly unconvincing to be told that the sole point or purpose of punishment is simply that it implements the "necessary law of retaliation" and ensures that we return "evil for evil done". So described, punishment has no point or value at all.[27] Smith's efforts to account for the *indirect* utility of such practices, it may be argued, indicate that he is himself aware of the "gap" in his account. This appeal to considerations of indirect utility is, however, beside the point. As we have already noted, according to Smith, it is *irrelevant*, from a justificatory point of view, that our retributive practices turn out to be of (indirect) utility. Clearly, therefore, Smith and his followers remain entirely committed to the view that such institutions and practices are just and proper, *irrespective of their consequences.*[28] Seen from the perspective of Hume's alternative views on this subject, however, this claim, so presented, is highly suspect. It is suspect because, as I have suggested, it leaves the "justificatory gap" entirely unbridged.

Hume's complex theory of punishment makes it possible for us to see our way past an apparent paradox in this sphere. On the face of it, there appears to be a conflict or tension between the fundamental tenets of naturalistic theory of responsibility and the claim that punishment requires a teleological element in its justification. More specifically, there appears to be a conflict between: the claim—as expressed by Strawson—that "the whole framework" of our moral sentiment requires no "external rational justification" (because it is a "given" or our human nature regarding which we have no choice) and the claim—as expressed by Hart—that punishment requires some adequate "general justifying aim" (because it is not a "given" of human nature and is, thus, a matter over which we *do* have choice).[29] Smith and his followers would eliminate this apparent tension by rejecting the suggestion that punishment requires some general justifying aim. From their perspective, our retributive practices, no less than the whole framework of our moral sentiments, are a given of human nature and, as such, are neither capable of nor require any "external rational justification".[30] Hume's complex theory succeeds, I believe, in providing us with a more satisfactory solution to this problem. By drawing a sharper distinction between our moral sentiments and our retributive practices, and by offering an alternative account of the relations between them, the complex theory enables us to explain how it is that consequentialist considerations are called for with regard to the latter but not the former. That is, although it is essential, on this account, that *punishment* be justified in terms of consequences, no such rationale is required for the framework of our moral sentiments. Clearly, once these points are established, it is possible to reconcile the prima facie conflicting demands of a naturalistic account of responsibility with a teleological element in the justification of punishment. In general, an understanding of the significance of this gap between our moral sentiments and our retributive practices is crucial if we are to avoid drawing the mistaken conclusion that a naturalistic theory of responsibility necessarily commits us to some strong form of positive retributivism.

Our analysis of the "justificatory gap" between blame (resentment) and punishment reveals a further point of disagreement between Hume and Smith. Lying behind their divergent views on the justificatory issue is a more fundamental disagreement concerning moral psychology. It is disagreement at this level which explains their more obvious disagreement at the level of justification. Smith's position involves two distinct, but intertwined, claims. First, as has been noted, Smith claims that punishment may be justified without reference to its consequences. Second, Smith also suggests—although this claim is not so clearly developed—that punishment is embedded in our human nature in such a way that we are left, in some important sense, with no choice in the matter. That is to say, Smith speaks of punishment as the "natural consequence of resentment" (TMS, 79) and thus as something which is (for us), in the relevant circumstances, a practical or psychological necessity. In other words, for Smith, retributive practices are, in some sense, "built into" our human nature. "As every man doth, so shall it be done to him, and *retaliation seems to be the great law which is dictated to us by nature*" (TMS, 82; my emphasis). This claim allows for two quite different interpretations. On the strong interpretation, Smith can be read as arguing that in respect of our will our retributive practices are on the same footing as our (reactive) moral sentiments. That is, Smith may be understood to be claiming that our retributive practices are essentially involuntary or spontaneous in the sense that they are not a matter of decision or choice *at all*. A few of Smith's remarks lend themselves to this interpretation, perhaps, but on the whole it is clear that this (self-evidently implausible) view is not what he has in mind.[31]

On the weak interpretation, Smith may be taken to acknowledge or recognize that our retributive practices are indeed voluntary and, in some measure, depend on our choices or willings. That is, our retributive practices, on this account, are a matter of deliberation and choice in a way that our moral sentiments clearly are not. However, the scope for deliberation is, nevertheless, severely limited. In this respect, Smith draws a useful analogy between our desire for retaliation and other "original and immediate instincts", such as our desire for food, water, and sex (TMS, 77–78). The general point of this analogy seems to be that our natural desire for retaliation is so fundamental to our human nature that it inevitably shapes our will and leads to action. It is inconceivable, in other words, given our human nature, that these desires could be rendered "inert" in actual practice. Although there may be some scope for choice in *shaping* and *directing* these practices, there is, on this account, no question of our suspending or abandoning these practices, altogether. Such practices, it is suggested, are simply too deeply embedded in our human nature for such an option to arise. Clearly this view of things blocks all proposals to eliminate—or even radically reform—our practice of punishment (i.e. on the ground that given our human nature such proposals are impracticable). In short, Smith is understood, on this account, to be arguing that we can no more choose to suspend or abandon our retributive practices as a whole than we can choose to abandon the whole framework of our moral sentiments. On the contrary, our natural human commitment to the latter ensures that we are inescapably committed to the former. Hence, within this sphere, there are natural limits to what we may decide or choose to do.[32]

The point at which Hume and Smith differ regarding the relation between the will and our retributive practices should now be quite clear. From a Humean perspective, Smith's model of how the practice of punishment is embedded in human nature substantially misrepresents the facts. The crucial point here is not simply that practices of this nature involve the intentional infliction of suffering and pain and hence must be *chosen*—this, as I have indicated, is a point which Smith can concede (i.e. on the weaker interpretation). Rather, the crucial point, from a Humean perspective, is that our commitment to the whole framework of the moral sentiments is not such that it is psychologically or practically impossible for us to free ourselves of retributive practices. That is to say, however natural retributive feelings and desires may be, we have no reason to regard our will as dominated and controlled by them. On the contrary, it is the sign of a civilized and humane mind (or society) that such retributive impulses are controlled and curbed in such a way that we can ensure that they serve only socially desirable ends.[33] Where they do not serve or secure such ends, they must be checked, and to that extent suspended or abandoned where necessary. This difference in our practical situation in respect of punishment accounts for the fact that it requires a further *level* of justification (and that it is at this level that consequentialist or forward-looking considerations come into play). Above all, from a *practical* point of view, we may not regard ourselves as "victims" of our own moral sentiments. Although we do not choose our moral sentiments, we do choose whom, and when, to punish. In this respect, we stand in an utterly different position in relation to the practice of punishment than we do to our essentially spontaneous or involuntary emotional reactions to the moral qualities of other people. There is, then, on this account, sufficient scope for us to choose to suspend or abandon our retributive practices in circumstances in which we can see that they secure no socially desirable ends.

There is much to be said for this Humean reply to Smith. Nevertheless, I have one or two reservations which I will briefly describe. First, even if we concede that it is possible for us to "check" our desire for retaliation in light of utilitarian considerations, such a policy seems to encourage and condone widespread hypocrisy and insincerity. That is to say, if we are constantly deciding whether or not to *express* our moral sentiments, in word or deed, on the basis of (forward-looking) utilitarian considerations, then it seems clear that we will frequently have reason *not* to express our true or sincere sentiments toward one another. In these circumstances, whereas our moral sentiments will be conditioned by backward-looking considerations, our actual treatment of the individuals who are the objects of these sentiments will be shaped (at least in part) by forward-looking considerations. This discrepancy between, on the one hand, the way we think and feel about one another and, on the other hand, the way we treat one another—if it is livable—will require a considerable loss of spontaneity. Moreover, on the basis of such a policy, we may find ourselves treating individuals in inconsistent ways. For example, in certain circumstances, utilitarian considerations may dictate that we punish some individuals for relatively minor failings whereas other individuals, whom we more strongly disapprove of, go unpunished (because punishment would serve no further purpose in their case). Similarly, we may find that two individuals who are the objects of similar negative moral sentiments should nevertheless be treated differently in respect of punishment, because it will be of utility to punish one but not the other. Such circumstances might be unlikely or improbable, but it is equally clear that they could well arise. In short, it may be argued that even if we concede to Hume that it is possible to curb our retributive practices in the way that he suggests, we will, nevertheless, have to pay a high price for such a policy in terms of hypocrisy, insincerity, and inconsistency. We should be reluctant, the critic might argue, to allow such a large discrepancy between our thought and action, feeling and practice, to develop.

Second, the critic might continue to be unconvinced by the Humean account of the relation between retributive practices and the will. That is, it remains far from obvious that it is possible to disengage our (natural) retributive feelings and desires from retributive practices in the way that Hume's theory presupposes. It is possible, perhaps, for some (few) individuals to master their retributive sentiments and desires in such a way that they could abandon or suspend their retributive practices. (We may view such individuals as "Spinozists" in practice, if not in thought.) Similarly, it is possible that all of us are, in some measure, capable of checking or curbing our retributive practices. Nevertheless, it is quite another thing to suggest that we are all (or even a sizable minority of us) capable of entirely suspending or abandoning our retributive practices. Granted that our moral sentiments are inescapable features of human life, it is, surely, demanding too much of human nature to claim that we could—despite this burden—simply suspend or abandon our retributive practices if we so chose. Our moral sentiments and our retributive practices are too closely bound up with each other for that to be possible. Considerations of this general nature, it may be argued, suggest that the psychological foundations of Hume's complex theory of punishment are themselves suspect.

It seems clear, in light of the foregoing analysis, that both Hume and Smith encounter difficulties with their naturalistic approach to the problem of punishment. Moreover, as it stands, it is not evident that either strategy can overcome all of the difficulties which lie in their respective paths. In several respects, as I have indicated, Hume's theory is both more plausible and more satisfactory than Smith's (strong) positive retributivism. Nevertheless, whatever the merits of Hume's account, there remains a serious tension between the claim that we are naturally and inescapably committed to our moral sentiments and the supposition that we may suspend or abandon our retributive practices when they prove to be of no social utility. Moreover, it may also be argued that whatever the shortcomings in Smith's account, at least it does not license a radical discrepancy between our moral evaluations of people and how we treat them. Clearly, then, difficulties arise for Hume as well as Smith.

Those thinkers who want to take a naturalistic approach to the problem of responsibility along the lines of Strawson should pause to consider the difficulties that Hume and Smith run into in this sphere. In particular, they should ask themselves where Strawson stands on these issues. Would he, for example, accept the Humean view that there exists a "justificatory gap" between our moral sentiments and our retributive practices—or would he follow Smith in rejecting this claim? Similarly, would Strawson accept the Humean view that our retributive practices, unlike our moral sentiments, are *not* inescapable features of human life? All this remains unclear. Finally, as I have suggested, it may be argued that if it is indeed impossible to reconcile a naturalistic approach to responsibility with a credible and coherent theory of punishment, then we have, on the face of it, strong grounds for rejecting such an approach. It is, accordingly, crucial that those who find merit in Strawson's discussion give further consideration to the rival strategies which Hume and Smith provide us with.

IV

My first objective in this chapter has been to articulate Hume's theory of punishment. There are, I claim, two particularly notable features of Hume's discussion. First, his theory rests on the foundations of a naturalistic theory of moral responsibility. Second, on the basis of this naturalistic foundation, he develops a "mixed" or teleological, retributivist account of punishment. These two elements of Hume's theory serve to distinguish his position from, on the one hand, those of Hobbes and Schlick and, on the other hand, from those of Smith and his followers. So interpreted, Hume's theory of punishment is, I have argued, not only distinctive, but also far richer and more complex than has hitherto been recognized.

My second objective has been to show that the contemporary interest of Hume's discussion lies primarily with his naturalistic approach to the problem of punishment. In particular, I have argued that Hume's discussion brings to light a number of interesting and important problems for Strawson's influential and very similar naturalistic account of responsibility. In more general terms, Hume's attempt to interpret the implications of a naturalistic theory of responsibility for the problem of punishment, I maintain, sheds considerable light on the wider issue concerning the relationship between responsibility and punishment. Within this general framework, Hume's contribution is, I suggest, as illuminating as it is distinctive.

Notes

1. See, e.g., T, 410: "Tis indeed certain . . ."; EU, 97–98: "All laws being founded . . .";
T, 609: "Men have observ'd . . ."; EM, 187: "When any man . . .".

2. See esp. *Treatise*, III, ii, 7. Some commentators, probably with these passages in mind, interpret Hume's views on punishment as being fundamentally utilitarian and thus "as necessitating the rejection of desert" (Kleinig, *Punishment and Desert*, 49). By and large, however, commentators on Hume's philosophy have little or nothing to say on this subject. We find, in other words, that the thinness of Hume's remarks on punishment is reflected in the relevant secondary literature.

3. See, in particular, Hobbes's *Leviathan*, chp. 28; Schlick, "When Is a Man Responsible?" 60.

4. One reason why Hume's views on punishment are generally associated with those of Hobbes and Schlick is that it is widely supposed (i.e. on the classical interpretation) that they all share similar views on free will and responsibility. Although Hume's remarks on punishment are rather slight, both Hobbes and Schlick do indicate, in some detail, the relevance of their views on free will to the problem of punishment. The fundamental point which both Hobbes and Schlick are concerned to make is that rewards and punishments serve to *cause* people to act in some ways and not in others and are, hence, of considerable social utility (cf. Hume, T, 410). Schlick, as we have noted, goes so far as to analyse responsibility in these terms.

5. See, more generally, *Treatise*, II, ii, 6. Other relevant passages can be found at T, 348, 376–77, 418, 439, and 605; EM, 302; and DP, 139.

6. Raphael, "Hume and Adam Smith on Justice and Utility", 99.

7. Hume repeatedly points out the difficulties involved in attributing human passions or sentiments to God: *Dialogues*, 156, 212, 226. See also Hume's letter to William Mure, LET, I/51 (#21).

8. Of course, this is a separate issue from the question concerning the *utility* of (religious) *belief* in the existence of such a future state. That is to say, as Hume recognized, many would claim that we have utilitarian reasons to promote and encourage belief in the doctrine of future rewards and punishments. In reply to this (distinct) claim, Hume maintains that beliefs of this general nature are, at best, of little social utility and that they in fact tend to undermine our natural human commitment to morality and the laws of society (D, 219–24; see also EU, 147).

9. My approach here draws heavily on Hart's influential statement of the teleological, retributivist (i.e. "mixed" or "reconciliationist") theory of punishment in "Prolegomenon to the Principles of Punishment", 1–27.

10. Cf. T, 348: "Nothing is more evident, than that any person acquires our kindness, or is expos'd to our ill-will, in proportion to the pleasure or uneasiness we receive from him, and that the passions keep pace exactly with the sensations in all their changes and variations."

11. Hume's position on this issue may be contrasted with Duncan-Jones's account of Butler's position. He reports Butler as taking the view that the notion of desert suggests "*both* that a man's conduct is bad *and* that to penalize him is useful, or *both* that his conduct is good *and* to praise or reward him is useful" (*Butler's Moral Philosophy*, 140; my emphasis).

12. Rawls, "Two Concepts of Rules", 144–70.

13. In light of these observations, it can be argued that, insofar as Hume's views on *punishment* have been misunderstood and misrepresented, the root difficulty lies with confusion about his views on *responsibility*. More specifically, the general tendency to place Hume squarely in the classical compatibilist tradition, alongside Hobbes and Schlick, has led commentators to overlook Hume's concern with the role of moral sentiment in this sphere. Clearly, as our analysis reveals, without an adequate interpretation of Hume's views on responsibility, it is impossible to develop a proper understanding of his position on punishment.

14. Suffice it to note that Schlick's account is widely thought to be vulnerable on precisely this point. See, e.g., Campbell's objections to "Schlick's essentially 'forward looking' interpretation of punishment and responsibility": "Is 'Freewill' a Pseudo-Problem?" 112–18.

15. Smith states (TMS, 77): "Let it be considered too, that the present inquiry is not concerning a matter of right, if I may say so, but concerning a matter of fact. We are not at present examining upon what principles a perfect being would approve of punishment of bad actions; but upon what principles so weak and imperfect a creature as man actually and in fact approves of it." (Along with *The Theory of Moral Sentiments*, also relevant is Smith's *Lectures on Jurisprudence*, hereafter abbreviated as LJ.)

16. On Smith's account, we sympathize with another person when we imaginatively place ourselves in his position and feel what he feels (i.e. we find that our sentiments "correspond" with those of the person involved). In these circumstances, we regard his sentiments as proper or appropriate to their object, and thus we approve of them.

17. Smith's views on this issue, it should be noted, are not entirely uniform. More specifically, Smith does say that on some occasions "we both punish and approve of punishment, *merely from a view to the general interest of society*, which, we imagine, cannot be otherwise secured" (TMS, 90; my emphasis; see also LJ, 105). It is not entirely obvious, however, how we are supposed to interpret such exceptional cases; nor how Smith's remarks in this direction square with his analysis of the standard case. On this, see Raphael, "Hume and Adam Smith", 96–97.

18. LJ, 104. Here Smith probably has Hume primarily in mind—although it is "Grotius and other writers" to whom he actually refers. See the editor's remarks at TMS, 87–88.

19. It may be noted that Smith's claims regarding the *indirect* utility of retributive practices are highly questionable. That is, Smith claims that the "law of retaliation" will effec-

tively "regulate" punishment in such a way that it indirectly secures our utilitarian ends (deterrence, reform, etc.). At least two difficulties arise for this claim: (a) in many cases such practices might serve no such ends—they might even be counterproductive; (b) from a utilitarian perspective, there might be *more effective* alternative strategies available to us.

20. Within the present confines, it is not possible to explore the significance which this general interpretation of Hume's theory has for the more specific or narrower remarks Hume makes on the subject of punishment. Two passages, however, merit brief comment. First, at T, 608–9 Hume argues, as was noted in the previous chapter, that a distinction can be drawn between moral qualities and natural abilities insofar as moral qualities, but not our natural abilities, "may be chang'd by the motives of rewards and punishments, praise and blame". I have argued that there is much in this account to question. However, Hume's position on this more specific issue is, I suggest, more intelligible when considered within the framework of his general theory of punishment. Second, at EM, 322—developing points raised from the passage at T, 608–9 (taking issue, in particular, with the suggestion that the distinction between voluntary and involuntary be made the foundation of a theory of morals)—Hume objects to those philosophers or divines who treat "all morals as on a like footing with civil laws, guarded by the sanctions of reward and punishment". The general point Hume is concerned with here is that it is crucial to distinguish between situations in which our moral sentiments have been legitimately aroused and those in which we are justified in distributing rewards and punishments on the basis of these sentiments. This fundamental point is firmly embedded in Hume's general theory of punishment. Indeed, it lies at the heart of his objections to the theological doctrine of future rewards and punishments.

21. "Savage or civilized", Strawson claims, "we have some belief in the utility of the practices of condemnation and punishment . . ." (FR, 78). For Strawson, however, this is not the central issue. Rather, the point which Strawson is concerned to establish is that "to speak in terms of social utility *alone* is to leave out something vital in our conception of these practices" (viz. our moral sentiments).

22. Even though "Freedom and Resentment" has generated a great deal of comment and criticism, very little has been said about the problem of punishment as it arises for Strawson. Instead, commentators have focussed their attention, almost exclusively, on the narrower issues of freedom and responsibility. This situation is particularly surprising in light of the fact that Smith (in whose footsteps Strawson clearly follows) devotes a great deal of his attention to the problem of punishment. It is fair to say, I believe, that this is indicative of the extent to which Strawson's naturalistic theory of responsibility has been cut off from its historical roots.

23. Whereas Hume's views on the subject of punishment have received little attention over the years, Smith's naturalistic account of positive retributivism has succeeded in attracting a number of followers. The most important of these have been Westermarck (*Ethical Relativity*, see esp. chp. 3) and, more recently, Mackie ("Morality and the Retributive Emotions"). The Smithian flavour of Mackie's general position is quite obvious—indeed it can be traced directly to Smith via Westermarck. In order to preserve the coherence and direction of my own discussion, however, I will continue to focus attention on Smith's views.

24. According to Hume, our moral sentiments arise out of our beliefs about people's pleasurable or painful qualities of mind or character. These sentiments, as I have explained, may be said to be *indirectly* reasonable or unreasonable, justified or unjustified, on this basis. The crucial point, therefore, is that according to Hume *our* moral sentiments are not to be justified in terms of *their* future consequences or utility. Whether or not such sentiments are of utility, they will naturally arise in the relevant circumstances. In this sense, they are neither capable of, nor require, a consequentialist rationale.

25. Regarding the relationship between blame and punishment, see, e.g. Squires, "Blame", 204–11, and Wasserstrom, "Some Problems in the Definition and Justification of Punish-

ment", 307–8. (Wasserstrom, I note in passing, raises several interesting objections against the sort of "mixed" or teleological, retributivist theory of punishment which I attribute to Hume. Suffice it to say, in this context, that I am not persuaded that his objections tell against Hume's position.)

26. Consider the following tale told about Zeno of Citium, a necessitarian, by Diogenes Laertius: "We are told that [Zeno] was once chastising a slave for stealing, and when the latter pleaded that it was his fate to steal, 'Yes, and to be beaten too,' said Zeno" (*Lives of Eminent Philosophers*, II, 135).

27. Smith may be understood to be suggesting—in a more utilitarian vein—that the point of punishment is that it gratifies our desire for retribution. This line is pursued by Stephen (*Liberty, Equality, Fraternity*, 152). Stephen argues that common crimes are punished, "not only because they are dangerous to society, but also for the sake of gratifying the feeling of hatred—call it revenge, resentment or what you will". It follows, Stephen suggests, that the criminal law is "an emphatic assertion of the principle that the feeling of hatred and the desire to for vengeance . . . are important elements of human nature which ought in such cases to be satisfied in a regular public and legal manner."

28. Consider, for example, the theological implications of Smith's account and how it contrasts with Hume's position. That is, granted the ontology presupposed in the doctrine of a future state, Smith *cannot* follow Hume in regarding the existence of Hell as a barbarism without point or purpose. Indeed, Smith takes quite the opposite view. See TMS, 91 and 163f. (Although Smith would grant, no doubt, that Hell involves the *excessive* punishment of the guilty.)

29. Strawson, FR, 78; Hart, "Prolegomenon", 8–11.

30. This theme is pursued in some detail in Mackie, "Morality and the Retributive Emotions".

31. Implausible as this strong view might be, several of Mackie's comments ("Morality and the Retributive Emotions", 216–19) lend themselves to this interpretation. In general, Mackie blurs the distinction between retaliating without a view to consequences and retaliating spontaneously or instinctively without making any "conscious choice" on the matter.

32. So described, Smith's position may be (loosely) interpreted in terms of Frankfurt's account of free will ("Freedom of the Will and the Concept of a Person"). That is, our desire for retaliation is such that, whatever our reflective attitude might be with respect to these desires, they will nevertheless be effective in leading to action. In other words, it is impossible for us to restructure our will in such a way that our resentment does not lead to retaliation or retribution. We cannot alter or change our will in this respect. This is consistent with the (obvious) fact that retaliatory actions are done of our own will, and thus we enjoy freedom of action in respect of them.

33. Clearly, for Hume, someone who is willing to intentionally inflict pain and suffering for no purpose other than vengeance is simply vicious. See especially T, 605–6, where Hume notes that although "anger and hatred are passions inherent in our very frame and constitution" (and the "want of them . . . may even be a proof of weakness and imbecillity"), when these passions "rise up to cruelty, they form *the most detested of all vices*" (my emphasis). It is *cruel*, on Hume's account, to intentionally inflict suffering on any person—whatever we feel about his character—simply to satisfy our sense of hatred and anger.

11

Pride, Fortune, and the Godless Man

A desire of fame, reputation, or a character with others, is so far from being blameable, that it seems inseparable from virtue, genius, capacity, and a generous or noble disposition.

Hume, *An Enquiry concerning the Principles of Morals*

But even though superstition or enthusiasm should not put itself in direct opposition to morality; the very diverting of the attention, the raising up a new and frivolous species of merit, the preposterous distribution which it makes of praise and blame, must have the most pernicious consequences, and weaken extremely men's attachment to the natural motives of justice and humanity.

Hume, *Dialogues concerning Natural Religion*

Any adequate theory of responsibility must provide some account of the sanctions that attach to morality and make us aware of ourselves as objects of moral evaluation or assessment. Related to this, a theory of responsibility must describe to what extent the virtuous can legitimately and reasonably expect some measure of happiness as their due reward (in this life or the next). Hume's approach to these issues downplays the importance of a system of legal rewards and punishments. Furthermore, Hume firmly rejects any system of divine rewards and punishments in a future state.[1] His alternative approach to these matters does, however, place considerable weight on the importance of "pride and humility" in moral life. It is these emotions, Hume claims, which are the principal instrument through which we attach some measure of happiness to virtue and misery to vice. In this chapter, I explain these features of Hume's system and show how they are related to his wider philosophical outlook concerning the relationship between religion and morality.

I

In his influential chapter called "Moral Relations", in the second Book of *An Essay concerning Human Understanding*, Locke suggests that there are three different kinds of moral law, each of which has its own peculiar system of sanctions (*Essay*, 352–57 [II, xxviii, 7–13]). First, there is the "Law of God", on the basis of which people believe they will receive "happiness, or misery, from the hands of the Almighty" (p. 352).[2] Second, there is the civil law or "Rule set by the Commonwealth". "This

154

Law", says Locke, "no body over-looks: the Rewards and Punishments, that enforce it, being ready at hand" (p. 352). Finally, there is "the Law of Opinion or Reputation", which is backed up by the approbation and dislike of the people in our own society (pp. 353–54). Locke continues,

> I think, I may say, that he, who imagines Condemnation and Disgrace, not to be strong Motives on Men, to accommodate themselves to the Opinions and Rules of those, with whom they converse, seems little skill'd in the Nature, or History of Mankind: the greatest part whereof he shall find to govern themselves chiefly, if not solely, by this Law of Fashion." (pp. 356–57)

Many people, Locke observes, believe they can evade or escape punishment from God and the commonwealth, but this is not true of the "Law of Fashion".

> No Man scapes the Punishment of their Censure and Dislike, who offends against the Fashion and Opinion of the Company he keeps, and would recommend himself to. Nor is there one of ten thousand, who is stiff and insensible enough, to bear up under the constant Dislike, and Condemnation of his own Club. He must be of a strange, and unusual Constitution, who can content himself, to live in constant Disgrace and Disrepute with his own particular Society. Solitude many Men have sought, and been reconciled to: But no Body, that has the least Thought, or Sense of a Man about him, can live in Society, under the constant Dislike, and ill Opinion of his Familiars, and those he converses with. This is a Burthen too heavy for humane Sufferance. (p. 357)

Hume would likely have been familiar with this important passage in Locke's *Essay*. More important, he agrees with Locke's claim that the "Law of Reputation" is a stronger motive to morality (i.e. virtue) than either the "Law of God" or the "Civil Law". Hume explains these principles of the human mind in terms of the workings of the indirect passions—in particular, in terms of our feelings of pride and humility.[3]

"The happiest disposition of the mind", says Hume, "is the virtuous" (ESY, 168 [Sceptic]; cf. EU, 140: "I acknowledge . . ."). How is it that virtue secures happiness for us? The general outline of Hume's reply seems quite clear. Pride is a pleasurable emotion, and humility is painful. Those qualities and objects that belong to, or attach to, us that are independently pleasurable give rise to pride, and those that are painful give rise to humility. Of all the causes of pride and humility, virtue and vice are "the most obvious" (T, 295; DP, 146). Virtue enables a person to take pleasure in himself, just as vice makes it painful for a mind to "bear its own survey" (T, 620). Our moral qualities, then, not only arouse love and hate in others—which in itself secures treatment from them, which makes us happy or miserable—but also arouse self-esteem or self-hatred (i.e. pride or humility). In this way, we naturally become an object of moral assessment to ourselves (T, 292), and this, typically, becomes an important source of happiness or unhappiness for us.

Hume emphasizes the social context in which we develop our sense of pride and humility. More specifically, the principles of sympathy largely account for the manner in which virtue secures happiness and vice brings us unhappiness. This occurs at two levels, which Hume distinguishes as the "original" and "secondary" causes of pride and humility (T, 316). The original causes of pride are virtue, beauty, and riches. These, however, may be further supported or reinforced by our "reputation", or "name", among our fellows (T, 316, 320, 331–32, 501, 571; EM, 276). The original causes of pride secure love and praise from other people. In the case of virtue, it produces approval and moral praise. This approval or love which is aroused in others becomes a separate (i.e. secondary) cause of pride for the possessor of virtue. Hume points out that reputation and love of fame is of great importance to human beings and that it does much to support moral life.[4]

> Another spring of our constitution, that brings a great addition of force to moral sentiments, is the love of fame; which rules, with such uncontrolled authority, in all generous minds, and is often the grand object of all their designs and undertakings. By our continual and earnest pursuit of a character, a name, a reputation in the world, we bring our own deportment and conduct frequently in review, and consider how they appear in the eyes of those who approach and regard us. This constant habit of surveying ourselves, as it were, in reflection, keeps alive all the sentiments of right and wrong, and begets, in noble natures, a certain reverence for themselves as well as others, which is the surest guardian of every virtue. (EM, 276)

It is evident, then, that according to Hume we want not only to merit approval and praise, but to have that merit *socially recognized and acknowledged* (because this brings us a separate and further pleasure). Indeed, as I will explain, on Hume's account the pleasure that we take in our merit depends to a great extent on that merit's being recognized and acknowledged by others.

Hume puts emphasis on the point that our *self*-evaluations depend very largely on the judgments of others.

> But of all our opinions, those, which we form in our own favour; however lofty or presuming; are, at bottom, the frailest, and the most easily shaken by the contradiction and opposition of others. Our great concern, in this case, makes us soon alarmed, and keeps our passions upon the watch: Our consciousness of partiality still makes us dread a mistake: And the very difficulty of judging concerning an object, which is never set at a due distance from us, nor seen in a proper point of view, makes us hearken anxiously to the opinions of others, who are better qualified to form just opinions concerning us. Hence that strong love of fame, with which all mankind are possessed. (DP, 152; cf. T, 321; EM, 276)

Our self-evaluations are, then, supported or undermined by the influence of society and sympathy. This influence varies depending on who these other individuals are and how they stand to us. Most important, "we receive a much greater satisfaction from the approbation of those whom we ourselves esteem and approve of, than of those whom we contemn and despise" (DP, 152–53; cf. T, 321). In other words, approval and praise is valued by us in direct proportion to the extent to which we respect and approve of those who are judging us. Similarly, we receive very little pleasure from the praise of others when we judge that it is not well founded (T, 322, 324; DP, 153). It follows, then, that the virtuous person receives the greatest pleasure or happiness from his virtue when it is recognized by other people who the virtuous person holds in esteem and who, he believes, have an accurate assessment of his character.

The value of pride, Hume suggests, is that it is, first, "immediately agreeable" to its possessor and, second, of utility insofar as "it capacitates us for business" (T, 600).

In respect of its utility, Hume points out that (due) pride or self-esteem "makes us sensible of our own merit, and gives us a confidence and assurance in all our projects and enterprises" (T, 596–97). Indeed, Hume suggests "that all those great actions and sentiments, which have become the admiration of mankind, are founded on nothing but pride and self-esteem" (T, 599). Many of the most noble virtues—for example, courage, ambition, magnanimity—rest on the foundation of well-regulated pride (T, 599–600). However, when pride breaks "its just bounds", it loses these advantages. It may lead the person (and those who follow him) into folly and catastrophe (T, 600–601). Moreover, excessive pride and self-concern shows an insensitivity to the feelings and sentiments of others and is rightly condemned. It is important, therefore, that our pride be both well regulated and "decently disguised" (EM, 265; cf. T, 596–98). None of this, however, requires that a person be "ignorant of his own merits and accomplishments" (EM, 265).

Virtue, Hume argues, is not fully rewarded unless it is recognized and acknowledged by others. In his essay "The Stoic", he makes this point directly:

> But where is the reward of virtue? And what recompence has nature provided for such important sacrifices, as those of life and fortune, which we must often make to it? . . . GLORY is the portion of virtue, the sweet reward of honourable toils, the triumphant crown, which covers the thoughtful head of the disinterested patriot, or the dusty brow of the victorious warrior. Elevated by so sublime a prize, the man of virtue looks down with contempt on all the allurements of pleasure, and all the menaces of danger. Death itself loses its terrors, when he considers, that its dominion extends only over part of him, and that, in spite of death and time, the rage of the elements, and the endless vicissitudes of human affairs, he is assured of an immortal fame among all the sons of men. (ESY, 153–54)

Hume points out that a person must *already* be virtuous in order to benefit and receive the "portion of Glory" that nature has provided for its "favourite child"—virtue (ESY, 153). Vice manifests itself by an uncaring attitude to reputation and name (i.e. shamelessness). The virtuous person loves virtue and virtuous actions "for their own sake", but this, Hume observes, is thoroughly "mixed" with love of fame and reputation (ESY, 86 [Dignity of Human Nature]).[5]

Hume's overall position on this matter can be summarized as follows. The natural reward for virtue is happiness, and the natural punishment for vice is unhappiness. The principal mechanism which secures these natural rewards and punishments is that of the indirect passions. Through sympathy and our basic human needs and emotions, human beings are bound together in their thoughts and feelings.[6] One of our greatest sources of happiness or unhappiness is how other human beings with whom we have contact think and feel about us—because this directly affects how we think and feel about ourselves. In order to feel good about ourselves, others must support our positive self-evaluation. Praise and approval from those whom we do not respect, or whom we believe are misinformed about us, bring us much less happiness than the approval and praise of those we respect and believe to be well informed and good judges of character. In short, for the happiness due to virtue, it suffices neither that we view ourselves as praiseworthy nor that we are simply approved of, and praised by, others. Virtue secures steady and reliable happiness for us only when we believe that we merit approval *and* those we have contact with and hold in esteem support our positive self-evaluation. Failing either of these conditions, virtue will not fully secure its natural reward.[7]

II

Virtue receives the reward of happiness secured through self-esteem and supported by our good name and reputation among our fellows. These aspects of human nature, as described by Hume, are brought into line or rendered consistent with our natural desire that those we love and approve of be happy and those we hate and disapprove of be miserable (T, 368). The system of nature, however, is not a perfect mechanism for distributing happiness as determined purely by moral merit. Many philosophers maintain, in light of this, that a perfect distribution of this sort can be achieved or realized only in a future state that is governed and maintained by God—indeed, they claim that this is a requirement or presupposition of moral life and practice.[8]

A number of Hume's psychological observations concerning our reactions to virtue and vice explain much of the attraction of the theological doctrine of rewards and punishments in a future state. The virtuous can, for example, on this account, rely on the all-knowing and perfect judgment of God to support and maintain their own (moral) self-esteem—however unreliable the imperfect and corrupted judgment of other human beings might be. Beyond this, the existence of a future state, and an all-powerful God governing it, guarantees that the virtuous get the happiness that we (naturally) wish for them and that the vicious are rendered appropriately miserable, as is required to satisfy our retributive desires. Such a scheme, some suppose, stands to realize a "perfect" distribution of happiness among human beings (i.e. considered from an impersonal and purely moral point of view). Certainly, considered from this perspective—a perspective Hume plainly does not share—it seems clear that God and a future state are required to achieve a perfect distribution of justice so conceived.

Hume holds that the doctrine of future rewards and punishments is of little practical force or influence in human life, and, more important, insofar as it has some influence and effect on moral practice it is largely corrupting. In a variety of contexts, Hume maintains that, in actual practice, most people—including those who profess to be religiously inclined or inspired—are little influenced by considerations concerning a future state: "Men are always more concern'd about the present life than the future; and are apt to think the smallest evil, which regards the former, more important than the greatest, which regards the latter" (T, 525).[9] In the *Dialogues*, he takes up the issue at greater length. Philo says,

> Consider . . . the attachment, which we have to present things, and the little concern which we discover for objects so remote and uncertain. When divines are declaiming against the common behaviour and conduct of the world, they always represent this principle as the strongest imaginable (which indeed it is) and describe almost all human kind as lying under the influence of it, sunk into the deepest lethargy and unconcern about their religious interests. Yet these same divines, when they refute their speculative antagonists, suppose the motives of religion to be so powerful, that, without them, it were impossible for civil society to subsist; nor are they ashamed of so palpable a contradiction. It is certain, from experience, that the smallest grain of natural honesty and benevolence has more effect on men's conduct,

than the most pompous views suggested by theological theories and systems. (D, 220–21)[10]

Hume argues, beyond this, that the religious doctrine of future rewards and punishments, where it does have some influence, is largely corrupting, because it tends to weaken or sever our (human) attachment to "the natural motives of justice and humanity". Moreover, in its place, the religious system raises up "a new and frivolous species of merit" (D, 222). Where this corruption of morality takes root, we find that the distribution of praise and blame is based on "monkish virtues"—which are truly vices—such as celibacy, fasting, penance, self-denial and solitude. This is a "moral" system which, from any reasonable and natural perspective, simply encourages pernicious vices that "harden the heart" and "sour the temper" (EM, 270). On top of all this, these principles of "superstition", being generally weak and unreliable as practical motives, encourage hypocrisy and fraud (D, 222).

Hume objects to the doctrine of a future state conceived in terms of the divide between Heaven and Hell, on the ground that it presupposes a flawed understanding of the nature of moral merit. From a Humean perspective, a doctrine of this kind inevitably distorts and oversimplifies moral experience and feeling. In particular, it mistakenly suggests that individuals can be placed, systematically, into one of two distinct moral categories: the "wicked" ("sinful", "criminal", etc.), who have violated some set of rules or laws, and the "righteous" ("law-abiding", "devout", etc.), who have followed and maintained the system of rules.

> Heaven and hell suppose two distinct species of men, the good and the bad. But the greatest part of mankind float betwixt vice and virtue.
>
> Were one to go round the world with an intention of giving a good supper to the righteous and a sound drubbing to the wicked, he would frequently be embarrassed in his choice, and would find, that the merits and demerits of most men and women scarcely amount to the value of either. (ESY, 594–95 [Immortality])

These remarks draw attention to the complexity and diversity of the moral personality and the significance of this fact for any sound assessment of moral merit.[11] The crude moral outlook suggested by the doctrine of Heaven and Hell—reducing, as it does, the entire (moral) population to the categories of the "good" and the "bad"— has its roots in an account of moral life that emphasizes "commandments" or "laws" that are supposed to produce obedience.[12] It is precisely this sort of morality which Hume rejects. In its place, he advances a virtue-based morality that depends primarily on a system of honour, rather than a system of divine rewards and punishments, for its support and foundation.[13] In general, then, Hume regards the whole substance of the doctrine of future rewards and punishments as flawed and ill conceived. We have, he maintains, overwhelming reason to discard this doctrine and prevent it from corrupting and distorting our moral attitudes and practices.

According to Hume, there is no sign of a perfect distribution of justice in this world. Virtue is not *always* rewarded with happiness nor vice always punished with unhappiness and misery. In respect of this matter, fortune holds sway over human affairs. Although virtue is "undoubtedly the best choice, when it is attainable; yet such is the disorder and confusion of human affairs, that no perfect or regular distribution of happiness and misery is ever, in this life, to be expected" (ESY, 178 [Sceptic]). He continues, "Not only the goods of fortune, and the endowments of the body (both of which are important), . . . are unequally divided between the virtuous and vicious, but even the mind itself partakes, in some degree, of this disorder, and the most worthy character, by the very constitution of the passions, enjoys not always the highest felicity". The fact of the matter, therefore, is that a number of varied factors contribute to human happiness. Virtue certainly is an important and significant source of happiness, but it is far from being the *only* factor that shapes and affects our happiness. Bad health or a "gloomy disposition" can render even the most virtuous person entirely miserable. Moreover, all people form close attachments to other people in their family and social circles—people with whom they strongly sympathize—and their welfare and condition will directly influence each person's own happiness or misery. It is evident, then, that no person can rely on virtue alone to provide and secure her happiness.

Arguably, the most disconcerting observation Hume has to make on this subject is that the very mechanism which serves to attach happiness to virtue and misery to vice—that is, the mechanism of the indirect passions as governed by the principles of sympathy—can fail its usual effect because of the influence of fortune. More specifically, as Hume's analysis suggests, the pride that we take in virtue is vulnerable to the influence of other people's evaluations—particularly, the evaluations of those people we care about and respect. Even the most virtuous people, therefore, can find themselves in circumstances in which their self-esteem and happiness is undermined by the (illegitimate) adverse judgments of those whom they come in contact with and rely on. These "frowns of fortune" (T, 600) constitute one of the most severe tests of virtue. It is a notable merit of Hume's system that he can explain why this is so.

Hume's outlook on the relationship between virtue and happiness is neither pessimistic nor optimistic. On the whole, virtue is much more conducive to happiness than vice is.[14] Nevertheless, there is no guarantee that virtue will receive the happiness which is its natural due. Human life, Hume points out, is governed by fortune, and thus the happiness of any person can be interrupted or disturbed at any time by a turn of events or by some underlying condition that makes the person miserable. The role of philosophy is not to offer consolation by painting a picture according to how humankind might like things to be in some idealized universe.[15] Rather, philosophers must take human nature and the human condition as they find it. We must try to understand and accurately describe moral life as we see and experience it in order to guide our practices and structure our institutions in a way that is suitable to our human needs and limitations. The natural connexion between virtue and happiness, Hume argues, is strong and steady enough to support moral life and the bonds of society.[16] Any effort to supplement or ground it in the doctrines of religion is, in any case, more likely to corrupt than console. The life we lead, he suggests, will be happier when we reconcile ourselves to these facts about the human condition.

III

In the *Treatise*, Hume argues that one of the reasons "why the doctrine of liberty [of indifference] has generally been better receiv'd in the world, than its antagonist [the doctrine of necessity], proceeds from *religion*, which has been very unnecessarily interested in this question" (T, 409). He goes on to argue "that the doctrine of necessity, according to my explication of it, is not only innocent, but even advantageous to religion and morality". When Hume came to present his views afresh in the *Enquiry* (Sect. 8), he was less circumspect about his hostile intentions with regard to "religion".[17] In the parallel passage (EU, 96–97), he again objects to any effort to refute a hypothesis "by a pretence to its dangerous consequences to *religion and morality*" (my emphasis). He goes on to say that his account of the doctrines of liberty and necessity "are not only consistent *with morality*, but are absolutely essential to its support" (E, 97; my emphasis). By this means, he makes it clear that he is not claiming that his position is "consistent" with *religion*. In the final passages of the *Enquiry* discussion of liberty and necessity (EU, 99–103)—passages which do not appear in the original *Treatise* discussion—Hume makes it plain exactly how his necessitarian principles have "dangerous consequences for religion".[18]

Hume considers the following objection:

> It may be said, for instance, that, if voluntary actions be subjected to the same laws of necessity with the operations of matter, there is a continued chain of necessary causes, pre-ordained and pre-determined, reaching from the original cause of all to every single volition of every human creature. . . . The ultimate Author of all our volitions is the Creator of the world, who first bestowed motion on this immense machine, and placed all beings in that particular position, whence every subsequent event, by an inevitable necessity, must result. Human action, therefore, either can have no moral turpitude at all, as proceeding from so good a cause; or if they have any turpitude, they must involve our Creator in the same guilt, while he is acknowledged to be their ultimate cause and author. (EU, 99–100)

In other words, the doctrine of necessity produces an awkward dilemma for the theological position: Either the distinction between (moral) good and evil collapses, because everything is produced by a perfect being who intends "nothing but what is altogether good and laudable" (EU, 101), or we must "retract the attribute of perfection, which we ascribe to the Deity" on the ground that he is the ultimate author of moral evil in the world.

Hume treats the first horn of this dilemma at greatest length. He draws on his naturalistic principles to show that the conclusion reached (i.e. that no human actions are evil or criminal in nature) is absurd. There are, he claims, both physical and moral evils in this world that the human mind finds naturally painful, and this affects our sentiments accordingly. Whether we are the victim of gout or of robbery, we naturally feel the pain of such evils (EU, 101–2). No "remote speculations" or "philosophical theories" concerning the good or perfection of the *whole universe* will alter these natural reactions and responses to the particular ills and evils we encounter. Hence, even if we were to grant that this is indeed the best of all possible worlds— and Hume clearly takes the view that we have no reason to suppose that it is (D, 212; EU, 137–42)—this would do nothing to undermine the reality of the distinction we draw between good and evil (i.e. as experienced on the basis of "the natural sentiments of the human mind" [EU, 103]).[19]

What, then, of the alternative view, that God is "the ultimate author of guilt and moral turpitude in all his creatures"? Hume offers two rather different accounts of this alternative—although he does not distinguish them properly. He begins by noting that if some human actions "have any turpitude, they must involve our Creator in the *same guilt*, while he is acknowledged to be their *ultimate* cause and author" (EU, 100; my emphasis). This passage suggests that God is *also* blameworthy for criminal actions in this world, since he is their "ultimate author". At this point, however, there is no suggestion that the particular human agents who commit these crimes (as preordained by God) are not accountable for them. In the passage that follows this is the position taken.

> For as a man, who fired a mine, is answerable for all the consequences whether the train he employed be long or short; so wherever a continued chain of necessary causes is fixed, that Being, either finite or infinite, who produces the first, is likewise the author of all the rest, and must both bear the blame and acquire the praise which belong to them. (EU, 100)

Hume goes on to argue that this rule of morality has even "greater force" when applied to God, since he is neither ignorant nor impotent and must, therefore, have *intended* to produce those criminal actions which are manifest in the world.[20] Granted that such actions are indeed criminal, it follows, says Hume, "that the Deity, not man, is accountable for them" (EU, 100; cf. EU, 101).[21]

It is evident that Hume is arguing two points. First, if God is the creator of the world and preordained and predetermined everything that happens in it, then the (obvious) existence of moral evil is attributable to him, and thus "we must retract the attribute of perfection" which we ascribe to him. Second, if God is indeed the ultimate author of moral evil, then no individual human being is accountable for the criminal actions he performs. The second claim does not follow from the first. Moreover, it is clearly inconsistent with Hume's general position on this subject. As has been noted, in this same context, Hume has also argued that no speculative philosophical theory can alter the natural workings of our moral sentiments. The supposition that God is the "ultimate author" of all that takes place in the world will not, on this view of things, change our natural disposition to praise or blame our fellow human beings. *Whatever* the ultimate causes of a person's character and conduct, it will (inevitably) arouse a sentiment of praise or blame in other humans who contemplate it. This remains the case even if we suppose that God also deserves blame for the "moral turpitude" we find in the world. In general, then, Hume's first formulation of the second alternative (i.e. that God must *share* the blame for those crimes that occur in the world) is more consistent with his naturalistic principles.[22]

What is crucial to Hume's polemical purpose in these passages is not the thesis that if God is the author of crimes then his human creations are not accountable for them. Rather, the point Hume is concerned to make (since he does not, in fact, doubt the inescapability of our moral accountability to our fellow human beings) is that the religious hypothesis leads to the "absurd consequence" that God is the ultimate author of sin in this world and that he is, accordingly, liable to some appropriate measure of blame. Hume, in other words, takes the (deeply impious) step of showing that if God exists, and is the creator of the universe, then he is no more free of sin than man is. According to Hume, we must judge God as we judge human beings, on the basis of his effects in the world, and we must then adjust our sentiments accordingly. Indeed, there is no other natural or reasonable basis on which to found our sentiments toward God. In certain respects, therefore, we can make better sense of how we (humans) can hold God accountable than we can make sense of how God is supposed to hold humans accountable (i.e. since we have no knowledge of his sentiments, or even if he has any; cf. D, 156, 212, 226; ESY, 594; but see also LET, I/51). It is, of course, Hume's considered view that it is an egregious error of speculative theology and philosophy to suppose that the universe has been created by a being that bears some (close) resemblance to humankind. The question of the origin of the universe is one that Hume plainly regards as beyond the scope of human reason (see, e.g., EU, 11–13, 137–42, 144–47, 165; D, 134–36, 186–87, 205). Nevertheless, Hume's point is plain: On the basis of the (limited) evidence that is available to us, we must suppose that if there is a God, who is creator of this world and who orders all that takes place in it, then this being is indeed accountable for all the (unnecessary and avoidable; D, 205) evil that we discover in it.[23]

IV

It is clear that there is a very close connexion between Hume's theory of responsibility and his wider interests in problems of religion. The question arises, therefore, precisely what is the nature of this relationship between Hume's naturalistic account of responsibility and his scepticism about matters of religion, and how should this relationship be understood when considered in terms of the development of Hume's fundamental philosophical ideas and intentions? A puzzle in respect of these issues immediately presents itself.

Hume's most detailed and complete account of his position on the subject of moral responsibility is presented in the *Treatise*. This was, moreover, the context in which Hume first presented his theory. It is, however, widely held that the philosophy in the *Treatise* is *not* directly or significantly concerned with problems of religion. Hume's principal concerns in this work, it is claimed, lie elsewhere.[24] According to this view of things, Hume turned to problems of religion in a direct and detailed fashion only in his later writings—beginning with some of the later essays in the first *Enquiry*. This perspective on the *Treatise* clearly suggests that the discussion of responsibility, as presented in this work, has no substantial or intimate connexion with the anti-Christian philosophical themes that Hume presented and pursued in his later works. In other words, Hume's most elaborate and detailed account of the nature and conditions of moral responsibility was, according to this view, presented independently of his major sceptical attacks on the principles and dogmas of the Christian religion. Insofar as the relationship between his theory of responsibility and his views on matters of religion are worked out and clarified, this job was addressed and completed only in the more mature works (i.e. *Enquiries*, *Dialogues*, etc.). In my view, this general interpretation misrepresents how the theory of responsibility is related to Hume's fundamental intentions in the *Treatise*, and it also misrepresents the philosophical source and context of Hume's thinking on this subject.

In order to clarify these matters, we need to take up the following issue: What role does the theory of responsibility play in relation to Hume's wider intentions in the *Treatise*? For our present purposes, it will suffice simply to sketch an outline of my reply to this question. In a series of papers, I have argued for an "atheistic" or anti-Christian interpretation of Hume's fundamental intentions in the *Treatise*.[25] The gist of this interpretation may be summarized as follows: What is crucial for an adequate understanding of Hume's intentions in the *Treatise* is a proper appreciation of his fundamental concern with matters of religion. That is to say, it is problems of religion, broadly conceived, which hold the contents of the *Treatise* together as a unified work. More specifically, the direction and structure of Hume's thought in the *Treatise* is shaped by his attack on Christian metaphysics and morals and by his effort to construct, in its place, a secular, scientific account of morality. Hume believed that moral and political philosophy must proceed on the same methodology as that which is appropriate to the natural sciences. This scientific investigation of morals must begin with an examination of human thought and motivation—it being assumed that "the minds of all men are similar in their feelings and operations" (T, 575). The metaphysical foundation of this project is Hume's naturalistic and necessitarian conception of humankind.[26]

According to this view, the constructive or "positive" side of Hume's thought in the *Treatise*—his "science of man"—must be interpreted in terms of his concern to establish a plausible, scientifically grounded, secular morality. The destructive or critical side of the philosophy of the *Treatise* is simply the other side of the same anti-Christian coin. That is to say, in order to clear the ground to build the edifice of a secular morality, Hume had to undertake a sceptical attack on those theological doctrines and principles which threatened such a project. The varied and apparently disparate sceptical arguments which Hume advances in the *Treatise* are in fact very largely held together by this overarching concern to discredit and refute Christian metaphysics and morals. Among the specific doctrines Hume was especially concerned to refute was that of free will—a doctrine which the most prominent Christian moralists and divines of Hume's time had maintained was essential to both religion and morality.[27]

Viewed from the general perspective of the "atheistic" interpretation of Hume's intentions in the *Treatise*, the naturalistic theory of responsibility is, clearly, a particularly important part or aspect of Hume's wider effort to establish a secular, scientifically based account of moral life. One of the central lessons of Hume's theory of responsibility, as presented in the *Treatise*, is that we can make sense of issues of responsibility only within the framework or fabric of human nature and human society. What is required in order to understand and explain the nature and conditions of moral responsibility, therefore, is an accurate and detailed description of its foundations in human thought and sentiment.

This (naturalistic) framework explicitly excludes not only the metaphysics of libertarianism (e.g. agent causation and noumenal selves) but also all (further) theologically inspired metaphysics that generally accompanies it (i.e. God, the immortal soul, a future state, and so on).[28] The metaphysics of religion, Hume suggests, serves only to confuse and obscure our understanding of these matters and to hide their true foundation in human nature. So interpreted, Hume's general account of responsibility in the *Treatise* is, evidently, profoundly "atheistic" or anti-Christian.[29]

The metaphysics of responsibility, as laid out in the *Treatise*, is the metaphysics of a godless man. In his later writings, as we have noted, Hume was more open in his attacks on the Christian religion. Throughout his life, Hume's philosophical interests and concerns were very largely dominated and directed by his fundamental concern with the issue concerning the relationship between religion and morality. It is this general issue which unifies not only Hume's thought in the *Treatise* but his philosophical development and outlook taken as a whole. A basic theme in Hume's philosophy, so considered, is his effort to demystify morality and release it from the metaphysical trappings of "superstition". The core thesis of Hume's *Treatise*—indeed, of his overall ("atheistic") philosophical outlook—is that moral and social life neither rests on nor requires the dogmas of Christian metaphysics. Hume's empirical and scientific approach to the issue of moral responsibility is the very pivot on which this fundamental thesis turns.

Notes

1. In a variety of contexts, Hume does, of course, present himself as accepting or endorsing the orthodox Christian view on this subject (e.g. T, 410–11). Clearly, however, as the discussion in the previous chapter makes plain, Hume's remarks to this effect are patently insincere and motivated by considerations of prudence (which was, indeed, required of "freethinkers" at this time).

2. "That God has given a Rule whereby Men should govern themselves, I think there is no body so brutish as to deny. He has a Right to do it, we are his Creatures . . . and he has a Power to enforce it by Rewards and Punishments, of infinite weight and duration, in another Life" (Locke, *Essay*, 352).

3. Most expositions and discussions of Hume's views on pride are concerned with analysis of the elements and causal conditions of pride, rather than with his account of the role that pride plays in moral and social life. Two exceptions to this are Whelan, *Order and Artifice in Hume's Political Philosophy*, 173–77, and Baier, *A Progress of Sentiments*, 206–10.

4. The role of pride and love of fame in relation to morals was a much-discussed issue in the early eighteenth century. The most important and influential contribution on this subject came from Mandeville, who argued, famously, that "the moral virtues are the political offspring which flattery begot upon pride" (*Fable of the Bees*, in Raphael, ed., *British Moralists*, I, 234). Other important sources on this subject for Hume and his contemporaries include Spinoza, Bayle, Shaftesbury, and Hutcheson.

5. "If I have no vanity, I take no delight in praise" (EM, 301). In more general terms, the point Hume is concerned to make is that virtue and our desire to do what is honourable are not only compatible with our (independent) interest in happiness, they actually *promote* it. These concerns become "mixed" in the mind of the virtuous person and are difficult to disentangle. This analysis does not imply, however, that it is considerations of prudence (i.e. the desire for happiness) which is the sole or principal motive to virtue. On the contrary, on Hume's account, this cannot be the case if virtue is to secure the happiness that we desire from it. This is so because the pleasure we take in the virtuous person generally depends on the fact that the virtuous person acts on something *other* than (purely) prudential considerations. Hume observes, however, that this fact is consistent with the further fact that virtue brings us happiness (i.e. through pride and self-esteem).

6. See, e.g., T, 363: "This is still more conspicuous in man, as being the creature of the universe, who has the most ardent desire of society".

7. Hume's position on this subject contrasts in important respects with that of both Mandeville and Smith. Mandeville argues that people are virtuous only because they have a love of praise and flattery. Following Hume, Smith argues (in direct and explicit opposition

to Mandeville) that we seek not only to be praised but also, more important, to be *praiseworthy*. Unlike Hume, however, Smith argues that the desire to be worthy of approval does not require further support and confirmation from our fellows in order for it to be fully satisfied. The self-approbation of the wise person, he says, "stands in need of no confirmation from the approbation of other men. It is alone sufficient, and he is contented with it. This self-approbation, if not the only, is at least the principal object, about which he can or ought to be anxious. The love of it, is the love of virtue" (TMS, 117; cf. 297–98). Smith, therefore, distinguishes the "desire of doing what is honourable and noble" from "the love of true glory" (i.e. "the love of well-grounded fame and reputation") and argues that, for the virtuous person, the former is largely independent of the latter (TMS, 309). Although love of fame is "inferior" to love of doing what is honourable, it is not, on Smith's account, to be confused with pernicious vanity. The latter is a desire for praise either for qualities which are not praiseworthy or for qualities we do not possess, or it is a desire for an excessive show or exhibition of praise and "marks of respect" (TMS, 310). The general drift of Smith's discussion is to render the virtuous person as independent as possible from the judgments and evaluations of others. Hume is, in my view, rightly sceptical about this effort to insulate self-assessment from the assessments of others.

8. This is, for example, a central theme in the philosophy of Samuel Clarke and Bishop Butler—two of the most important and influential Christian moralists in the first half of the eighteenth century, and two thinkers in whose writings Hume had a very strong interest. See Clarke, *Discourse*, Pt. 2, "The Evidence of Natural and Revealed Religion", props. 3, 4, and 5 (*Works*, II, 641–56); and Butler, *Analogy of Religion: Natural and Revealed*, chps. 1–5. See also Berkeley, *Alciphron*, 3rd dialogue.

9. Hume points out in a number of different contexts that humankind is naturally constituted so as to be more concerned with this life than the next. See, e.g., T, 113–15, 428–38; EU, 140–42, 146–47; EM, 343. Indeed, in the context of his discussion of justice, Hume points out that our inclination "to prefer whatever is present to the distant and remote" (T, 536–38) is a problem that arises *within this life*, and it requires the institutions of political society to overcome it.

10. Philo continues: "This is well understood in the world; and none but fools ever repose less trust in a man, because they hear, that, from study and philosophy, he has entertained some speculative doubts with regard to theological subjects. And when we have to do with a man, who makes a great profession of religion and devotion; has this any other effect upon several, who pass for prudent, than to put them on their guard, lest they be cheated and deceived by him."

11. See, e.g., Hume's observations concerning the way Hannibal combined "great virtues" with "great vices" (EM, 320). Similarly, Hume also points out that virtuous individuals, such as Caesar and Cato, can vary greatly in the *kinds* of virtue they possess—one being "amiable" and the other "awful" (T, 607–8; EM, 316). Virtue and vice, in other words, can manifest themselves in different ways and in different combinations. No adequate theory of morality, he suggests, can overlook facts of this nature.

12. Baier has recently pointed out that Hume rejects conceptions of morality that "typically take the form of commandments or laws, which are supposed to produce obedience". Hume's version of morality, she says, is concerned to "minimize flat prohibitions" and thus emphasizes virtues and vices rather than "laws" and "obligations" (*A Progress of Sentiments*, 169, 184, 195).

13. Hume explicitly contrasts his own moral system, which views well-grounded pride as one of its principal supports, with the morality of the Christian religion, "which places humility in the rank of the virtues" (T, 600) and regards all pride as sinful. Closely related to the Christian emphasis on the place of humility in moral life is the general view of human

nature as "fallen", imperfect, and corrupted. This linkage is, as Hume notes, quite apparent in the writings of such Christian thinkers as Pascal (EM, 342–43).

14. "I acknowledge, that, in the present order of things, virtue is attended with more peace of mind than vice, and meets with a more favourable reception in the world. I am sensible, that, according to the past experience of mankind, friendship is the chief joy of human life, and moderation the only source of tranquillity and happiness. I never balance between the virtuous and the vicious course of life; but am sensible, that, to a well-disposed mind, every advantage is on the side of the former" (EU, 140).

15. "All doctrines are to be suspected, which are favoured by our passions" (ESY, 598 [Immortality]).

16. It is, clearly, Hume's view that not every virtuous person will be happy, nor every vicious individual miserable. He holds, however, that the relationship between virtue and happiness is generally reliable enough to support moral life and the social fabric. To expect more than this is neither necessary nor achieveable. (These issues are, of course, pursued in some detail in the work of Hobbes, Spinoza, Bayle, Shaftesbury, and others.)

17. However, even in the *Treatise* passage cited above, Hume makes little effort to conceal his actual views on this matter. He notes, for example, that we cannot show that an opinion is false because of its "dangerous consequences" to religion and morality but that an opinion is certainly false when it leads to "absurdities" (T, 409; cf. EU, 96). In the *Enquiry*, he specifies what absurdities we are led into by the religious hypothesis (cf. E, 100: "An absurd consequence . . ."). (Note Hobbes's similar sentiments in *Liberty and Necessity* [in Raphael, ed., *British Moralists*, I, 62]: "what use soever be made of truth, yet truth is truth, and now the question is not, what is fit to be preached, but what is true".)

18. It is quite possible that this passage of the *Enquiry* was one of the "nobler parts" of the *Treatise* which Hume deleted out of "prudence" (cf. LET, I/25; LET, I/106, 111).

19. At EU, 101, Hume refers to the Stoics' efforts to show "that those ills under which they laboured were, in reality, goods to the universe"; but at D, 194 [X], he also refers to Leibniz's "bold and paradoxical opinion" that denies the reality of "human misery".

20. At T, 249, Hume considers the doctrine of "Malebranche and other Cartesians" who assert that God is the only *real* agent in the world (cf. T, 159–60; EU, 71–72). He points out that this doctrine leads to "the grossest impieties and absurdities", because it suggests that "the supreme being is the real cause of all our actions, bad as well as good, vicious as well as virtuous". Clearly, in these circumstances, so interpreted, God is the *immediate* and *sole* cause of all criminal actions (as human beings are conceived of as entirely inactive and thus incapable of producing criminal conduct). However, in the situation examined at EU, 99–103, God is neither the immediate nor the sole cause of criminal conduct but is only its *ultimate* cause—which is (at least) a different matter.

21. For further discussion of these passages in the *Enquiry*, see, e.g., Flew, *Hume's Philosophy of Belief*, 160–65, and Gaskin, *Hume's Philosophy of Religion*, 69–73.

22. Significant difficulties are apparent in Hume's discussion of this matter. In general, Hume takes the view that character and conduct naturally gives rise to moral sentiment *whatever* the nature of the particular causes that produce it. His remarks in the passage under consideration indicate, however, that he wavers on this issue when the (ultimate) cause of a person's character and conduct is supposed to be *another agent* who *controls* (i.e. intentionally, with design and purpose) the volitions and actions of the person concerned. Within the confines of his own system, Hume cannot allow that human agents subject to the control of "superior beings" cease to be accountable. To concede this point would involve a much more basic challenge to the general assumption that the *way* that character and conduct is conditioned (including its ultimate source) is irrelevant to the responsibility of the agents concerned. For a contemporary perspective on this important matter, see Dennett, *Elbow Room*, esp. chps. 1 and 3.

23. In the final paragraph of Sec. 8 of the first *Enquiry*, Hume firmly and tersely closes the door on the most obvious alternative route of escape for the theist. That is, he argues that if the theist tries to avoid these (absurd) consequences by rejecting the doctrine of necessity in favour of that of indifference, then we simply run into another set of absurdities. In this case, the impossibility of reconciling "the indifference and contingency of human actions with [God's] prescience" (EU, 103). Having established these points, Hume suggests that we drop these (theologically inspired) "obscurities and perplexities" and return to "the examination of common life".

24. A particularly explicit statement of this view can be found in Flew, *Hume's Philosophy of Belief*, 7–12. Flew argues that one significant difference between the *Treatise* and the first *Enquiry* is that in the earlier work "there is no hint at all" of Hume's aggressive polemics against the theological speculations of religious philosophers. Mossner's standard biography of Hume lends some credence to this claim. Mossner suggests that when Hume published the *Treatise* he was counting on a "serious consideration of his philosophy as philosophy, rather than as religious controversy" (*Life of David Hume*, 113). In recent years, several influential studies of Hume's philosophy have appeared which discuss the central doctrines of the *Treatise* (i.e. scepticism, naturalism, etc.) but nevertheless have little or nothing to say about their relevance to matters of religion. See, e.g., Stroud, *Hume*; and Fogelin, *Hume's Skepticism*.

25. These papers include "Hume's *Treatise* and Hobbes's *The Elements of Law*"; "Skepticism and Natural Religion in Hume's *Treatise*"; "'Atheism' and the Title-Page of Hume's *Treatise*"; "A Hobbist Tory: Johnson on Hume"; "Epigram, Pantheists, and Freethought in Hume's *Treatise*"; "Hume's *Treatise* and the Clarke-Collins Controversy". In these papers, I show that Hume's anti-Christian project in the *Treatise* draws from an "atheistic" tradition of thought that includes, most notably, Hobbes and Spinoza. Related to this, the most prominent and consistent target of Hume's battery of sceptical, antirationalist arguments in the *Treatise* is Samuel Clarke. Clarke was the most eminent Newtonian philosopher in early eighteenth-century Britain, and he was a severe critic of Hobbes and Spinoza. In his highly influential Boyle Lectures of 1704–1705 (i.e. his *Discourse Concerning the Being and Attributes of God*), Clarke sought to *demonstrably* refute the "atheistic" philosophy of "Hobbes, Spinoza And their Followers" and to *prove* the "truth and certainty" of the Christian religion. It is, I maintain, this debate between "atheists" and defenders of the the Christian religion that is fundamental to understanding Hume's basic intentions in the *Treatise* and, indeed, his philosophical development as a whole.

26. The "plan" and structure of Hume's *Treatise* is modelled after Hobbes's works—specifically, *The Elements of Law* and the first two parts of *Leviathan*. For further details and evidence concerning this relationship, see my "Hume's *Treatise* and Hobbes's *The Elements of Law*".

27. This is an important theme in the writings of Butler, Berkeley, and especially Clarke. See Butler, *Analogy*, chp. 6, esp. p. 115, where Butler states that "the opinion of Necesssity seems to be the very basis, upon which infidelity grounds itself". Berkeley, *Alciphron*, 7th dialogue, secs. 17–19. Clarke's writings on this subject were enormously influential throughout the eighteenth century. Clarke vigorously attacked the necessitarianism of Hobbes, Spinoza, and their "followers" and sought to defend the free will position. (This was part of his larger project to demonstrably refute the "atheistic" philosophy of Hobbes, Spinoza, and their followers.) Clarke's views on free will are presented in the *Discourse*, Pt. 1, "A Demonstration of the Being and Attributes of God", esp. prop. 9 (*Works*, II, 548–53); and also in his series of philosophical exchanges with Anthony Collins, published under the title *A Letter to Mr. Dodwell* and reprinted in the *Works*, III, 719f. See esp. pp. 851 and 905–6, where Clarke argues that the doctrine of liberty is required for religion and morality. (Cf. Hume's comments on

this subject at T, 409, and EU, 96–97.) For further discussion, see my "Hume's *Treatise* and the Clarke-Collins Controversy".

28. Hume's attack on the doctrine of the immortality of the soul is presented in the *Treatise* at I, iv, 5 and 6. Clarke and Butler are, again, particularly prominent and obvious targets of Hume's sceptical arguments in this context. Hume's contemporaries were perfectly aware of Hume's anti-Christian intentions in these passages and, indeed, throughout the *Treatise*. See, e.g., the charges raised against Hume as presented in *A Letter from a Gentleman* (i.e. "universal scepticism", "atheism", "denying the immateriality of the soul, and the consequences flowing from this denial", etc.). These issues are discussed at further length in my "Skepticism and Natural Religion in Hume's *Treatise*" and in "Hume's *Treatise* and the Clarke-Collins Controversy".

29. Hume's anti-Christian view is well expressed by Nietzsche in the following (sharp) terms: "In Christianity neither morality nor religion come into contact with reality at any point. Nothing but imaginary *causes* ('God', 'soul', 'ego', 'spirit', 'free will'—or 'unfree will'): nothing but imaginary *effects* ('sin', 'redemption', 'grace', 'punishment', 'forgiveness of sins'). A traffic between imaginary *beings* ('God', 'spirits', 'souls'). . . . This purely fictitious world . . . falsifies, disvalues and denies actuality" (*The Anti-Christ*, sec. 15).

12

Responsibility Naturalized:
A Qualified Defence of Hume

Men are now cured of their passion for hypotheses and systems in natural philosophy, and will hearken to no arguments but those which are derived from
experience. It is full time they should attempt a like reformation in all moral
disquisitions; and reject every system of ethics, however subtle and ingenious,
which is not founded on fact and observation.

Hume, *An Enquiry concerning the Principles of Morals*

The hypothesis which we embrace is plain. It maintains that morality is determined
by sentiment. . . . If you call this metaphysics, and find anything abstruse here,
you need only conclude that your turn of mind is not suited to the moral sciences.

Hume, *An Enquiry concerning the Principles of Morals*

Throughout this study, I have been concerned to draw attention to the significance
of what I have termed the "naturalistic" aspects of Hume's theory of responsibility.
There are, I have argued, two related senses in which Hume's theory is naturalistic
(see chp. 4, sec. 3). First, Hume insists on an empirical, descriptive approach to this
issue. An adequate theory of responsibility, it is held, must be based on an informed
and plausible moral psychology. With this in view, Hume locates the foundation of
moral responsibility in the observable features of human nature. Second, Hume's
theory is also naturalistic in the sense that it places emphasis on the role of emotion
in this sphere. Specifically, responsibility has to be explained in terms of the structure of human feeling. These closely related aspects of Hume's approach may be
distinguished as his "scientific" and "feeling" naturalism. In the preceding chapters,
I have described the significance of these naturalistic aspects of Hume's theory of
responsibility in relation to the details of his system. In this concluding chapter, I
consider the wider and more general significance of Hume's naturalistic approach to
the problem of responsibility. I am especially concerned to explain the relevance of
Hume's naturalism about responsibility to his views regarding moral freedom.

I

According to the classical interpretation, Hume approaches the issue of responsibility primarily through the free will problem. It is also claimed that Hume's general

strategy or approach is essentially conceptual or "verbal". I have argued that it is a mistake to interpret Hume's views on this subject in these terms. Nevertheless, so interpreted, Hume is presented as taking what may be described as a *rationalistic* approach to the problem of responsibility. We can appreciate the general significance of Hume's naturalism more fully by explaining how it contrasts with the rationalistic approach.

By and large, the major parties in the free will dispute (i.e. libertarians, compatibilists, and moral sceptics) share fundamental rationalistic assumptions. In particular, what they share is the assumption that we must begin our investigations by way of *reflecting* on, or *thinking about*, the concept (idea, notion, etc.) of responsibility and its immediate relatives (e.g. freedom). Having started from the concept, it is argued, we must *then*, on this basis, proceed to see if that concept has any application. In this way, the rationalistic approach suggests that our investigations must be separated into two distinct steps. The first step involves an a priori articulation—or, perhaps more accurately, an a priori construction—of the concept of responsibility and the conditions required for its application. At this stage, an effort is made to identify some specific property, power, or quality in virtue of which an agent may be said to be responsible. It is, generally speaking, a further unchallenged assumption of the rationalistic approach that the key element in question must be some particular mode of freedom. Accordingly, these philosophers see a very intimate link between these two concepts.[1] Second, on the basis of this theoretical construct, the rationalist then proceeds to examine the human condition, both its internal and external circumstances, to see if we are in fact ever justified in applying this concept.

Corresponding to these two stages of the rationalistic approach, there are two areas of potential sceptical crisis. First, the sceptic might claim that analysis reveals the concept of responsibility to be, in some way, irredeemably "incoherent", "obscure", or "meaningless". In these circumstances, it is argued, we have no choice—insofar as we hope to maintain the integrity of our moral language—but to jettison this concept in favour of some suitably emended version which we can make some sense of. Second, the sceptic might argue that, although this concept is perfectly coherent and intelligible in itself, it nevertheless lacks any application to human beings as we find them. Thus it might be argued that, if we look at the human condition and consider carefully the limitations of human nature, then we must conclude that we lack the requisite powers, capacities, or qualities which this concept demands of us. It is important to note that these two sceptical challenges raise quite distinct sorts of difficulties and that these difficulties correspond to two quite distinct stages in the rationalistic approach.[2]

When we start from this rationalistic position, we are, from the very beginning, in constant danger of falling prey to the sceptic's doubts. We might find either that this concept has no coherent content or that it has no application in practice. Clearly, then, as soon as we embark on the rationalistic approach, we begin moving along a path that takes us right up to the precipice of scepticism. In response to this situation, the rationalistic philosophers divide into two camps. Some of them, the rationalistic sceptics, take the leap. Others, the rationalistic antisceptics, desperately cling to the ledge. What these two parties share, however, is their understanding of what is required of any adequate (philosophical) justification of responsibility. That is to say, for these philosophers, an adequate justification of responsibility must proceed through the two stages of the rationalistic approach described above. According to them, such a justification requires the following: (1) a coherent and intelligible concept of responsibility and an account of its conditions of applicability; (2) that we show that this concept does indeed have some application (to human beings); *and* (3) that we tackle this problem in this order—from the concept to its application. The maxim of the rationalistic approach may thus be characterized as "think, *then* look". A rationalistic approach to responsibility of this nature presupposes that the entire framework of responsibility requires some general justification of this kind.

Unlike the rationalistic sceptic, the rationalistic antisceptic believes he can provide an adequate justification for responsibility—that is, one which succeeds in overcoming *both* of the hurdles which the sceptic might throw in their path. Philosophers in this tradition view the sceptic's challenge as a very real threat to the integrity of our moral life. For this reason, they view their philosophical objective as nothing less than the defence and preservation of the whole edifice of human responsibility and freedom. This edifice, they believe, is constantly in danger of collapse as a result of the corroding and undermining work of the philosophical sceptic.[3] When it comes to presenting their own justifications of responsibility, however, the rationalistic antisceptics have encountered seemingly intractable problems.[4]

In response to the sceptic's challenge, the rationalistic antisceptic tradition has developed two dominant strategies: traditional libertarianism and classical compatibilism. Both these strategies constitute an attempt to "justify responsibility". That is, they both seek to preserve the whole edifice of responsibility and freedom by way of shoring up its (supposed) foundations. Generally speaking, the libertarian begins with an attempt to articulate a fully adequate account of responsibility and freedom. On the libertarian account, responsibility demands "free will" or "categorical freedom". In response to these difficulties associated with the dilemma of determinism, libertarians have had to construct their own distinctive metaphysics.[5] On the whole, they recognize that without some relevant metaphysical apparatus, they will remain firmly impaled on the protruding horn of chance. In many respects, the classical compatibilist strategy is the reverse of that of the libertarian. That is to say, compatibilists approach the enterprise of justifying responsibility with most of the key elements of their metaphysical base *already* clearly defined. To this extent, the compatibilist project seems to start from somewhat surer foundations. Here, however, the compatibilist's difficulties begin. Their account of responsibility and freedom must be constructed from *within* the constraints and limitations imposed by their preestablished metaphysical base. Furthermore, their construction must not only remain true to its metaphysical base but must also keep the compatibilist a safe distance from the apparent dangers posed by the horn of necessity.[6]

The most common charge levelled against the libertarian strategy is that it ultimately depends on what Strawson describes as "obscure and panicky metaphysics" (FR, 80). In order to avoid impaling themselves on the horn of chance, libertarians must construct a metaphysical base whose very *coherence* is in doubt. On the other hand, compatibilists, in order to avoid impaling themselves on the horn of necessity, must rest satisfied with notions of responsibility and freedom whose *adequacy* is in doubt. That is to say, it is argued that the success of the compatibilist project depends entirely on an appeal to notions which are mere shadows of those which we ordinarily employ and appeal to.[7] In this way, when we embark on the project of "justifying responsibility", we find ourselves either having to appeal to notions which have the appearance of being irredeemably obscure, or else, having set ourselves to eliminate such obscurities, we find that all we have succeeded in defending and preserving is an inadequate conception of responsibility and freedom which is incapable of doing the work we demand of it. In short, the rationalistic antisceptic's project of justifying responsibility appears to oscillate between incoherence and inadequacy and therefore falls to its knees as soon as it encounters the very first hurdle. It would seem, then, that we are quite unable to articulate a credible notion of responsibility and freedom by way of the rationalistic approach. Clearly, an incoherent notion has no intelligible conditions of application. It is also clear that the justified application of an impoverished notion of responsibility will hardly satisfy those who have sought to preserve and defend the full-blooded original.[8]

Neither sceptical nor antisceptical arguments of the rationalistic variety have had a great impact on our actual practice. These arguments are rather like gears that spin and turn but fail to engage the rest of the machinery. We find that the other gears, outside of philosophical life, continue to operate smoothly and efficiently no matter what direction these philosophical gears may move in. On the whole, the ordinary person carries on as before and takes little notice of the philosophical battles which rage in other quarters. By and large, these individuals are neither comforted nor disturbed by the "proofs" which rationalistic philosophers have pulled out of their hats. It would be quite wrong, however, to conclude that in ordinary life we find that most people are unconcerned with the rationale which lies behind their day-to-day ascriptions of responsibility. On the contrary, such individuals often display great sensitivity and sophistication when it comes to noticing significant distinctions and relevantly different cases or circumstances, and they judge the individuals concerned accordingly. In light of this, it may be argued that the problem of responsibility as the rationalist conceives of it is not so much *intractable* as simply *misconceived*. For this reason, we may call into question the rationalist's general approach to "the problem of responsibility".

II

The wider methodological significance of Hume's naturalistic approach can be judged in terms of the philosophical impasse which the rationalistic approach has reached on the free will issue. According to Hume, we must eschew rationalistic, a priori investigations into the nature and conditions of responsibility in favour of a more empirical approach. More specifically, we must carefully examine and describe the attitudes, sentiments, and practices associated with responsibility *as we find them*. Only then will we be in a position to effectively criticize and evaluate the rationality of the attitudes, sentiments, and practices in question. Moreover, it is by this route that we will be able to discover *what sort* of justifications are actually required (or not required) in this sphere.

Whereas the rationalist starts from the concept of responsibility, the naturalist starts from the *fact* of responsibility. That is, our attitudes, sentiments, and practices in this sphere present themselves as objects for our observation. It is an error of the rationalist's procedure to treat these objects as idealized entities to be theorized over and perfected in a Platonic heaven and then brought back down to earth to see how they "fit". The naturalist, unlike the rationalist, examines responsibility as she finds it. Its foundations are rooted not in the realm of concepts but rather in human nature and the human condition.

The naturalistic philosopher proceeds to evaluate *critically* the rationale of responsibility as already embodied in moral life. If this rationale suffers from incoherence or inconsistency, then it is an incoherence or inconsistency which can be identified and located in our actual practice. Accordingly, naturalists do not ask, "Does the concept of responsibility have any application to human beings?" Rather, they ask, "Do the attitudes, sentiments, and practices *which are constitutive of responsibility* have any adequate or proper justification?" With their procedure and task formulated in this manner, naturalistic philosophers are in a position to examine the nature and adequacy of the justifications involved. In this way, it should be clear that the naturalistic approach is in no way committed to "leaving everything as it is". There is no reason whatsoever why the naturalistic philosopher should be committed to the view that the attitudes, sentiments, and practices in question are in all respects perfectly reasonable. Furthermore, where these faults and weaknesses are identified, the naturalistic philosopher is well placed to suggest how, and when, they can be removed or remedied. Hence, this approach to responsibility in no way assumes that the entire superstructure of responsibility is entirely sound. What it does assume, contrary to the rationalistic approach, is that we must begin our investigation from *within* this structure. If alterations have to be made, then they have to be made from *inside*.[9]

Barry Stroud makes the following observation concerning Hume's overall naturalistic approach to the study of humankind:

> [Hume] thought we could understand what human beings do, and why and how, only by studying them as part of nature, by trying to determine the origins of various thoughts, feelings, reactions and other human 'products' within the familiar world. The abstract study of such things as 'meanings', 'concepts' and 'principles' was to be engaged in only in so far as they could be grounded in *what people actually think, feel and do in human life*. (*Hume*, 222; my emphasis)[10]

In a similar vein, Alasdair MacIntyre states that "the virtue of Hume's ethics, like that of Aristotle and unlike that of Kant, is that it seeks to *preserve morality as something psychologically intelligible*".[11] The dominant trends in twentieth-century, English-speaking philosophy have been fundamentally hostile to the naturalistic outlook. More specifically, for the better part of this century, moral philosophy has been primarily concerned with the study of moral language and with the formal features of moral reasoning. This "abstract" approach to moral life (to use Stroud's term) has strongly encouraged philosophers to embrace the rationalistic rather than the naturalistic approach to the problem of responsibility. There are, nevertheless, clear signs in the past decade or so that the "rationalistic" approach to moral life is less dominant than it once was. It is noticeable, for example, that more recent work in moral philosophy tends to reflect a stronger interest in the relevance of moral psychology and moral development. To this extent contemporary ethics has taken something of "a Humean turn". For this reason, therefore, the time may be ripe for a better appreciation of the naturalistic aspects of Hume's approach to responsibility.[12]

The inadequacies and weaknesses of the rationalistic approach to responsibility provide some insight into the more general and more fundamental weaknesses of the rationalistic approach to morals.[13] In this context, however, the point I am especially concerned to emphasize is that the naturalistic approach has the enormous merit of endeavouring to reunite the study of moral philosophy with the study of human psychology. It invites us to view moral responsibility as something that must be understood in terms of a human nature that has, as Murdoch puts it, "certain discoverable attributes".[14] This is, as I have indicated, a theme that is of considerable significance for Hume's entire approach to moral life.

III

Corresponding to the "feeling" dimension of Hume's naturalism, there is an opposing antinaturalistic outlook. This is the philosophical view that reason alone, as opposed to feeling and emotion, must provide us with our understanding of the nature and conditions of responsibility. Accordingly, insofar as rival theories of responsibility tend to overlook or dismiss the role of feeling and emotion in this sphere, then they may be described as rationalistic in this further sense of the term. In highlighting the role of feeling and emotion in the sphere of responsibility, Hume's naturalistic approach once again touches on a theme of much wider and deeper significance in moral philosophy.

Just as moral philosophy in this century has tended to approach its subject matter abstractly, so, too, it has tended to downplay, or ignore, the role of emotion and feeling in moral life. This aspect of the rationalistic outlook, however, has also had its critics.[15] Indeed, some philosophers have been concerned to argue that these shortcomings of modern moral philosophy have very deep roots. Many years ago, John MacMurray diagnosed the lure and danger of this aspect of the rationalistic outlook in terms of what he described as "the modern dilemma". His remarks are in several respects very Humean, and they are therefore worth quoting at length.

> The tradition of our civilization is heavily biased in favour of the intellect against the emotions. We think that it is wise to trust our minds, and foolish to trust our feelings. We consider that it is the human intellect that raises man above the level of the animal creation, while the emotional movements in us are what gives us kinship with the animals. We behave in terms of that bias. Faced with a problem, we invariably turn to the intellect to solve it for us. . . . As a result we admire and rely upon all those expressions of human life which are intellectual . . . and we spend much time and labour on the task of developing our intellects and training our capacity to think; while we hardly ever think it necessary, or even possible, to train our capacity for feeling. (*Freedom in the Modern World*, 44–45)

MacMurray goes on to note that this bias in favour of the intellect has a long history. Its roots, he suggests, "lie in that very ancient doctrine that teaches the evil of desire and the necessity of subduing desire". He proceeds to argue that these observations shed light on the modern predicament.

It is a commonplace that you cannot argue any man into a real belief if his feelings are set against it. I want you to consider the consequences of this with me for a little, for it is the heart of the modern dilemma. A merely intellectual force is powerless against an emotional resistance. . . . Unless the emotions and the intellect are in harmony, rational action will be paralyzed. . . . In the modern period, that is to say since the break-up of the mediaeval world, there has been an immense development of knowledge. There has, however, been no corresponding emotional development. As a result we are intellectually civilized and emotionally primitive. . . . We have set the intellect free and kept emotion in chains. That is a summary of the inner history of the modern world. (*Freedom in the Modern World*, 46–48)[16]

MacMurray's comments were written well over half a century ago. They are, however, still as pertinent today as they were when they were first written.

It is particularly important to note that MacMurray is concerned to describe a crisis in our self-understanding, one which affects our whole practical perspective on the world. In this way, it may be argued that the general aversion to a proper recognition of the role of feeling and emotion in morals is a deeply ingrained feature of the modern outlook and is a source of many of the seemingly intractable perplexities of modern life. Clearly, then, as long as we continue to overintellectualize human nature and disparage the emotions, we will not only retard and distort our emotional development but find it impossible to achieve the sort of self-understanding on which progress in moral philosophy must depend.[17] This state of affairs is of considerable relevance to the problem of responsibility. Given the widespread tendency to disparage the emotions—both in moral philosophy and beyond—it is, once again, less than surprising to find that many contemporary philosophers remain inclined to embrace a rationalistic rather than a naturalistic approach to responsibility.

I have argued that corresponding to the two dimensions of Hume's naturalism (i.e. his "scientific" and "feeling" naturalism), there exist two opposing dimensions in the rationalistic outlook: disdain for the empirical study of human nature and (and related to this) lack of concern with the role of feeling and emotion in the sphere of responsibility. This opposition in outlook and approach, I maintain, touches on problems that cut much deeper and wider in moral philosophy. Throughout most of this century, the dominant outlook in moral philosophy has been rationalistic in both senses of the term described above. This explains in some measure the continuing appeal of the rationalistic approach to responsibility. Nevertheless, as I have already indicated, the tide seems to be turning against the rationalistic approach, and thus what Hume has to say on the subject of responsibility may find an increasingly receptive audience.

IV

I have argued that it is, generally speaking, an unquestioned assumption—we might say a dogma—of the rationalistic approach that the key item for any adequate analysis of responsibility is the concept of freedom. It is thus a commonplace to find that philosophers analyse the concept of responsibility directly in terms of freedom.[18] The classical interpretation, as I have indicated, presents Hume as committed to a rationalistic strategy of this kind. According to this view, the central feature of Hume's theory of responsibility is his account of freedom, in particular his (conceptual) distinction between "liberty of spontaneity" and "liberty of indifference". Hume, it is claimed, takes the view that responsibility is, quite simply, a matter of acting freely (i.e. "voluntarism"). The difficulty for Hume, therefore, is to state accurately what is required for free action.[19] The naturalistic interpretation makes plain that this account of Hume's position is fundamentally misleading and that it fails, in particular, to provide an adequate account of Hume's understanding of the relationship between responsibility and freedom.

What is central to Hume's theory of responsibility is his *descriptive* account of the workings of moral sentiment. Hume's approach to the narrower issue of "free will" can be properly understood only within this wider framework. More specifically, Hume's arguments concerning the relevance of the distinction between the two kinds of "liberty" and the indispensability of "necessity" to ascriptions of responsibility are intimately tied to his descriptive account of the mechanism which generates the moral sentiments. The relevance of his "definitions" of "liberty" and "necessity" must be understood in these terms. It is evident, then, that in the absence of a clear account of the naturalistic elements of Hume's system, it is not possible to grasp why Hume believes that it is "only upon the principles of necessity, that a person acquires any merit or demerit from his actions" (T, 411); nor is it possible to explain properly why he believes that liberty of indifference would entirely "subvert" morality (T, 410–11). On Hume's account, therefore, an adequate understanding of the *sort of* freedom that is required for responsibility depends on a *prior* description of the workings of moral sentiment.

Related to this, it is a fundamental insight of Hume's discussion of these matters that issues of responsibility are not *reducible* to the problem of "free will". Action is, of course, especially important because it reveals an agent's will and intention. However, it constitutes just one kind of "sign" of a person's character or mental qualities. Desires and feelings, as well as natural abilities, Hume holds, can also manifest pleasurable or painful qualities of mind, even though they are not (typically) under the control of the agent's will and can, indeed, be expressed involuntarily. We are accountable for these aspects of mind, he maintains, even though they arise involuntarily and may be manifested involuntarily. In this way, according to Hume, we can hold people responsible for qualities of mind that they have no control over and that are indicative of neither their will nor their intentions. Liberty of spontaneity or freedom, therefore, is not always necessary for responsibility. All that is necessary is that the agent manifest (signs of) pleasurable or painful qualities of mind, because these will naturally arouse moral sentiments of the appropriate kind.

The fact that it is moral sentiment, rather than freedom, that is fundamental to Hume's theory of responsibility is especially apparent when we compare Hume and Smith on this subject. Hume and Smith, as I have pointed out, agree on the fundamental principle of the naturalist's position, namely, that responsibility must be interpreted in terms of the working of moral sentiment. There is, moreover, no *disagreement* between Hume and Smith on the subject of free will. The reason for this is that Smith is *silent* on this matter—even though he has a great deal to say about issues of responsibility.[20] Nevertheless, as we have noted, despite the significant affinities between Hume and Smith on this subject, there are a whole range of quite basic differences between their positions. They differ, for example, about whether it is (beliefs about) particular actions or their underlying character traits that arouse moral sentiment (i.e. the sense of merit or demerit); they disagree about whether the consequences of action, in themselves, affect our moral evaluation of an agent; they disagree about whether a person can be held accountable merely for feelings and desires; and they disagree about the relationship between our moral sentiments and our retributive practices. All of these are matters of fundamental importance. Disagreement on these matters, however, does not reflect any disagreement on the narrower question of free will. The significance of all this is that it shows that a common commitment to the naturalistic approach allows for considerable disagreement and divergence on a wide range of issues that are of basic importance for our understanding of responsibility. It also shows that the conception of freedom, important as it is, does not lie at the heart of the naturalistic approach. Indeed, it is possible to agree about the basic principles of the naturalistic approach and nevertheless to disagree about the nature of moral freedom and its relation to responsibility.[21]

We can shed further light on the specific significance of Hume's account of freedom in relation to his (naturalistic) theory of responsibility by comparing Hume's views with those of Hobbes and Schlick. Hume's definition of freedom (T, 407–8; EU, 95) is essentially that of both Hobbes and Schlick (i.e. understood as an absence of external impediments to action). So they are, indeed, generally agreed about what *freedom* (i.e. "liberty") consists in.[22] Clearly, however, as I have explained in some detail, they are not agreed about wider issues concerning the nature and conditions of responsibility—because neither Hobbes nor Schlick allows for any role for moral sentiment in this sphere. For this reason, although Hume has a similar conception of freedom, his understanding of its *significance* in relation to responsibility is wholly different from the sorts of accounts that Hobbes and Schlick have put forward. More specifically, according to Hume, we cannot explain *why* freedom, so interpreted, is of importance to ascriptions of responsibility—nor why libertarian conceptions must be rejected—until we can explain its relevance to the working of the mechanism that produces the moral sentiments. Freedom, in short, has a quite different *role* to play in the framework of Hume's moral system. This is true even though Hume does not disagree with Hobbes and Schlick about the *nature* of freedom and what it consists in.

Clearly, then, it is a radical mistake to assimilate Hume's theory of moral responsibility with the positions of Hobbes and Schlick simply on the ground that they all have a shared conception of freedom. Unlike Hobbes and Schlick, Hume holds that issues of responsibility must be interpreted in terms of our natural human propensity to entertain moral sentiments toward our fellow human beings. Questions concerning moral freedom—and the general relationship between freedom and moral responsibility—must be considered inside this naturalistic context. Any effort to address the free will problem outside this framework is bound to mislead and perplex us. This is a theme of fundamental importance for Hume's moral philosophy.

The upshot of these (historical) comparisons is evident. The essential feature of Hume's theory of responsibility (i.e. its "naturalism") is independent of the account of freedom (i.e. liberty of spontaneity). It is possible to embrace the naturalistic aspect of the theory of responsibility without being committed to the suggested account of freedom (e.g. Smith, Butler), and, similarly, it is possible to embrace Hume's account of freedom without being committed to his naturalistic theory of responsibility (e.g. Hobbes, Schlick). What is distinctive and interesting about Hume's strategy is how he combines these specific elements and how he explains their relationship. These aspects of Hume's strategy are wholly obscured by the classical interpretation.

V

My remarks in this chapter make clear that I am broadly sympathetic to Hume's naturalistic approach to responsibility. I am also sympathetic, more specifically, to Hume's general understanding of the place of the free will problem in relation to the wider issue of responsibility. That is to say, I believe Hume is correct in holding that the issue of responsibility is not reducible to the free will problem and that the whole question of free will needs to be addressed within the framework of an account of the workings of moral sentiment. However, beyond this, I have also argued, in various passages of this book, that Hume's naturalistic theory of responsibility suffers from several serious shortcomings, or flaws, and that one of the most important of these is his "thin" account of moral freedom. (See my remarks at the end of chp. 5.) This is a weakness that relates to two other shortcomings in Hume's position: his (inadequate) account of moral capacity and his (mistaken) account of moral virtue.

As I have explained, according to the classical interpretation, Hume's account of freedom is the central feature of his theory of responsibility. Although this claim is, in my view, wholly mistaken, it is nevertheless true that, historically speaking, it is this aspect of Hume's discussion that has been especially influential. This is unfortunate, because (as Stroud notes) Hume's remarks on this matter are not very original, and, more important, they are clearly inadequate.

The freedom to act according to the determinations of our own will is, of course, a necessary capacity for a person to be a moral agent. Indeed, without such a capacity, a person cannot be an *agent* at all. However, such a capacity (i.e. to act according to the determinations of our desires and willings) is possessed by many individuals who are clearly not *moral* agents (e.g. children, animals, the mentally ill). It follows, then, that "liberty of spontaneity" does not suffice to distinguish moral from nonmoral agents—that is, it does not serve to identify individuals we may legitimately regard as objects of moral sentiment. What, then, is missing from Hume's account? The libertarian answer is straightforward: *Moral* agents require a capacity for free will (i.e. liberty of indifference, rather than mere liberty of spontaneity). This response, as we have discussed, has its own well-known difficulties. The question remains, however: How are we to distinguish moral from nonmoral agents if not on the basis of the capacity for free will?

There is, evidently, an intimate link between the issue of moral freedom and moral capacity. Libertarians claim that our distinguishing moral capacity is the capacity of free will (however it may be explained). On any account, therefore, naturalists like Hume require *some* relevant and plausible description of the sorts of capacities that render a person an appropriate object of *moral* sentiment. Hume's effort to deal with this matter, I have argued, is not acceptable (chp. 6, sec. 2). That is, Hume holds that what makes a person an object of moral sentiment is that he is judged to possess pleasurable or painful qualities of mind. Any person who has such qualities is, on this view, an appropriate (i.e. natural) object of moral sentiment. This would render (very young) children, the mentally ill, the mentally disabled, and other such individuals (fully) morally accountable. Beyond this, it is, Hume claims, simply an ultimate fact about human beings that we do not entertain moral sentiments toward (other) animals—even though they, too, might possess pleasurable or painful qualities of mind. Clearly, Hume's account is incapable of drawing required distinctions in this sphere. What is needed, therefore, is an alternative description of the sorts of moral capacities required for the naturalistic theory. Elsewhere in this work, I have sketched what I take to be the basic elements of such an alternative account (chp. 6., sec. 2; chp. 9., sec. 2).

Hume's failure to (properly) describe the sort(s) of capacities required to render a person an appropriate object of moral sentiment is related to his faulty account of moral virtue. According to Hume, a virtue is simply a pleasant quality of mind. To be capable of moral virtue, therefore, requires nothing more than possessing traits or qualities of this kind. Again, as I have argued before, this account will not do—because it is much too wide in scope (chp. 6, sec. 2; chp. 8, sec. 3; chp. 9, sec. 1). Pleasurable and painful qualities of mind do not, as such, constitute moral virtues and vices (although virtues and vices might well be pleasurable or painful). What is essential to the capacity for moral virtue, in very general terms, is that a person be capable of manifesting a particular mode or way of *valuing* the interests and concerns of others, as well as herself; and that the person be capable of becoming aware or self-conscious about these modes of desire and conduct, and aware of how such dispositions influence the moral sentiments of those that she is dealing with. Such an individual requires a capacity for language and, through this, self-understanding and self-criticism. As capacities of this kind develop, a person will become, by degrees, a full member of the moral community and an appropriate object of moral sentiment.[23] Capacities of this general kind seem, at the very minimum, necessary for a person to participate fully in the moral life of the community and to be recognized as an individual who stands in the relevant relations to her fellows.

This sketch suggests that there is a close connexion between Hume's difficulties in respect of his understanding of moral virtue and his lack of any adequate account of moral capacity. Let us return to the issue of the relation between moral capacity and moral freedom. Clearly, it is possible to give a more adequate description of the nature of moral capacities which distinguish responsible from nonresponsible agents without any appeal to the "free will" metaphysics of libertarianism. More specifically, what is required is that we carefully describe the (sophisticated and complex) capacities of moral agents: their capacity to articulate their desires and intentions, to reflect on their character and the structure of their will, and to alter or amend them on this basis. This provides us with an account of moral capacity that is entirely consistent with the principles of naturalism and with the metaphysics of determinism. More important, it lays the foundations for a more adequate understanding of moral *freedom*. Within this framework, we can intelligibly consider problems of freedom that extend well beyond mere freedom of *action*. Specifically, this account suggests how agents can find "internal" barriers to their freedom (e.g. in the form of having a will they do not want or do not value). It also explains how we can distinguish human agents who, although they *act* freely, are incapable of exercising the sort of higher activities required for (full) moral responsibility (e.g. critical self-reflection). These sorts of considerations about the nature of moral capacity suggest that the naturalistic approach Hume recommends requires a much richer description of the nature of moral freedom and that this description must be rooted in a more adequate account of moral capacity. A strategy of this sort will not give libertarians and incompatibilists everything they want, but it will go a long way toward addressing their *legitimate* concerns.

Clearly, then, as many critics of Hume have argued, we do require a more sophisticated account of moral freedom than that of "liberty of spontaneity". Related to this, the naturalistic theory of responsibility requires a more plausible and more substantial account of moral capacity than Hume provides us with. It is, I have argued, possible to provide such an account without any appeal to the (obscure) "free will" metaphysics of libertarianism. These observations plainly suggest that there are serious weaknesses and shortcomings in Hume's system in respect of these issues. However, they do not discredit the very fundamental insights that emerge from Hume's discussion. In particular, the fact that we require a more *elaborate* account of moral freedom and moral capacity does not discredit the view that the problem of freedom is best understood through a naturalistic approach to responsibility. On the contrary, the nature of the problem of freedom is significantly clarified on this approach (although, evidently, more work needs to be done on this). More generally, whatever difficulties remain with Hume's account, he has, nevertheless, provided us with strong reasons for thinking that many philosophers have misconceived the relationship between responsibility and freedom, and that, standardly, they exaggerate the importance of voluntariness and control for moral evaluation.[24]

VI

In a short story entitled "The Metaphysician's Nightmare", Bertrand Russell claims that in Hell there is "a particularly painful chamber inhabited solely by philosophers who have refuted Hume".[25] For many philosophers, the route to that "particularly painful chamber" has begun with the misinterpretation of Hume's views. In this work, it has been my particular concern to show that, in both matters of detail and broad strategy, the classical or received interpretation of Hume on the subject of responsibility and freedom seriously misrepresents his position. What is at stake here is not simply a matter of narrow scholarly debate and exegesis. On the contrary, the contemporary interest of Hume's views on this subject lies primarily with that very aspect of his general strategy which the classical interpretation ignores—namely, his naturalism. If we neglect this aspect of his discussion then, I maintain, we will overlook those very elements and features of his discussion that are particularly illuminating in respect of the ongoing debate concerning responsibility and freedom.

Hume's detailed description of the mechanism of responsibility, and the way in which it depends on both moral sentiment and necessity, serves as the bridge over which he travels from metaphysics to morals, and it does much to bind the various elements of his philosophy into a connected and coherent whole. Moreover, his description of the nature and conditions of moral responsibility serves as the very foundation on which he builds his secular and scientific account of moral and social life—a project that is of the very essence of his anti-Christian fundamental intentions. Quite simply, then, it is not possible to acquire an adequate appreciation of Hume's overall moral philosophy, nor of his philosophy in general, unless these basic elements are properly understood.

I take the core of Hume's "science" of responsibility to be this. Moral responsibility is a given of human nature. It is constituted by, and takes the form of, moral sentiment. A moral sentiment is a mode of love or hate, or of pride or humility. These sentiments are the chains of our humanity. In the form of love or hate, they may hold us together or pull us apart. In the form of pride or humility, they may carry us through life or weigh down upon us. With every relationship we form, new links in these chains are forged. These are bonds that we can never free ourselves from. Our happiness depends in large measure on how we carry this burden in life. Be this as it may, whether we find the load heavy or light, these chains remain the bonds of our humanity and the indelible mark of our moral accountability. Beyond this, however, these chains do not extend to a future state nor bind us to any superior being. When, finally, we slip loose from all such human ties, we return to the condition from which we arose and are lost, again, in "the immense ocean of matter" (ESY, 176 [Sceptic]).

Notes

1. See, e.g., the article by Kaufman in *The Encyclopedia of Philosophy* ("Responsibility, Moral and Legal", vol. 7, 183–84). In a section entitled "Meaning and 'moral responsibility'", he writes, "Most persons would accept the following form of definition . . . . : A person is regarded as morally responsible for some act or occurrence x if and only if he is believed (1) to have done x, or to have brought x about; and (2) to have done it or brought it about freely." Kaufman goes on to note, however, that "Philosophers have too often supposed that the concept of 'freedom' essential to moral responsibility can be fixed independently of what it is to be responsible, and that only after the meaning of 'freedom' is specified can we determine whether and under what circumstances a person is responsible. But in fact what a person means by 'free,' 'freely,' or 'freedom' will reflect his moral convictions, and especially his views about justice, in the same way and for the same reasons that his conception of 'moral responsibility' will reflect these views".

2. In general, there is a fundamental difference between circumstances in which we have, on examination, no coherent and intelligible concept to apply, and circumstances in which we are unable to discover any cases in which the application of the concept would be justified. In the first case, our sceptical doubts are generated at the initial stage of critical reflection on our concepts; in the second case, they are generated when we attempt to "carry our concepts over to the world" and apply them. In the first case, the concept is revealed as empty, because it cannot be articulated—the difficulty lies in the concept itself. In the second case, the concept is revealed as empty, because we discover, on empirical investigation, that there are no objects in the world to which we would be justified in applying the concept. (Cf. Hobbes's remark: "I acknowledge this liberty, that I can do if I will; but to say, I can will if I will I take to be an absurd speech" (*Of Liberty and Necessity*, in Raphael, ed., *British Moralists*, I, 61–62).

3. The apparent significance of this task, and the threat the sceptic is taken to pose for it, perhaps explains why these issues arouse such passion and heat. The sceptical challenge in this sphere is viewed—at least by the (philosophical) antisceptic—as one which can affect

not just philosophical theory but also, far more importantly, concrete *moral practice*. To this extent the moral sceptic is regarded with a seriousness which few other sceptics receive. Unlike the philosopher who denies the existence of the external world or other minds, the moral sceptic is rarely viewed as a figure of mirth. In this sense, the free will issue is not regarded as "merely verbal" by the philosophical parties concerned. Ironically, however, although it is hotly debated within the philosophical community, the free will debate remains a rather remote and "academic" issue from the perspective of those outside the philosophical community—an observation that is perhaps of some significance.

4. In particular, these philosophers have found themselves unable to escape from the clutches of the dilemma of determinism. See chp. 1, sec. 1 in this volume.

5. The most influential and extreme version of this is to be found in Kant's system.

6. These observations suggest that although the libertarian and compatibilist are pursuing the same fundamental objective (viz. justifying responsibility), they are, nevertheless, in certain important respects, moving in opposite directions. More specifically, whereas libertarians seem to be willing to adapt their metaphysics to the requirements of their views on responsibility and freedom, compatibilists are inclined (or compelled) to adapt their views on responsibility and freedom to the requirements of their metaphysics. Historically speaking, this contrast is perfectly intelligible. Libertarians have generally been especially concerned to defend the integrity of our moral life, as they understand it, against what they take to be the illegitimate encroachment of the scientific worldview. By contrast, compatibilists have generally been concerned to push forward the ascendant scientific outlook in the face of what they perceive to be an essentially antiquated and irrational view of our moral life. In both cases, however, those concepts which are articulated first tend to place severe constraints on those deemed to be of secondary importance.

7. The force of claiming that these notions are somehow "inadequate" lies in the suggestion that they fail to support our supposition that human beings possess a certain "dignity" in virtue of which they are due "respect". Hence, these inadequacies have fatal consequences for any project which seeks to protect the integrity of our moral life.

8. It may be argued that it does not entirely do justice to the classical compatibilist tradition to overlook the empirical features of its strategy and to present it as "rationalistic". Certainly if we compare the classical compatibilist strategy with, for example, Kantian libertarianism—that is, a doctrine which "justifies" responsibility by appealing to the freedom of our noumenal (i.e. nonphenomenal) or rational selves—then there is something to be said for this claim. Nevertheless, in the twentieth century, with the general reorientation of the empiricist tradition from "psychologism" to "logical empiricism", there has been a tendency to place particular emphasis on the logical or conceptual features of the compatibilist strategy. Most important, it is almost always assumed by philosophers in this tradition that the "analysis" of (the concept of) responsibility primarily concerns the problem of free will.

9. We should not conclude from this—as Strawson appears to do (FR, 68, 70, 74)— that the sceptical challenge poses no *real* threat to the entire edifice of responsibility (i.e. that we will continue to hold other people responsible *whatever* sceptical arguments are put to us). As Nagel notes, criticisms that are "internal" to the whole superstructure of responsibility (i.e. internal to the "web" of moral sentiment) can *spread* and become comprehensive (*The View from Nowhere*, 125; cf. my "Strawson's Way of Naturalizing Responsibility"). Clearly, then, the naturalistic approach cannot *insulate* us from all forms of sceptical challenge. On the contrary, from any perspective, the sceptical challenge is both "real" and "legitimate"— the question is how to *meet* it.

10. It is, of course, ironic that Stroud makes this point—indeed, it constitutes a central theme of his interpretation of Hume's philosophy—given that Stroud entirely overlooks these features of Hume's system when it comes to issues of freedom and responsibility.

11. MacIntyre, "Hume on 'Is' and 'Ought'", 264. MacIntyre continues, "For the tradition which upholds the autonomy of ethics from Kant to Moore to Hare, moral principles are somehow self-explicable; they are logically independent of any assertion about human nature. Hume has been too often presented recently as an adherent of this tradition".

12. A number of works could be cited as evidence of this "Humean turn". See, e.g., Flanagan, *Varieties of Moral Personality*, and Gibbard, *Wise Choices, Apt Feelings*.

13. We may remember Bertrand Russell's observation that if the moralist ignores human nature, then "it is likely that human nature will ignore the claims of the moralist" (*Human Society in Ethics and Politics*, 18).

14. Murdoch's expression appears in the following context: "Human nature, as opposed to the nature of other hypothetical spiritual beings, has certain discoverable attributes, and these should be suitably considered in any discussion of morality" (*The Sovereignty of Good*, 78). It is important to note that moralists who are agreed that moral philosophy must be grafted onto an account of human nature might nevertheless be deeply divided about *what sort* of account of human nature is called for. In particular, there is a fundamental divide between those who believe that we require a teleological account of human nature in the Aristotelian tradition and those who demand a "mechanistic", nonteleological conception of human nature in the tradition of Hobbes, Spinoza, and Hume. (On this subject, see MacIntyre, *After Virtue*, chps. 4–6.)

15. Among our own contemporaries, Bernard Williams has probably been the most influential of these critics. Thirty years ago, Williams pointed out that "recent moral philosophy in Britain has not had much to say about the emotions". He went on to argue that, although emotions play a large part in moral thought, this "has not adequately been mirrored in the recent concerns of moral philosophers" ("Morality and the Emotions", 207). Clearly, however, this is changing. Along with the greater interest in moral psychology and moral development, more recent work in moral philosophy displays a great deal more understanding of the importance of emotion in moral life.

16. It should be noted that MacMurray's discussion is presented from a Christian perspective and is, therefore, in this respect, profoundly *non*-Humean. However, for our purposes, this is of little consequence. MacMurray elaborates on his views on this subject in *Reason and Emotion*, esp. 13–65.

17. The theme MacMurray touches on has, of course, deep roots that stretch beyond Hume to other thinkers, the most important of whom is probably Spinoza. A number of contemporary writers, outside of philosophy, have also commentated on these matters. See, e.g., Saul Bellow's remarks in the opening section of his early novel *Dangling Man*: "this is an era of hardboileddom. . . . Do you have feelings? There are correct and incorrect ways of indicating them. Do you have an inner life? It's nobody's business but your own. Do you have emotions? Strangle them. To a degree, everybody obeys this code. . . . Most serious matters are closed to the hard-boiled. They are unpracticed in introspection, and therefore badly equipped to deal with opponents whom they cannot shoot like big game or outdo in daring".

18. See note 1 above.

19. See, e.g., MacNabb, *David Hume*, 201–2, and Ayer, *Hume*, 77–78.

20. It is an important aspect of Hume's general account of responsibility to explain why "necessity" and "liberty" (properly understood) are "essential" to ascriptions of responsibility—i.e. to the generation of moral sentiment. Smith does not pursue these specific matters. He provides no account of either necessity or liberty. It is, however, worth noting that Smith describes the workings of desire, sentiment, and action in the "mechanical" language of "cause" and "effect" (see, e.g., TMS, 18, 67, 79, 82). (Beyond this, see also TMS, 289, where Smith describes "the whole machine of the world" as "that great chain of causes and effects which

has no beginning, and which will have no end". In general, Smith tacitly embraces a necessitarian outlook that is much influenced by Stoic philosophy.)

21. I note above, for example (chp. 5, sec. 4), that Hume and Strawson provide rather different accounts of moral freedom—even though their naturalistic approaches to responsibility are very similar. More significant, a moralist like Butler also takes a naturalistic approach to responsibility (see, e.g., "Nature of Virtue", in Raphael, ed., *British Moralists*, I, 378–86) but adheres to firmly libertarian principles on the matter of free will (*Analogy*, pt. 1, chp. 4).

22. Hobbes, *Of Liberty and Necessity*, in Raphael, ed., *British Moralists*, I, 68: "A *free agent* is he that can do if he will, and forbear if he will; and . . . *liberty* is the absence of external impediments"; Schlick, "When Is a Man Responsible?" 59: "A man is *free* if he does not act under *compulsion*, and he is compelled or unfree when he is hindered from without. . . . [A] man will be considered quite free and responsible if no such external compulsion is exerted upon him".

23. It is an interesting feature of moral development in the individual that as a person becomes increasingly able to *understand why* people entertain moral sentiments toward her, so that person becomes an increasingly *appropriate* object of such sentiments. Being legitimately held responsible, therefore, depends on the development of our capacity to be aware that we are an object of sentiments of this kind. In other words, we must not only be able to interpret our own desires, feelings, and conduct, but also be able to interpret the sentiments they arouse in others (chp. 6, note 14; chp. 8, sec. 1).

24. Compare Nietzsche's interesting and relevant remarks on this general theme (i.e. overcoming the prejudices of traditional morality) in *Beyond Good and Evil*, sec. 32.

25. Bertrand Russell, *Nightmares of Eminent Persons*.

Bibliography

When the original date of publication is relevant and diverges from the edition cited,
it is indicated in square brackets following the title.

Adams, Robert, "Involuntary Sin", *Philosophical Review*, 94 (1985), 3–31.

Alston, William, "Emotion and Feeling", in Edwards, ed., *The Encyclopedia of Philosophy*, vol. 2.

Anscombe, G. E. M., "Causality and Determinism", in E. Sosa, ed., *Causation and Conditionals* (Oxford: Oxford University Press, 1975).

Árdal, Páll, *Passion and Value in Hume's Treatise* (Edinburgh: Edinburgh University Press, 1966).

———, "Another Look at Hume's Account of Moral Evaluation", *Journal of the History of Philosophy*, 15 (1977), 405–21.

Aristotle, *Nicomachean Ethics*, trans. T. Irwin (Indianapolis: Hackett, 1985).

Ayer, A. J., "Freedom and Necessity", in Watson, ed., *Free Will*.

———, *Hume* (Oxford: Oxford University Press, 1980).

Baier, Annette, *A Progress of Sentiments: Reflections on Hume's Treatise* (Cambridge, Mass.: Harvard University Press, 1991).

Bayle, Pierre, *Historical and Critical Dictionary* [1702], selections and trans. by R. H. Popkin (Indianapolis: Bobbs-Merrill, 1965).

Bayles, Michael, "Hume on Blame and Excuse", *Hume Studies*, 2 (1976), 17–35.

Beauchamp, T. L., and A. Rosenberg, *Hume and the Problem of Causation* (Oxford: Clarendon Press, 1981).

Bennett, Jonathan, "Accountability", in van Straaten, ed., *Philosophical Subjects*.

Berkeley, George, *Alciphron* [1732], in A. C. Fraser, ed., *The Works of George Berkeley*, 4 vols. (Oxford: Oxford University Press, 1901).

Berlin, Isaiah, *Four Essays on Liberty* (Oxford: Oxford University Press, 1969).

Berofsky, Bernard, ed., *Free Will and Determinism* (New York: Harper & Row, 1966).

Bradley, F. H., *Ethical Studies*, 2nd ed. (Oxford: Oxford University Press, 1927).

Bricke, John, "Hume on Freedom to Act and Personal Evaluation", *History of Philosophy Quarterly*, 5 (1988), 141–56.

Butler, Joseph, *The Works of Joseph Butler*, 2 vols. (Oxford: Oxford University Press, 1849).

Campbell, C. A., "Is 'Freewill' a Pseudo-Problem?", in Berofsky, ed., *Free Will and Determinism*.

Chappell, V. C., ed., *Hume* (London: Macmillan, 1968).

Clarke, Samuel, *The Works of Samuel Clarke* [1738], 4 vols. (New York and London: Garland, 1978).

Collins, Anthony, *A Philosophical Inquiry Concerning Human Liberty* [1717], in J. O'Higgins, ed., *Determinism and Freewill* (The Hague: Nijhoff, 1976).

Davidson, Donald, "Actions, Reasons, and Causes", in *Actions and Events*.

————, "Freedom to Act", in *Actions and Events*.

————, "Mental Events", in *Actions and Events*.

————, "Psychology as Philosophy", in *Actions and Events*.

————, *Actions and Events* (Oxford: Clarendon Press, 1980).

Davie, William, "Hume on Morality, Action and Character", *History of Philosophy Quarterly*, 2 (1985), 337–48.

Dennett, Daniel, *Elbow Room: The Varieties of Free Will Worth Wanting* (Oxford: Clarendon Press, 1984).

Diogenes Laertius, *Lives of Eminent Philosophers*, 2 vols. (London: Loeb, 1925).

Double, Richard, *The Non-Reality of Free Will* (New York and Oxford: Oxford University Press, 1991).

Dray, W. H., "Historical Explanation of Actions Reconsidered", in P. Gardiner, ed., *The Philosophy of History* (Oxford: Oxford University Press, 1974).

Duncan-Jones, Austin, *Butler's Moral Philosophy* (Harmondsworth, Middx.: Penguin, 1952).

Edwards, Paul, ed., *The Encyclopedia of Philosophy*, 8 vols. (New York: Macmillan, 1967).

Fields, Lloyd, "Hume on Responsibility", *Hume Studies*, 14 (1988),161–75.

Fischer, John Martin and Mark Ravizza, eds., *Perspectives on Moral Responsibility* (Ithaca and London: Cornell University Press, 1993).

Flanagan, Owen, *Varieties of Moral Personality: Ethics and Psychological Realism* (Cambridge, Mass.: Harvard University Press, 1991).

Flew, Antony, *Hume's Philosophy of Belief* (London: Routledge & Kegan Paul, 1961).

————, "Paul Russell on Hume's 'Reconciling Project'", *Mind* 93 (1984), 587–88.

————, *David Hume: Philosopher of Moral Science* (Oxford: Blackwell, 1986).

Fogelin, Robert, *Hume's Skepticism in the Treatise of Human Nature* (London: Routledge & Kegan Paul, 1985).

Foot, Philippa, "Free Will as Involving Determinism", in Berofsky, ed., *Free Will and Determinism*.

Frankfurt, Harry, "Freedom of the Will and the Concept of a Person", in Watson, ed., *Free Will*.

Gaskin, John, *Hume's Philosophy of Religion*, 2nd ed. (London: Macmillan, 1988).

Gibbard, Allan, *Wise Choices, Apt Feelings: The Theory of Normative Judgment* (Cambridge, Mass.: Harvard University Press, 1990).

Glover, Jonathan, *Responsibility* (London: Routledge & Kegan Paul, 1970).

Hampshire, Stuart, *Thought and Action* (London: Chatto & Windus, 1959).

Hampton, Jean, and Jeffrey Murphy, *Forgiveness and Mercy* (Cambridge: Cambridge University Press, 1988).

Hardie, W. F. R., *Aristotle's Ethical Theory*, 2nd ed. (Oxford: Oxford University Press, 1980).

Hart, H. L. A., "Prolegomenon to the Principles of Punishment", in *Punishment and Responsibility: Essays in the Philosophy of Law* (Oxford: Oxford University Press, 1968).

Helm, Paul, "Hume on Exculpation", *Philosophy*, 42 (1967), 265–71.

Hendel, Charles, *Studies in the Philosophy of David Hume* (Princeton: Princeton University Press, 1925).

Hobbes, Thomas, *The Elements of Law* [1650], F. Tonnies, ed. (Cambridge: Cambridge University Press, 1928).

————, *Leviathan* [1651], R. Tuck, ed. (Cambridge: Cambridge University Press, 1991).

————, *Of Liberty and Necessity* [1654]. Selections reprinted in Raphael, ed., *British Moralists*, vol. 1.

————, *The English Works of Thomas Hobbes*, 11 vols., W. Molesworth, ed. (London: Bohn, 1839–1845).

Honderich, T., ed., *Essays on Freedom of Action* (London: Routledge & Kegan Paul, 1973).

————, *The Consequences of Determinism: A Theory of Determinism*, vol. 2 (Oxford: Clarendon Press, 1990).

————, *How Free Are You?: The Determinism Problem* (New York and Oxford: Oxford University Press, 1993).

Hook, Sidney, ed., *Determinism and Freedom in the Age of Modern Science* (New York: Collier, 1961).

Hospers, John, "What Means This Freedom?", in Hook, ed., *Determinism and Freedom*.

Johnson, Clarence, "Hume's Theory of Moral Responsibility: Some Unresolved Matters", *Dialogue*, 31 (1992), 3–18.

Kames, Lord (Henry Home), *Essays on the Principles of Morality and Natural Religion* [1751] (New York and London: Garland, 1983).

Kant, Immanuel, *Critique of Practical Reason and Other Works*, 6th ed., trans. by T. K. Abbott, (London: Longmans, 1909).

Kaufman, Gerald, "Responsibility, Moral and Legal", in Edwards, ed., *Encyclopedia of Philosophy*, vol. 7.

Kemp Smith, Norman, "The Naturalism of Hume" [1905], in A. Porteous, A. MacLennan, and G. Davie, eds., *The Credibility of Divine Existence: The Collected Papers of Norman Kemp Smith* (New York: Macmillan, 1967).

————, *The Philosophy of David Hume* (London: Macmillan, 1941).

Keynes, J. M., and P. Sraffa, introduction to David Hume, *Abstract of a Treatise of Human Nature* (Cambridge: Cambridge University Press, 1938).

King, William, *An Essay on the Origin of Evil* [1702] (New York and London: Garland, 1978).

Kleinig, John, *Punishment and Desert* (The Hague: Nijhoff, 1973).

La Rochefoucauld, Francois de, *Maxims*, trans. L. Tancock (Harmondsworth, Middx.: Penguin, 1959).

Leibniz, Gottfried Wilhelm, *Theodicy: Essays on the Goodness of God, the Freedom of Man and the Origin of Evil* [1710], A. Farrer, ed. (London: Routledge & Kegan Paul, 1951).

Locke, John, *An Essay Concerning Human Understanding* [1700], 4th ed., P. Nidditch, ed. (Oxford: Clarendon Press, 1975).

Lyons, John, *Emotion* (Cambridge: Cambridge University Press, 1980).

MacIntyre, Alasdair, "Hume on 'Is' and 'Ought'", in Chappell, ed., *Hume*.

————, *After Virtue* (Notre Dame: University of Notre Dame Press, 1981).

Mackie, J. L., *The Cement of the Universe* (Oxford: Clarendon Press, 1974).

————, *Ethics: Inventing Right and Wrong* (Harmondsworth, Middx.: Penguin, 1977).

————, "Morality and the Retributive Emotions", in *Persons and Values: Philosophical Papers*, vol. 2 (Oxford: Clarendon Press, 1985).

MacMurray, John, *Freedom in the Modern World*, 2nd ed. (London: Faber, 1935).

————, *Reason and Emotion*, 2nd ed. (London: Faber, 1961).

MacNabb, D. G. C., *David Hume: His Theory of Knowledge and Morality*, 2nd ed. (Oxford: Blackwell, 1966).

Malebranche, Nicolas, *The Search After Truth, with Elucidations* [1674], trans. T. M. Lennon and P. J. Olscamp (Columbus: Ohio State University Press, 1980).

————, *Dialogues on Metaphysics and on Religion* [1688], trans. M. Ginsberg (London: Allen & Unwin, 1923).

Mandeville, Bernard, *Fable of the Bees* [1714]. Selections reprinted in Raphael, ed., *British Moralists*, vol. 1.

McIntyre, Jane, "Character: A Humean Account", *History of Philosophy Quarterly*, 7 (1990), 193–206.

Mill, John Stuart, *A System of Logic*, 8th ed. (London: Longmans, Green & Co., 1898).

Moore, G. E., *Ethics* (Oxford: Oxford University Press, 1912).

Mossner, Ernest, "Philosophy and Biography: The Case of David Hume", in Chappell, ed., *Hume*.

————, *The Life of David Hume*, 2nd ed. (Oxford: Clarendon Press, 1980).

Murdoch, Iris, *The Sovereignty of Good* (London: Routledge & Kegan Paul, 1970).

Nagel, Thomas, "Moral Luck", in Watson, ed., *Free Will*.

———, *The View from Nowhere* (New York and Oxford: Oxford University Press, 1986).

Neu, Jerome, *Emotion, Thought and Therapy* (London: Routledge & Kegan Paul, 1978).

Nietzsche, Friedrich, *Beyond Good and Evil: Prelude to a Philosophy of the Future*, trans. W. Kaufmann (New York: Vintage, 1966).

———, *Twilight of the Idols and The Anti-Christ*, trans. R. J. Hollingdale (Harmondsworth, Middx.: Penguin, 1968).

Nowell-Smith, Patrick, "Freewill and Moral Responsibility", *Mind*, 57 (1948), 45–61.

O'Connor, D. J., *Free Will* (Garden City, N.Y.: Doubleday, 1971).

Parfit, Derek, "Later Selves and Moral Principles", in A. Montefiore, ed., *Philosophy and Personal Relations* (London: Routledge & Kegan Paul, 1973).

———, *Reasons and Persons* (Oxford: Clarendon Press, 1984).

Penelhum, Terence, *Hume* (London: Macmillan, 1974).

———, "Hume's Moral Psychology", in D. F. Norton, ed., *The Cambridge Companion to Hume* (Cambridge: Cambridge University Press, 1993).

Pitson, Antony E., "The Nature of Humean Animals", *Hume Studies*, 19 (1993), 301–16.

Raphael, D. D., ed., *British Moralists: 1650–1800*, 2 vols. (Oxford: Clarendon Press, 1969).

———, "Hume and Adam Smith on Justice and Utility", in *Justice and Liberty* (London: Athlone, 1980).

Rawls, John, "Two Concepts of Rules", in P. Foot, ed., *Theories of Ethics* (Oxford: Oxford University Press, 1967).

Reid, Thomas, *Active Powers of the Human Mind* [1788] (Cambridge, Mass., and London: MIT Press, 1969).

Ross, Ian, *Lord Kames and the Scotland of His Day* (Oxford: Clarendon Press, 1972).

Russell, Bertrand, "On the Notion of Cause", in *Mysticism and Logic and Other Essays*, 2nd ed. (London: Allen & Unwin, 1917).

———, *Human Society in Ethics and Politics* (London: Allen & Unwin, 1954).

———, *Nightmares of Eminent Persons and Other Stories* (Harmondsworth, Middx.: Penguin, 1962).

Russell, Paul, "On the Naturalism of Hume's 'Reconciling Project'", *Mind*, 92 (1983), 593–600.

———, "Hume's 'Two Definitions' of Cause and the Ontology of 'Double Existence'", *Hume Studies*, 10 (1984), 1–25.

———, "Sorabji and the Dilemma of Determinism", *Analysis*, 44 (1984), 166–72.

———, "Hume's 'Reconciling Project': A Reply to Flew", *Mind*, 94 (1985), 587–90.

———, "Hume's *Treatise* and Hobbes's *The Elements of Law*", *Journal of the History of Ideas*, 46 (1985), 51–64.

———, "'Atheism' and the Title-Page of Hume's *Treatise*", *Hume Studies*, 14 (1988), 408–23.

———, "Causation, Compulsion and Compatibilism", *American Philosophical Quarterly*, 25 (1988), 313–21.

———, "Skepticism and Natural Religion in Hume's *Treatise*", *Journal of the History of Ideas*, 49 (1988), 247–65.

———, "A Hobbist Tory: Johnson on Hume", *Hume Studies*, 16 (1990), 75–79.

———, "Hume on Responsibility and Punishment", *Canadian Journal of Philosophy*, 20 (1990), 539–64.

———, "Strawson's Way of Naturalizing Responsibility", *Ethics*, 102 (1992), 287–302.

———, "Epigram, Pantheists, and Freethought in Hume's *Treatise*: A Study in Esoteric Communication", *Journal of the History of Ideas*, 54 (1993), 659–73.

———, "Hume's *Treatise* and the Clarke-Collins Controversy", *Hume Studies*, 21 (1995), 95–115.

———, "Smith on Moral Sentiment and Moral Luck", paper read at meeting on "The Scottish Tradition in Philosophy", The University of Aberdeen, Scotland; June, 1995.

Schlick, Moritz, "When Is a Man Responsible?" [1930], in Berofsky, ed., *Free Will and Determinism*.

Schlossberger, Eugene, "Why We Are Responsible for Our Emotions", *Mind*, 95 (1986), 37–56.

Shaftesbury, Third Earl of, *Characteristics: Of Men, Manners, Opinions, Times* [1711]. Selections reprinted in Raphael, ed., *British Moralists*, vol. 1.

Smart, J. J. C., "Free Will, Praise and Blame", in G. Dworkin, ed., *Determinism, Free Will and Moral Responsibility* (Englewood Cliffs, N.J.: Prentice Hall, 1970).

Smith, Adam, *Lectures on Jurisprudence*, R. Meek, D. Raphael, and P. Stein, eds. (Indianapolis: Liberty Classics, 1978).

Sorabji, Richard, *Necessity, Cause and Blame: Perspectives on Aristotle's Theory* (London: Duckworth, 1980).

Spinoza, Benedict, *The Chief Works*, 2 vols., trans. R. H. M. Elwes (New York: Dover, 1951).

Squires, J. E. R., "Blame", in H. B. Acton, ed., *The Philosophy of Punishment* (London: Macmillan, 1969).

Stalley, R. F., "The Will in Hume's *Treatise*", *Journal of the History of Philosophy*, 24 (1986), 41–53.

Stephen, James Fitzjames, *Liberty, Equality, Fraternity* [1873] (Cambridge: Cambridge University Press, 1967).

Strawson, Galen, *The Secret Connexion: Causation, Realism and David Hume* (Oxford: Clarendon Press, 1989).

Strawson, P. F., *Introduction to Logical Theory* (London: Metheun, 1952).

———, "P. F. Strawson Replies", in van Straaten, ed., *Philosophical Subjects*.

Stroud, Barry, *Hume* (London: Routledge & Kegan Paul, 1977).

Taylor, Charles, "Responsibility for Self", in Watson, ed., *Free Will*.

Taylor, Gabriele, *Pride, Shame and Guilt: Emotions of Self-Assessment* (Oxford: Clarendon Press, 1985).

Taylor, Richard, "Determinism and the Theory of Agency", in Hook, ed., *Determinism and Freedom*.

van Inwagen, Peter, *An Essay on Free Will* (Oxford: Clarendon Press, 1983).

van Straaten, Zak, ed., *Philosophical Subjects: Essays Presented to P. F. Strawson* (Oxford: Clarendon Press, 1980).

Wasserstrom, Richard, "Some Problems in the Definition and Justification of Punishment", in A. I. Goldman and J. Kim, eds., *Values and Morals* (Dortrecht and Boston: Reidel, 1978).

Watson, Gary, "Free Agency", in *Free Will*.

———, ed., *Free Will* (Oxford: Oxford University Press, 1982).

Westermarck, Edward, *Ethical Relativity* (London: Routledge & Kegan Paul, 1932).

Whelan, Frederick, *Order and Artifice in Hume's Political Philosophy* (Princeton: Princeton University Press, 1985).

Wiggins, David, "Towards a Reasonable Libertarianism", in Honderich, ed., *Essays on Freedom of Action*.

Williams, Bernard, "Morality and the Emotions" in *Problems of the Self* (Cambridge: Cambridge University Press, 1973).

———, *Descartes: The Project of Pure Enquiry* (Harmondsworth, Middx.: Penguin, 1978).

Wolf, Susan, *Freedom within Reason* (New York and Oxford: Oxford University Press, 1990).

Wright, John, *The Sceptical Realism of David Hume* (Manchester: Manchester University Press, 1983).

Index

Action: actions of the mind, 111, 123n26; and character, 59–64, 66, 80, 95–96, 101–2, 106n8, 107n13, 107n17, 110–13, 120n1; causal theory, 15, 17, 22n16, 22n17, 110–13; and consequences, 111, 113, 114, 121n8, 131–32, 135; interpretation and the role of intention, 96, 102, 106n8, 110–13, 118, 119, 120n6, 121n9, 180; and 'moral agency', 179; rational explanation of, 17, 22n16; and responsibility, 4, 6, 13–15, 17, 18–19, 22n17, 47–55, 57n12, 59–61, 63–64, 66–67, 95–109, 110–13, 131–33, 177

Adams, Robert, 121n15

Anscombe, G. E. M., 23n17, 56n8

Antilibertarian argument, 12; classical account of, 13–15, 47–48, 51–53, 98–99; and dilemma of determinism, 14–15, 17, 51–53; and libertarian replies, 17; and liberty of indifference in acting (LIA)/ liberty of indifference in willing (LIW), 18–19, 23n20; naturalistic account of, 60, 63–64, 66–67, 119, 123n27; and necessity argument, 54–55, 56n7, 60

Árdal, Páll, 68n4

Aristotle, 129, 135n16, 174

Association of Ideas/Impressions: and causation, 32–39; and indirect passions (moral sentiment), 62, 100, 112

Ayer, A. J., 3, 4, 8n3, 8n4, 20, 22n12, 48–49, 56n3, 184n19

Baier, Annette, 70n17, 93n1, 94n12, 120n5, 165n3, 166n12

Bayle, Pierre, 23n22, 165n4, 167n16

Bayles, Michael, 121n11, 123n28, 133n5

Beauchamp, Tom, 39n2, 82n6

Bellow, Saul, 184n17

Bennett, Jonathan, 83n14

Berkeley, George, 37, 166n8, 168n27

Berlin, Isaiah, 8n4, 134n8

Bricke, John, 107n11

Butler, Joseph, 70n20, 151n11, 166n8, 168n27, 169n28, 179, 185n21

Caesar, Julius, 166n11

Campbell, C. A., 22n11, 82n3, 82n4, 134n9, 151n14

Cato, 127, 134n8, 166n11

Causation: of action, 17, 32n17, 59–60, 63–64, 66–67, 110–13; and compulsion, 4, 13, 47–50, 51, 53, 56n3; 'contrary causes', 59, 125; and double existence, 25, 30–38; and freedom and responsibility, 4, 11–23, 43–57, 63–64, 66–67, 74, 79–81, 150n4; and God, 29, 40n10, 56n11, 167n20; Hume's two definitions, 31, 35–37; in matter (bodies), 24–26, 32–33, 34–37, 45–46; in mind (perceptions), 31–32, 35; necessity not essential to, 17, 22n17, 52, 56n8; object/relation distinction, 13, 49–52, 56n7; and paradox, 25, 38, 40n6; and passions, 58, 61–63, 65, 70n20, 78, 79–81, 87–88, 100–101, 112, 117; regularity theory, 20, 39n2, 44, 47–50, 57n12, 69n12; realist interpretation, 41n17; and scepticism, 29–30, 38, 41n11, 42n17; uniformity and universality of (determinism), 79. *See also* Chance; Necessity